"Stephen Haynes has written a must-read Bonhoeffer book. Tracing Bonhoeffer's American reception over time through scholarship, op-ed pieces, blogs, documentaries, artistic presentations, and more, Haynes uncovers—with striking clarity—the range of images of Bonhoeffer and his legacy, paying particular attention to the evangelical appropriation of that legacy and its role in current political realities. I cannot commend this book highly enough."

— Lori Brandt Hale
Augsburg University

"Highly visible US evangelicals endorsed and still support Donald Trump, some doing so in the name of Dietrich Bonhoeffer, to the horror of the vast majority of serious students of the great German theologian and resister. Stephen Haynes long ago carved out a niche as the single best scholarly interpreter of the American reception of Bonhoeffer. Here he not only updates his scholarly work but also enters the Bonhoeffer-Trump-evangelicals debate himself with an impassioned warning to evangelicals to reverse their surrender to Trump before it is too late. This is a riveting book that every US Christian should read—immediately."

— David P. Gushee
Center for Theology & Public Life, Mercer University

THE BATTLE FOR BONHOEFFER

Stephen R. Haynes

William B. Eerdmans Publishing Company
Grand Rapids, Michigan

Wm. B. Eerdmans Publishing Co.
4035 Park East Court SE, Grand Rapids, Michigan 49546
www.eerdmans.com

Published 2018
Printed in the United States of America

27 26 25 24 23 22 21 20 19 18 1 2 3 4 5 6 7 8 9 10

ISBN 978-0-8028-7601-0

Library of Congress Cataloging-in-Publication Data
Names: Haynes, Stephen R., author.
Title: The battle for Bonhoeffer / Stephen R. Haynes.
Description: Grand Rapids : Eerdmans Publishing Co., 2018. | Includes bibliographical references and index.
Identifiers: LCCN 2018022306 | ISBN 9780802876010 (pbk. : alk. paper)
Subjects: LCSH: Bonhoeffer, Dietrich, 1906-1945.
Classification: LCC BX4827.B57 H359 2018 | DDC 230/.044092—dc23
LC record available at https://lccn.loc.gov/2018022306

Contents

PART TWO:
BONHOEFFER AND HOMEGROWN HITLERS

Foreword

In the decades since he was executed on Hitler's orders for the crime of high treason in the concentration camp in Flossenburg on April 9, 1945, Dietrich Bonhoeffer has become one of the most widely read and influential religious thinkers of our time. His story brings together people from diverse ecumenical and religious traditions in shared admiration of an indisputably authentic witness. No other theologian of the modern era crosses quite so many boundaries—genres, cultures, and audiences—while yet remaining exuberantly, and generously, confessional.

In his protest against totalitarianism and xenophobia, his early and consistent support of the Jews and the other victims of Nazi brutality, his theological cosmopolitanism and evangelical humanism, Bonhoeffer is surely a Christian for our time, and an exemplar of righteous action. The British ecumenist and scholar Keith Clements has said that Bonhoeffer belongs "not first to church history or to the Christian camp but to the human race," standing, as he does, among those who represent "the further possibilities of the human spirit."[1]

It is understandable then that readers with differing theological and ideological perspectives would desire to claim Bonhoeffer as their own. "Excerpting Bonhoeffer" has become a familiar exercise in each team's efforts *to win*; a quick Google search of "A Bonhoeffer Moment"

1. Keith Clements, *What Freedom? The Persistent Challenge of Dietrich Bonhoeffer* (Eugene, OR: Wipf and Stock, 2011), 11.

will put you directly in the crossfire of liberals and conservatives each laying claim to the great Christian martyr. Who would not wish to believe that a person we so greatly admire sees the world as we do? Not since the postwar debates over Bonhoeffer between the Federal Republic of Germany (West Germany) and the German Democratic Republic (East Germany) has Bonhoeffer's legacy been more contested.[2]

As I write this foreword in the summer of 2018, with the nation transfixed by horrific images of children in cages and ProPublica recordings of toddlers separated from their families sobbing in ICE gulags—the work of the Trump-Nielson-Miller-Sessions zero-tolerance immigration policy—most of us who position ourselves outside the provenance of "Fox News evangelicals" indulge in what-about-Bonhoefferisms and partisan proof texting. Prophetic judgment with invocations of the Confessing Church and German Resistance has rarely been more tempting. We can produce, on demand, high-minded (often inaccurate) disputations on the "relevance of Barmen" and the shocking displays of cheap grace among Fox News evangelicals.

On the other end of the spectrum, Eric Metaxas, with his populist Bonhoeffer, takes willful misuse to its extreme. Not since the death-of-God movement of the late 1960s has anyone produced so flawed, or

2. Ulrich Lincoln, pastor of Dietrich Bonhoeffer Church in Forest Hill in Southeast London, writes: "The Protestant church in the West found in him a key figure to legitimize her own claim to be the moral watchdog and guardian for the democratic society. . . . To the wider public of the German society he was sold not so much as a conspirator but more as a moral example, as one of the good Germans during the Nazi years. . . . In East Germany . . . he became a leading inspiration for a church that found itself in a position of minority and opposition: In a country where the state's attitude towards the church was openly hostile, where the church's capability to work in public was restricted by a hostile ideology, Bonhoeffer's writing about radical discipleship and about the church's poverty as well as his personal witness and martyrdom proved to be a major inspiration for many." The East German churches took Bonhoeffer at his word "that the church always has to be a church 'for others' as a help for their own situation: 'A Church within Socialism.' . . . And some theologians certainly identified the socialist society with that world come of age that Bonhoeffer had written about so affirmatively in 1944." Ulrich Lincoln, "The Perception of Dietrich Bonhoeffer in Germany," https://www.projectbonhoeffer.org.uk/the-perception-of-dietrich-bonhoeffer-in-germany/.

so influential, an account of Bonhoeffer's thought. Like those excitable pranksters—Thomas Altizer, Bishop Robinson, Gabriel Vahanian, etc.—Metaxas ignored the parts of Bonhoeffer he didn't like and invented the parts he needed.[3] The death-of-God crowd read *Letters and Papers from Prison* and avoided the rest; Metaxas read portions of *Discipleship* and *Life Together* and not much else. Kudos for candor, I suppose: Metaxas dismissed the prison writings as an irrelevant distraction; or as he put it, a "few bone fragments . . . set upon by famished kites and less noble birds, many of whose descendants gnaw them still"—despite Bonhoeffer's own sense that these ponderous thoughts marked profound transformation, a new reckoning with Jesus Christ in the ruins of the German nation. "In the last few years," he wrote from Tegel prison to his friend Eberhard Bethge, "I have come to know and understand more and more the profound this-worldliness of Christianity. The Christian is not a *homo religiosus* but simply a human being, in the same way that Jesus was a human being. . . . I do not mean the shallow and banal this-worldliness of the enlightened, the bustling, the comfortable, or the lascivious, but the profound this-worldliness that shows discipline and includes the ever-present knowledge of death and resurrection."[4]

How fortunate we are that Stephen Haynes, a distinguished scholar of the Holocaust and public theologian, has intervened in the increasingly contentious debate over Bonhoeffer's legacy. For the past quarter century, Haynes has also been at the forefront of international Bonhoeffer scholarship, writing for scholarly and popular audiences and lecturing widely on religion, race, and violence in Hitler's Germany—and, as in his extraordinary *Noah's Curse: The Biblical Justification of American Slavery* (New York: Oxford University Press, 2002), the American South as well. Haynes skillfully and even-

3. Toward the end of Fritz Stern's book *No Ordinary Men: Dietrich Bonhoeffer and Hans von Dohnanyi, Resisters against Hitler in Church and State*, written with his wife Elisabeth Sifton, the renowned historian turned his attention to Metaxas's account only to note the "amazing ignorance of the German language, German history, and German theology." Elisabeth Sifton and Fritz Stern, *No Ordinary Men: Dietrich Bonhoeffer and Hans Von Dohnanyi, Resisters against Hitler in Church and State* (New York: New York Review of Books, 2013), 147.

4. Dietrich Bonhoeffer, *Letters and Papers from Prison*, 1st ed. (Minneapolis: Fortress, 2010), 541.

handedly analyzes the interpretive conflicts surrounding Bonhoeffer's inheritance in the United States. His intention is to understand Bonhoeffer for our cultural moment, and even more, to understand the cultural conditions that produce such incompatible, and often unsupportable, appropriations. Is it the arrogance of expertise? The contempt of the guild for popular readings? Have we been misled by a perceived open-endedness in Bonhoeffer's thought? Haynes treats the "Bonhoeffer phenomenon" to a much-needed acid bath, stripping away the accretions of partisan cherry-picking and wishful thinking to which we must all plead guilty. Still, *The Battle for Bonhoeffer* is more than an incisive account of interpretive conflicts and their repercussions for the church and the world; it also serves as a compass we will need to keep our bearings amid the confused and often colliding images of God in our perilous times.

The polarization of Bonhoeffer's thought is most vexing precisely because such efforts are rarely accompanied by attention to his own politics. Have you heard progressive Christians cite the passage in *Ethics* calling abortion "nothing but murder"?[5] Or recall Bonhoeffer's preference for monarchy over democracy? Or champion his odious portrayal of psychoanalysts as a "scenting and sniffing lot," ever "gnawing away at our confidence and security," "degenerates" all?[6]

Regarding the specifics of his political views, it might be helpful to recall that, during the only free election in which he participated, Bonhoeffer supported the Catholic Center Party. In a letter to his friend Hans Hildebrandt, who supported the Protestant Christians People's Party, Bonhoeffer said that only the Catholic Center Party

5. Dietrich Bonhoeffer, *Ethics* (Minneapolis: Fortress, 2005), 206.

6. Bonhoeffer, *Letters and Papers from Prison*, ed. Eberhard Bethge (New York: Simon and Schuster, 1997), 325–36. He calls them people who "regard themselves as the most important thing in the world, and who therefore like to busy themselves with themselves," a threat to the foundations of Christian culture, to the family, to the home, to the virtuous woman, to the strong man, and to the ordinary guy in the street, the one who "spends his everyday life at work and with his family"—on and on he goes. See Sander Gilman's book, *The Case of Sigmund Freud: Medicine and Identity at the Fin de Siècle* (Baltimore: Johns Hopkins University Press, 1993), for a helpful discussion of this and other anti-Semitic portrayals of psychoanalysis.

had half a chance of defeating Hitler.[7] While there is no easy parallel to American politics, the core convictions of the *Deutsche Zentrumspartei* would not seem to lend themselves to the prevailing "Republican misrule in Washington."[8] The Center Party was a heterogeneous people's party, attracting members from widely diverse backgrounds: aristocrats, priests, bourgeoisie, peasants, workers. While its membership was majority Roman Catholic, the Party remained interconfessional and committed to the democratic ideals of the Weimar Constitution. It adhered to a strict separation of church and state, to belief in strong government and the welfare state, and to the facilitation of nonpartisan policy making. Though the Center Party was not free from inner tensions and political fissures, it successfully presented itself as a party of the *Mitte* (the middle way), putting Christian social ethics in service to the commonweal of the "great German nation" in a manner that proved inclusive and flexible.[9] Over time, support for the party (along with support for the Weimar Republic) decreased gradually, from 21.2 percent in 1919 to 15.1 percent in 1930. When the Nazis came into power, the Zentrum was forced to dissolve itself as one of the last *bürgerliche* parties—not, alas, before signing the Enabling Act and thereby proving Bonhoeffer's argument against Hildebrandt to have been naïve.[10]

We also know—on the question of Bonhoeffer's politics—that he admired the work of the American religious Left and its innovations in social ministry, encountered during his year in the United States. Upon his return to Berlin in the summer of 1931, he told his social-

7. Theresa Clasen, "Notes on the Catholic Center Party" (unpublished report commissioned by the author, 2014).

8. George F. Will, "Vote against the GOP This November," *Washington Post,* June 22, 2018.

9. Zentrum became one of the ruling parties of the Weimar Republic, a compromising and reliable partner in almost all of the various Weimar coalitions. Conversation with Dr. Theresa Clasen, Berlin University.

10. The Center Party's support of the Enabling Act, as I understand it, was part of a deal to secure Hitler's support for the 1933 Concordat with the Vatican that would protect the rights of the Catholic Church from Nazi encroachment. I am grateful to my tenacious research assistant, Isaac May, a doctoral student at the University of Virginia in American religious history, for clarifications on this point. Any errors related to the above summary are solely mine.

ist brother Karl-Friedrich that Germany would need an ACLU of its own: the rights of conscientious objectors and protections for resident aliens from deportation mattered deeply.[11] With American professors and fellow students, he had discussed "labor problems, restriction of profits, civil rights, juvenile crime, and the activity of the churches in these fields" and the role of churches in selective buying campaigns and public policy.[12] He met with representatives of the National Women's Trade Union League, the NAACP, and the Workers Education Bureau of America, and, as he wrote in his notes, visited "housing settlements, Y.M. home missions, co-operative houses, playgrounds, children's courts, night schools, socialists schools, asylums, [and] youth organizations." Bonhoeffer discerned, and he experienced, the presence of Christ in these spaces of social healing existing within and beyond the walls of the parish church. He discovered a new way of pursuing the theological vocation.

In his immersions in African American Christianity, Bonhoeffer discovered a new way of being Christian. "I heard the Gospel preached in the Negro Churches of America," he said. The African American Christian story came as a refreshing breeze to a theological prodigy from Berlin who found himself completely uninspired by the plodding Lutheranism of the north German plains. From the diaspora through slavery, Jim Crow, segregation, and civil rights, the African American Christian witness has always "confronted the nation with troubling questions about American exceptionalism." The shameful practices of slavery, disenfranchisement, Jim Crow, and segregation "contradicted the mythic identity of Americans as a chosen people."[13] In the story of African American Christianity, chosenness meant, as Albert Raboteau eloquently surmised, "joining company not with the powerful and the rich but with those who suffer: the outcast, the poor, and the despised."[14] Bonhoeffer's encounter with "the church of the outcasts of America" came too as a call to discipleship and obedience.

11. Eberhard Bethge, *Dietrich Bonhoeffer: A Biography*, rev. ed., ed. Victoria J. Barnett (Minneapolis: Fortress, 2000), 162.

12. Bonhoeffer, cited in Mary Bosanquet, *The Life and Death of Dietrich Bonhoeffer* (New York: Harper and Row, 1968), 84.

13. Albert Raboteau, "American Salvation," *Boston Review*, Summer 2005.

14. Raboteau, "American Salvation."

Bonhoeffer did not write a political theology nor was he much given to discussing politics in his letters, sermons, and lectures. He has at times been criticized by scholars as apolitical—which is an odd claim to make of one of the few ministers murdered in the concentration camps on charges of political conspiracy. By the end of 1933, Bonhoeffer denounced the Nazi race statutes as heresy and insisted on the church's moral obligation to defend all victims of state violence, regardless of race or religion; these convictions alienated him from the *Deutsche Christen* and even from some fellow resisters. His political theology clusters around his theological practices; living with "a view from below," from a higher satisfaction; bearing witness to Jesus Christ through prayer and righteous action; attending with compassion to "those who have been unjustly silenced," encountering Christ in the excluded and the distressed,[15] "as a beggar among beggars, as an outcast among the outcast . . . a sinner among sinners."[16]

Still, he remained first and foremost an "ecumenical patriot"—as the theologian Larry Rasmussen has written in a passage cited by Haynes. Throughout the church resistance, Bonhoeffer believed that the best way to contest the Third Reich and its useful ecclesial idiots was by affirming and inhabiting the global, ecumenical church. He was—in Donald Shriver's words—an "honest patriot," a patriot whose historical memories and expectations are chastened by reality—by "the blood-stained face of history" (Camus). "Every time belief in the catholic church is confessed in the creed, every time we sing of the church being 'one' . . . patriotism is being put in its proper perspective," Keith Clements wrote. "We are also committing ourselves to face the scandalous inequalities and divisions of our world more intimately than ever before, because these inequalities and divisions do not stop outside the church door."[17] Can one really believe in the church universal and profess America First without offense to the body of Christ? At the same time, Bonhoeffer considered it an "An-

15. The phrase comes from the British Quaker theologian Rachel Muers in her marvelous book, *Keeping God's Silence: Towards a Theological Ethics of Communication* (Oxford: Clarendon, 2004), 219.

16. Dietrich Bonhoeffer Works, 12:356.

17. Keith Clements, *A Patriotism for Today: Love of Country in Dialogue with Dietrich Bonhoeffer* (London: Collins, 1984), 158.

glo-Saxon failing" to presume that the church should have an answer and a solution for every social problem.[18]

Thomas Merton would later say in a remarkable riff on the theme "religionless Christianity": "We are all under judgment. None of us is free and whole at the mere cost of formulating a just and honest opinion. Mere commitment to a decent program of action does not lift the curse. . . . The church has an obligation not to join in the incantation of political slogans and in the concoction of pseudo-events, but to cut clear through the deviousness and ambiguity of both slogans and events by her simplicity and her love."[19] Bonhoeffer pondered the shape of Christian witness amid the ruins of the church in a montage of images, in lightning flashes of insight, in a barrage of unexpected questions, all the while illuminating a style of theological writing graced by *hilaritas*. Indeed, Bonhoeffer's enduring contributions to Christian faith and practice are found as much in the power of his questions as in the eloquence of his answers. "What is Christianity, or who is Christ for us today?" "If religion is only the garb in which Christianity is clothed—and this garb has looked very different in different ages—what then is religionless Christianity?" "How can Christ become Lord of the religionless as well?" "Are we still of any use?" "Religionless Christianity," which Karl Barth dismissed as but a "catchy phrase," was the framework of discipleship, obedience to Jesus Christ: it was the necessary reckoning with domesticated, weaponized transcendence for the sake of the triune God.[20] "Had Jesus not lived," Bonhoeffer said, "then our life would be meaningless, despite all the other people we know, respect, and love."

CHARLES MARSH
June 29, 2018

18. Bonhoeffer, cited in Thomas Merton, *Violence and Faith: Christian Teaching and Christian Practice* (Notre Dame: University of Notre Dame Press, 1984), 145.

19. Thomas Merton, *Violence and Faith*, p. 161.

20. Bonhoeffer, "Prayers for Prisoners, Morning Prayer," in *Letters and Papers from Prison*, 194.

Acknowledgments

I SUSPECT THAT I AM attracted to Bonhoeffer for the same reasons most American Christians are. According to Keith L. Johnson, Bonhoeffer "just seems to see things differently than the rest of us, as if he instinctively knows something about God that most of us spend our lives seeking but can never quite find." These words speak for me as well. I am also drawn to Bonhoeffer because he cultivated the space between the worlds of the academy and the church in a way that, to quote Johnson again, made him "*more* rather than less faithful as a result of living with this tension."[1]

I would like to acknowledge those who allow and encourage me to explore Bonhoeffer's legacy in the liminal space between academy and church: colleagues at Rhodes College, members of Idlewild Presbyterian Church, and friends who wonder why I spend so much time thinking about someone who has been dead nearly eighty years. These include Oscar Carr, Stephen and Mary McIntosh, Casey West, Don McClure, Margaret Burnett, Philip Taylor, and Tim Huebner, among many others.

My family was extraordinarily supportive during the writing of this book, as they always are. As I rushed to complete it in the early weeks of 2018, they kept asking if I was "almost finished." Now that I am, I must admit that, given the nature of this study, it does not seem finished at all. As those who are concerned about the direction of our nation continue to try to make sense of what is happening around them, Bonhoeffer will continue to be our conversation partner. I hope that what I have written about the role of Bonhoeffer in our public discourse will have a positive impact on the role he plays in that conversation.

More than anyone else, Trevor Thompson deserves credit for this book. He read a piece I wrote about Bonhoeffer in the *Huffington Post* shortly after the 2016 election and saw the germ of a book. To be honest, I did not; but Trevor persisted and eventually convinced me that I had something to say that might advance the conversation. He was right, and I am thankful for his gentle persuasion, as well as his strong encouragement.

Finally, I would like to dedicate this book to the men of the Tuesday noon group. Keep coming back.

PART ONE

Exploring Bonhoeffer's American Reception

CHAPTER ONE

The Man, the Myth, the Battle

IN THE MID-1990S LEON HOWELL complained that Dietrich Bonhoeffer had not yet become a household name in America. Today such a complaint seems oddly quaint, for it is doubtful whether any educated American who is mildly curious has not heard of Bonhoeffer. That is not to say that Americans are likely to know much about him, let alone be familiar with his writings. Even so, they may be aware that Bonhoeffer is among the "modern martyrs" commemorated with a statue at London's Westminster Abbey and the first Christian whose martyrdom is officially recognized by the United Methodist Church. They may recall that in 2002 President George W. Bush called Bonhoeffer "one of the greatest Germans of the twentieth century." Or they may have attended a church program addressing some facet of Bonhoeffer's legacy.[1]

Even if they have not encountered Bonhoeffer in one of these ways, it is likely that if they spend time online, they have come across references to the German pastor-theologian in the blog posts or social media conversations where he is invoked on one side (and sometimes both sides) of contentious religious or political questions. If so, they have met Bonhoeffer where the contest to claim his legacy is the fiercest. This book is about the battle for Bonhoeffer that is waged in these and other venues, the shapes that battle has assumed during the first two decades of the twenty-first century, and the ways it influenced, and was influenced by, the 2016 American presidential election.

The habit of bringing Bonhoeffer into discussions of divisive social issues is not new. On the left, Bonhoeffer has been cited by Vietnam-era draft resisters, peace activists, and liberation theologians, while on the right he is looked to by Christian opponents of abortion and same-sex marriage. But since 9/11 the desire to harness Bonhoeffer's moral capital for partisan ends has intensified as knowledge of his life and witness has expanded, and as American society has grown more politically polarized. Given this growing cultural divide—and the growing ubiquity of social media—Americans are now as likely to encounter references to Bonhoeffer on Facebook and Twitter as in sermons or Christian publications.

The resulting democratization of Bonhoeffer's legacy is part of the broader story of his American reception, which I detailed in *The Bonhoeffer Phenomenon* (2004). In the years since that book appeared, Bonhoeffer's legacy has suffused American culture to the point that today cataloguing it would be a full-time job. To keep up with the task, one would need to note the emergence of retail establishments such as Bonhoeffer's Espresso & Café in Nashua, New Hampshire (which serves direct trade "coffee with a mission"), and financial services companies like Bonhoeffer Capital Management (whose "value-oriented" private hedge fund is named for the German pastor-theologian), not to mention religious organizations like the Bonhoeffer Institute (which offers one-day training conferences on "biblical values and public policy") and the Bonhoeffer Project (a ministry of "discipleship with accountability" inspired by Bonhoeffer's "Grand Experiment" at Finkenwalde).[2]

The Bonhoeffer Phenomenon described competing portraits of the German pastor-theologian that I labeled "radical," "liberal," "evangelical," and "universal." Careful attention to Bonhoeffer's legacy since 9/11 has convinced me to add a hybrid category I am calling the "populist Bonhoeffer," which actually preceded and anticipated the current populist moment in American politics. This populist portrait that has come to dominate Bonhoeffer's American reception in the twenty-first century reflects not only our polarized political climate and the role of social media in the exchange of information, but also the proliferation of popular versions of Bonhoeffer's life.

Although the populist Bonhoeffer was fashioned on the right, he has become the currency of writers across the political spectrum, if only because they are obliged to register dissent using the rhetorical forms in which the populist Bonhoeffer thrives and the media platforms where he is most accessible. Given how poorly these platforms accommodate genuine conversation, the "battle for Bonhoeffer" has become a rhetorical contest whose goal is to claim the pastor-theologian on one's own side of the American ideological divide. Thus when the populist Bonhoeffer is invoked, it is not as an invitation to thoughtful reflection but as a stake driven into contested ground. The point is not to consider what he might have to say to us in a particular situation, but to identify the current "Bonhoeffer moment"—the cultural *kairos* that summons true patriots and disciples to action.

Since the populist mood implies a suspicion of academic elites and other representatives of a corrupt "establishment," it is not surprising that shapers of the populist Bonhoeffer rarely defer to credentialed scholars. As a result, images of Bonhoeffer forged in recent years often bear a rather casual relationship to history. Indeed, the more Bonhoeffer's name proliferates in American public discourse, the more fuzzy become the details of his life and the more stubbornly errors attach themselves to his legacy.

For instance, reading recent claims for Bonhoeffer's relevance for the American political scene, one is surprised to learn that the theologian departed Germany to escape persecution in 1933 (it was actually six years later), returned to Germany in 1939 because "millions of European Jews were being slaughtered by Hitler's death squads" (the Final Solution did not commence until 1941), founded the Confessing Church (he was not actually present at the Barmen Synod where the group was born), was detained due to a failed attempt on Hitler's life (his involvement with the plotters was not known at the time of his arrest), wore a purple triangle (these were reserved for Jehovah's Witnesses), and died in the "death camp at Buchenwald," or a "Gestapo prison," or a "Nazi torture chamber" (it was actually Flossenbürg), where he was "hung with a noose of piano wire" (a persistent myth). When the aim is to use the German hero's gravitas to seize rhetorical high ground, the details of his life and death are simply not that important.

That such demonstrably false claims appear with regularity in appeals to Bonhoeffer no doubt reflects the absence of editorial oversight in many online forms of publication. Yet these errors could be avoided with a modicum of effort. That they are not avoided suggests the urgency with which Bonhoeffer is often carried into rhetorical combat. The same carelessness is reflected in some of the quotes that are frequently misattributed to Bonhoeffer. In the flood of sloppy attribution that has engulfed his reception in recent years, Bonhoeffer is repeatedly misidentified as the source of Martin Niemöller's famous lament about the results of complacency ("first they came for the Communists . . ."), as well as of the oft-repeated adage that "silence in the face of evil is itself evil. God will not hold us guiltless. Not to speak is to speak. Not to act is to act."

This "Bonhoeffer quote," which continues to circulate widely, has been traced to two sources—a 1971 book by Robert K. Hudnut and a 1998 article describing an exhibit at the Liberty Museum in Philadelphia, now defunct. From the museum it somehow migrated to the dust jacket of Eric Metaxas's *Bonhoeffer: Pastor, Martyr, Prophet, Spy* (2010), from which it made its way onto innumerable Twitter and Facebook accounts and lists of "Top 10 Best Dietrich Bonhoeffer Quotes," not to mention posters, T-shirts, and coffee mugs. During President Barack Obama's second term, the ubiquitous adage became a rallying cry for right-leaning Americans seeking to remind their fellow citizens what happens when good people ignore creeping tyranny. As such, the statement was featured in hundreds of sermons and speeches opposing abortion, gay marriage, and threats to "religious liberty," and even showed up several times in the Congressional Record, each time in speeches by Republicans, each time attributed to Bonhoeffer.[3]

Predictably, given the increasing politicization of Bonhoeffer's legacy, the quote figured on both sides of the 2016 presidential campaign. Socially liberal faith leaders utilized it in their opposition to Donald Trump's "bigotry," while pro-Trump forces adapted it—"not to vote is to vote," they warned—to mobilize Christians who were tempted to sit out the election. In the wake of white supremacists' descent on Charlottesville in August 2017, this "Bonhoeffer quote" about silence in the face of evil found new life when it was widely applied to President Trump's failure to unequivocally condemn those who had gathered to "unite the Right."[4]

It is appropriate that Eric Metaxas is the source for most invocations of this misquote since the details of the populist Bonhoeffer who today occupies such a large space in the American imagination were largely fashioned by him. Metaxas's Bonhoeffer biography topped the *New York Times* best-seller list for e-book nonfiction in 2011 and has reportedly sold over one million copies. As we will see, the populist Bonhoeffer has other sources, but Metaxas has given it momentum by advocating Bonhoeffer's liberation from the interpretive control of scholarly experts. In addition to disseminating the faux-Bonhoeffer "silence" quote with a posttruth nonchalance, Metaxas has sown distrust of Bonhoeffer scholars, whom he blames for perpetuating "a terrific misunderstanding" of the pastor-theologian's legacy.

Metaxas has expressed the hope that his biography would set the record straight, once and for all exploding legends perpetuated by the "secular Left." While it is natural for biographers to seek to revise the received portrait of their subject, Metaxas has effectively dismissed a generation of scholarly engagement with Bonhoeffer's life and thought, ignoring works that had hitherto been regarded as the starting point for serious reflection. Into the vacuum created by this summary rejection of mainstream Bonhoeffer scholarship, Metaxas has introduced assertions of "spectacular parallels" between Hitler's Germany and Obama's America.[5]

Metaxas repeated these claims so persistently in the months and years following *Bonhoeffer*'s publication that use of the phrase "Bonhoeffer moment" as a clarion call to conservative activism cannot be understood apart from his influence. The expression, in fact, was first uttered by Metaxas in his keynote address at the 2012 National Prayer Breakfast. Three years later it was being intoned by a variety of Christian leaders as the US Supreme Court prepared to rule in *Obergefell v. Hodges* on the constitutionality of state laws banning same-sex marriage. The proclamation of a "Bonhoeffer moment" in 2015 reflected not only Metaxas's usage but his vision of an American political landscape dominated by totalitarian threats analogous to those faced by Bonhoeffer himself. As we will see, however, Metaxas's most influential work as champion of the populist Bonhoeffer was still to come.

Just as the populist Bonhoeffer is not the sole creation of Eric Metaxas, neither is it an inevitable result of the rise of social media nor a direct reflection of posttruth sensibilities. Although affected by these forces, the populist Bonhoeffer has deeper roots in the interpretive diversity that has always defined Bonhoeffer's reception in America, as well as in the tendency for competing perceptions of the German pastor-theologian to be weaponized for interpretive battle. These trends are explicated in the chapters that make up the rest of part 1. Chapter 2, "Rorschach Test: American Bonhoeffers from Cox to Koehn," describes the diverse, sometimes incompatible, ways American interpreters have portrayed Bonhoeffer. Chapter 3, "Gradual Embrace: The Evangelical Bonhoeffer before Metaxas," offers an in-depth analysis of American evangelicals' engagement with Bonhoeffer prior to the publication of Metaxas's biography.

Before exploring the distinct portraits of Bonhoeffer that are the focus of these chapters, we should note the remarkable array of sources Americans have drawn on in developing them, which include critical editions of Bonhoeffer's works, biographies, historical novels, dramas, films, and devotional compilations. The richness of these scholarly and popular resources is evident even if we limit our focus to the past thirty years. For most of that time, scholars were at work on a seventeen-volume critical edition of the Dietrich Bonhoeffer Works in English (DBWE) that was finally completed in 2014. Meanwhile, dozens of biographical accounts of Bonhoeffer's life and thought were appearing as well.

Those seeking a scholarly perspective on Bonhoeffer have been treated to two recent biographies of the pastor-theologian—Friedrich Schlingensiepen's *Dietrich Bonhoeffer, 1906–1945: Martyr, Thinker, Man of Resistance* (2010) and Charles Marsh's *Strange Glory: A Life of Dietrich Bonhoeffer* (2014). Both authors possess the knowledge of German religious and cultural life required to present a fully contextualized portrait of Bonhoeffer. But these well-regarded biographies have had to compete not only with Metaxas's best-selling *Bonhoeffer* but with briefer biographical studies such as Michael Van Dyke's *Dietrich Bonhoeffer: Opponent of the Nazi Regime* (2001) and Susan Martins Miller's *Dietrich Bonhoeffer* (2002), books whose hagiographical character is indicated by their appearance in evangelical publishers' "heroes of the faith" series. Less hagiographical, but also less demanding of readers, than the biographies by Marsh and Schlingensiepen are *Dietrich Bonhoeffer: Called by God*, by Elizabeth Raum (a college librarian who also writes children's books), and *Till the Night Be Past: The Life and Times of Dietrich Bonhoeffer*, by Theodore J. Kleinhans (a retired pastor and air force chaplain), both published in 2002.[6]

Several authors of historical fiction have paid tribute to Bonhoeffer in recent years. Mary Glazener's *The Cup of Wrath* (1992), Denise Giardina's *Saints and Villains* (1998), and Paul Barz's *I Am Bonhoeffer: A Credible Life* (2008) are fictionalized accounts that apply a novelist's imagination to the raw materials of Bonhoeffer's biography. *Saints and Villains* received wide critical acclaim, and the paperback edition included a "reader's guide" designed for use in the book groups so popular in the United States. Authors of "Christian fiction" have also taken up the challenge of portraying Bonhoeffer for American audiences. In Michael Phillips's *The Eleventh Hour* (1993), Bonhoeffer plays an important secondary role, as he does in Suzanne Woods Fisher's *Copper Fire* (2008).[7]

For those seeking more succinct accounts of Bonhoeffer's vita, many catalogues of modern "saints" feature entries on the German pastor-theologian. These texts devoted to Christians who lived remarkable lives include Robert Ellsberg's *All Saints*, which devotes April 9 to "Dietrich Bonhoeffer theologian and confessor"; James C. Howell's *Servants, Misfits, and Martyrs*, which treats Bonhoeffer in chapters on "prisoners" and "martyrs"; *Cloud of Witnesses*, by Jim Wallis and Joyce Hollyday, which includes Bonhoeffer in its catalogue of "saints, prophets and witnesses"; William D. Apel's *Witnesses before Dawn*, in which Bonhoeffer is one of seven modern paragons of Christian discipleship; and Bernard Christensen's *The Inward Pilgrimage*, which treats *Life Together* alongside other Christian "spiritual classics." Perhaps the best-known work in this genre is Malcolm Muggeridge's *A Third Testament*, in which the author celebrates six heroes of the spirit—Augustine, Pascal, Blake, Kierkegaard, Tolstoy, and Bonhoeffer—who share a capacity "to relate their time to eternity."[8]

Admirers of Bonhoeffer now have a variety of cinematic depictions of his life from which to choose as well. These include dramas such as *Hanged on a Twisted Cross* (1996), *Bonhoeffer: Agent of Grace*

(2000), and *Come before Winter* (2017), and documentaries including *Bonhoeffer: Memories and Perspectives* (1983) and Martin Doblmeier's *Bonhoeffer* (2003), a feature-length film that turned rejection at the Sundance Film Festival into a grassroots following and a national television debut on the Public Broadcasting System in 2006.[9]

Bonhoeffer's story has long inspired playwrights, and over the past two decades new dramatic treatments of his life have proliferated. These include Nancy Axelrod's *Personal Honor: Suggested by the Life of Dietrich Bonhoeffer* (2009), Tim Jorgenson's *Bonhoeffer: An Introduction through Drama* (2002), Art Cribbs's *Awaiting Judgement* (2008), Mary Ruth Clarke's *Bonhoeffer's Cost* (2012), Elizabeth Avery Scott's *Lies, Love, and Hitler* (2013), Jürgen K. Tossman's *Bonhoeffer: The Last Encounter* (2015), and Cheri Costales's *The Shoe Room* (2017). In 2002 Peter Krummeck's one-man show titled *Bonhoeffer* took its place alongside Al Staggs's *A View from the Underside: The Legacy of Dietrich Bonhoeffer*, which has toured the United States since the mid-1990s.

When considering the sources through which Americans encounter Bonhoeffer, one must not overlook the growing number of editions of his writings packaged for inspiration, among them holiday "gift" books. Items of this type appearing since the mid-1990s include *Meditations on the Cross* (1996), *The Mystery of Holy Night* (1996), *The Mystery of Easter* (1998), *Voices in the Night: The Prison Poems of Dietrich Bonhoeffer* (1999), *The Wisdom and Witness of Dietrich Bonhoeffer* (2000), *Seize the Day with Dietrich Bonhoeffer* (2000), *My Soul Finds Rest: Reflections on the Psalms by Dietrich Bonhoeffer* (2002), *Reflections on the Bible* (2004), *Who Am I? Poetic Insights and Personal Identity* (2005), *Christmas with Dietrich Bonhoeffer* (2005), *Dietrich Bonhoeffer's Christmas Sermons* (2005), *A Year with Dietrich Bonhoeffer: Daily Meditations from His Letters, Writings, and Sermons* (2005), *Dietrich Bonhoeffer's Meditations on Psalms* (2005), *Wondrously Sheltered* (2006), *I Want to Live These Days with You: A Year of Daily Devotions* (2007), *God Is in the Manger: Reflections on Advent and Christmas* (2008), *Fifteen Days of Prayer with Dietrich Bonhoeffer* (2009), *Dietrich Bonhoeffer: Meditation and Prayer* (2010), *God Is on the Cross: Reflections on Lent and Easter* (2012), *Watch for the Light: Readings for Advent and Christmas* (2014), and *Wonder of Wonders: Christmas with Dietrich Bonhoeffer* (2015).

Repetition of the words "mystery," "meditation," "reflection," and "prayer" in these titles indicates that they are marketed to readers who are in search of spiritual edification. While there is plenty of spiritual edification to be found in Bonhoeffer's writings, it is probably safe to say that readers who know him primarily from such texts remain unfamiliar (and perhaps uninterested) in larger questions surrounding his theology and its intellectual and social contexts. In this sense, even though much of this recent devotional literature includes excerpts from new critical editions of his writings, its presentation of Bonhoeffer's thought makes readers susceptible to the sorts of decontextualized interpretations on which the populist Bonhoeffer thrives.

In fact, many of these biographical, fictional, artistic, and devotional sources have contributed to a distillation of Bonhoeffer's intellectual legacy into aphorisms that can be inserted into articles and social media posts and introduced with the formula "As the German theologian Dietrich Bonhoeffer once said. . . ." Since authors who garnish their writings with excerpts from Bonhoeffer's writings are using the theologian's moral authority to enhance their own, concern for context is generally lacking. Excerpting Bonhoeffer to make a point, which is the functional equivalent of biblical proof texting, has become more frequent as American social and political discourse has grown more rigid and polarized.

All this points to an ironic feature of Bonhoeffer's American reception: the better he becomes known, naturally the more his life and witness inspire publishers, novelists, artists, playwrights, storytellers, spiritual writers, essayists, bloggers, and social media posters. But the greater the number and variety of sources through which the public is likely to encounter Bonhoeffer, the more difficult it becomes to keep misconceptions (and misquotes) from spreading. In this sense, Bonhoeffer's very popularity has added momentum to populist versions of his life and legacy.

Given this situation, one would expect that conflicting, even contradictory, claims on Bonhoeffer would be a typical feature of his American reception. Indeed, such interpretive conflicts have become more and more common over the past decade. On the question of Bonhoeffer's role in the anti-Hitler resistance, for instance, a 2013 book titled *Bonhoeffer the Assassin?* attacked the "myth" that Bonhoeffer supported or was involved in any plot to assassinate Hitler. Yet in 2016, when Patricia McCormick recounted the story of Bonhoeffer's life for young adults, her book's title was *The Plot to Kill Hitler.* Similarly, Eric Metaxas's 2010 biography of Bonhoeffer claims in its subtitle that Bonhoeffer was a "righteous gentile"; however, the institution responsible for bestowing this designation, Yad Vashem in Jerusalem, has repeatedly denied that Bonhoeffer is deserving of the honor. And then there is the curious fact that in 2015, as conservative activists were using Bonhoeffer to rally resistance to same-sex marriage, a few scholars were arguing that Bonhoeffer himself may have been gay.

In this confusing morass of assertions and counterassertions, one is tempted to exclaim in exasperation: "Who is Bonhoeffer, anyway?" This book does not answer that question, but it attempts to shed light on some others, perhaps equally intriguing: Who do we *need* Bonhoeffer to be? And how is this need affected by the way "we" define ourselves and the threats we face? I hope the descriptions of the "battle for Bonhoeffer" in the pages that follow will illuminate these important questions.

CHAPTER TWO

Rorschach Test: American Bonhoeffers from Cox to Koehn

IN 1964 HARVEY COX likened disparate interpretations of Bonhoeffer to the results of a widely implemented Rorschach test. About the same time, another observer complained that not only was Bonhoeffer enlisted in support of one side of many questions, but he was frequently claimed by both sides. Half a century later, the range of interpretations applied to Bonhoeffer's life and thought has only expanded.[1]

This fact was brought home to me several years ago as I perused the religion section of a local bookstore. Two of the books I happened to open were *A New Christianity for a New World*, by John Shelby Spong, and *Jesus Freaks*, "stories of those who stood for Jesus," by the Christian rap group DC Talk. While it is difficult to imagine texts further apart on the spectrum of American Christian culture, Bonhoeffer was the point at which they overlapped: Spong's book began with an epigraph from Bonhoeffer's *Letters and Papers from Prison*, while *Jesus Freaks* included several references to the German martyr.[2]

Cox's observation that perceptions of Bonhoeffer represent a projective measure of viewers' concerns is accurate in another sense as well. As with interpretations of Rorschach's ink blots, responses to Bonhoeffer cluster in ways that reflect various "types." Just so, the bewildering diversity of interpretations applied to Bonhoeffer coalesce into distinguishable, though largely conflicting, portraits. Having described these portraits in *The Bonhoeffer Phenomenon* and *The Bonhoeffer Legacy*, I offer in this chapter an updated description of the liberal Bonhoeffer (or "Critical Patriot"), the post-Holocaust Bonhoeffer (or "Righteous Gentile"), and the universal Bonhoeffer (or "Moral Hero"). The evangelical Bonhoeffer will be explored in depth in the next chapter.[3]

Critical Patriot

For several decades Bonhoeffer has been something of a hero among American liberal Protestants, many of whom regard him as a model for Christians who wish to maintain a critical stance toward their own nation. In fact, the practice of utilizing Bonhoeffer in sustained critiques of the American government goes back at least to 1970, when Daniel Berrigan, SJ, went underground to elude the FBI after he destroyed military draft records to protest the Vietnam War.

In a published "review" of Eberhard Bethge's biography of Bonhoeffer, which Berrigan was reading while on the lam, the Jesuit fugitive made it plain that he viewed his antigovernment activism through the lens of Bonhoeffer's life. "I begin these notes on 9 April 1970," he wrote, having become a "fugitive from injustice" for disobeying a federal court order to begin a three-year sentence for destroying draft files. Berrigan noted the significance of the fact that it was "the twenty-fifth anniversary of the death of Dietrich Bonhoeffer in Flossenbürg prison for resistance to Hitler." To emphasize the connection between Bonhoeffer's struggle and his own, Berrigan referred to the Vietnam War as "a parable in its genocidal character to Hitler's war and his near extinction of the German Jews."[4]

In 1971 theologian Robert McAfee Brown offered a more systematic application of Bonhoeffer's legacy to the situation of the American church during a time of war. For Brown, Bonhoeffer's story took on new meaning as he came to believe that churchmen must be willing to oppose the evil policies of evil governments, including their own. "I have tried to resist making facile comparisons between Nazi Germany and the United States," Brown wrote, "but as the Vietnam War has mounted in intensity, the Bonhoeffer experience has seemed more and more relevant to the American experience."[5]

The image of Bonhoeffer as "critical patriot" received considerable elaboration during the 1980s, as American political culture shifted decidedly to the right. In *Liberating Faith: Bonhoeffer's Message for Today* (1984), Geffrey B. Kelly claimed that for Bonhoeffer the church fulfilled its calling only when it existed for others, even if this meant unflinchingly accepting "the 'death' of its present forms and the denial of some of its less-than-central aims." In *Dietrich Bonhoeffer—His Significance for North Americans* (1990), Larry Rasmussen decried the Reagan-Bush era's co-optation of "Judeo-Christian values" as a way to legitimate America as "a righteous empire in a world read largely in Manichean terms." According to Rasmussen, Bonhoeffer's contribution to North American Christianity was to help it "envision and embody a community of the cross with an ethic of imitation, or participation, as the church's societal vocation and presence."[6]

Concerned that Bonhoeffer's involvement in a political conspiracy had led Americans to assume that he would have approved opposition to Soviet totalitarianism by any means, G. Clarke Chapman in 1988 denied that the Soviet bloc presented a credible parallel with Nazi Germany and asserted that a clearer analogy with the fascist ideology Bonhoeffer opposed could be found in America's "brew of Messianic nationalism, injured innocence, and crusading confidence." The segment of Bonhoeffer's life most nearly matching "our situation" in the late 1980s, Chapman wrote, is not the violence-justifying Bonhoeffer of the conspiracy against Hitler but the "peacemaking" Bonhoeffer of the early 1930s. In Chapman's view, late 1980s America resembled Bonhoeffer's world not so much in its resistance to "godless communism" as in its embrace of nuclearism—an idolatry Chapman claimed was comparable with Nazism.[7]

During the Clinton era, Geffrey Kelly utilized Bonhoefferian insights to expose the "idolatries" underlying the Republican revolution of 1994. Among these, Kelly identified the worship of material prosperity, consumerism, callous disregard for the less fortunate, and the cult of violence associated with "national security." Bonhoeffer's theology represents a "prophetic critique" of such idolatrous behavior, Kelly maintained, precisely because mid-1990s America had so much in common with Hitler's Germany.[8]

"Ecumenical patriot" is the term coined by Larry Rasmussen to describe Bonhoeffer's commitment to Christ that transcended national allegiance. Through his involvement in the international ecumenical movement, Rasmussen contended, Bonhoeffer embodied this critical patriotism by "subordinat[ing] his national citizenship to membership in the transnational church." "What made Dietrich different than most of his countrymen," he noted, was his wide experience abroad and his habit of exploring "what were for him the margins in order to see the center from the edges and, if need be, to relocate his viewpoint."[9]

This survey of the liberal Bonhoeffer in America is far from complete, emphasizing as it does appeals to the theologian prior to the "war on terror," which are more fully explored in a subsequent chapter. But it indicates how tempting it has been for Americans, even prior to the degradation of public discourse in the Internet age, to combine considerations of Bonhoeffer's "critical patriotism" with allegations of America's resemblance to Nazi Germany.

Righteous Gentile

"When I give a public talk," Doris Bergen wrote in 2013, "the questions I am most often asked are about Dietrich Bonhoeffer and Pius XII," whom many consider "the opposite poles of Christian involvement with Nazism: success and failure, or put another way, martyrdom and silence." With this observation Bergen describes what for many is an essential aspect of Bonhoeffer's contemporary relevance—his identity as a Christian who understood the threat Hitler posed for Jews and vowed to protect them at the cost of his own life.[10]

Perceptions of Bonhoeffer as a crusader for Jewish rights have developed slowly in response to trends in Bonhoeffer scholarship and wider cultural tendencies. Just as consciousness of "the Holocaust" is a post-1960s cultural phenomenon, the image of Bonhoeffer as an advocate for Jews came into focus gradually beginning in the mid-1970s. For instance, while the proceedings of the inaugural Scholars Conference on the German Church Struggle and the Holocaust in 1970 included dozens of references to Bonhoeffer, none mentioned his relationship with Jews. By 1990, however, the *Encyclopedia of the Holocaust* declared that Bonhoeffer's "theological influence has been significantly instrumental in the post-Holocaust rethinking of Christian relationships with the Jewish people."[11]

This burgeoning interest in "Bonhoeffer and the Jews" was influenced, of course, by Christian efforts to grapple with the beliefs and attitudes that had made the Holocaust possible. These efforts, in turn, influenced the historiography of the German Church Struggle, which gradually overcame a "tendency to hagiography" in its exploration of the less heroic aspects of the church's career under Nazism. As scholars explored this dark chapter in church history, German Protestants who spoke up on Jews' behalf stood out. Evidence for judging Bonhoeffer's relationship with Jews was supplied by Eberhard Bethge's definitive biography, published in English in 1970, which Karl Barth credited with bringing to light Bonhoeffer's role as "the first and almost the only one to face and tackle the Jewish question so centrally and energetically."[12]

These scholarly developments illuminated the ways Bonhoeffer stood apart from his coreligionists, including leaders in the Confessing Church, by recognizing that the suffering of Nazism's victims, whether or not they were members of the church, must be of concern for Christians. But exploration of Bonhoeffer's career under Hitler also revealed troubling data, particularly in his essay "The Church and the Jewish Question" (1933). In addition to its bold assertion that Christians have an unconditional obligation to aid victims of the state, the essay gave credence to the ancient view that "the 'chosen people,' which hung the Redeemer of the world on the cross, must endure the curse of its action in long-drawn-out suffering." Furthermore, in this essay and another from September 1933 titled "Theses on the Aryan Paragraph in the Church," Bonhoeffer argued that a church that excludes Jewish Christians effectively becomes "a Jewish Christian church." In 1933, referring to one's ecclesiastical opponents as "Jewish Christians" was a clever rhetorical strategy, but it did nothing to protect German Jews.[13]

Despite this evidence of reflexive anti-Judaism in Bonhoeffer's initial response to Nazism and its Christian enablers, many scholars have followed Bethge in plotting a trajectory of growth in Bonhoeffer's perceptions of Jews, with a turning point coming around the time of *Kristallnacht* in November 1938. Bethge, in fact, came to portray Bonhoeffer as a post-Holocaust bridge between Christians and Jews and cited him as inspiration for his own involvement in efforts at reconciliation. During the 1980s and '90s, as the enormity of the Holocaust's challenge to the church became his "special passion," Bethge personally embodied the link between Bonhoeffer's legacy and Christian-Jewish rapprochement.[14]

Unfortunately, since the 1980s the image of Bonhoeffer as a friend of Jews and instinctive philo-Semite has encountered a stubborn rebuttal in the determinations of Yad Vashem: The World Holocaust Remembrance Center in Jerusalem. This is the organization responsible for recognizing men and women who rescued Jews from the Nazis and their collaborators as "righteous among the nations." After a process of rigorous vetting, these "righteous gentiles" are honored for their active involvement in saving Jews, at mortal risk to themselves and without material compensation. But on several occasions Yad Vashem has determined that Bonhoeffer does not belong among this select group of non-Jews.[15]

The case for Bonhoeffer's recognition as a "righteous gentile" focuses on his efforts in support of "Operation-7," a scheme devised by Bonhoeffer's brother-in-law Hans von Dohnányi and *Abwehr* admiral Wilhelm Canaris to supply fourteen German Jews (most of them Christian converts) with false papers and spirit them across the border to neutral Switzerland during August and September of 1942. Bonhoeffer aided the operation mainly by calling on his ecumenical contacts to arrange visas and sponsors for the rescuees.

In 1998 efforts to secure Bonhoeffer's recognition as a "righteous gentile" were bolstered by an affidavit from an "Operation-7" rescuee and a newly found copy of an indictment charging Bonhoeffer with trying to assist an imprisoned Jewish professor. Nevertheless, Yad Vashem concluded that Bonhoeffer did not qualify as a "righteous gentile" because there was no evidence of his personal involvement in assisting Jews at considerable personal risk or of his open defiance and condemnation of Nazi anti-Jewish policies; nor was there any "direct linkage," the organization concluded, between his arrest and his stance on the Jewish issue. Putting the matter succinctly, Mordecai Paldiel, director of the Yad Vashem's Righteous Among the Nations program, told a reporter that Bonhoeffer was not among the "non-Jews who specifically addressed themselves to the Jewish issue, and risked their lives in the attempt to aid Jews."[16]

Stinging as these statements have been for Bonhoeffer's admirers, Yad Vashem's verdict has not interfered with popular perceptions of Bonhoeffer as a friend of Jews whose early debt to theological anti-Judaism was transcended in his later sacrificial acts. This is partly because, as Doris Bergen suggests, for many Christians Bonhoeffer embodies a compelling model of heroic behavior during the dark days of the church's capitulation to Nazism. Although images of Bonhoeffer as someone who "struggled passionately on behalf of . . . Jews" persist even in scholarly works, they are more likely to be found in popular accounts of his life. The notion that Bonhoeffer "gave his life to save Jewish people" is particularly common in collections of Christian "hero stories" and works of historical fiction. An example of the former is *Hero Tales: A Family Treasury of True Stories from the Lives of Christian Heroes*, in which authors Dave and Neta Jackson relate the story of "Operation-7" in a way that suggests Bonhoeffer himself drove threatened Jews across the Swiss border.[17]

The most prominent example of historical fiction that highlights Bonhoeffer's identity as a friend of Jews is Michael Phillips's *The Eleventh Hour*. In 1937 Baron Heinrich von Dortmann, who has been auditing Bonhoeffer's lectures on the Sermon on the Mount at Finkenwalde, tells his wife that the young theologian "has been flying in the Nazis' face for years, making enemies with his bold pro-Jewish sentiments and his pronouncements to the church to awaken from its complacency." Later in the novel Bonhoeffer confides to von Dortmann that he has "prayed and prayed for years about what should be our response as Christians" to the Nazis and has concluded that "the Nazi evil against the Jews is of such magnitude that bringing force against it may be necessary."[18]

Another fictionalized account of Bonhoeffer's deeply felt affinity for German Jews appears in Michael Van Dyke's *Dietrich Bonhoeffer: Opponent of the Nazi Regime.* After naively asking the head of Tübingen University's Jewish student group if he would like to join his fraternity, Bonhoeffer is shocked to learn that the "Hedgehogs" do not accept Jews. Considering the charge that his fellow Hedgehogs are "truly haters of Jews," he recalls fraternity songs with lines celebrating "Germany, pure and strong" and "the blood of Christian men." In a moment of stunned recognition, Bonhoeffer's entire world seems to be crashing down. "He closed his philosophy book," Van Dyke writes, "laid his head down upon it, and began to weep softly."[19]

These and other popular treatments of Bonhoeffer's life often overestimate not only Bonhoeffer's personal efforts in defense of Jews but also the Nazi government's involvement in Protestant ecclesiastical affairs and the extent of the confessors' resistance to Nazism. Typical exaggerations include mischaracterizations of the Church Struggle as "the persecution of the church by Hitler" and of the Confessing Church as a "resistance movement," suggestions that Bonhoeffer was present at the Barmen Synod at which the Confessing Church was born, and claims that the declaration drafted at Barmen clarified the "errors introduced into the church by the Nazis."[20]

A detailed portrait of Bonhoeffer as pro-Jewish crusader is elaborated in Denise Giardina's biographical novel *Saints and Villains*. The book's opening chapter, in fact, suggests that Bonhoeffer's aversion to anti-Semitism was virtually innate. When Dietrich and his twin sister, Sabine, are caught in a snowstorm in the Thüringer Wald, a woman who shelters the teenagers remarks that their hometown of Berlin contains "too many Jews." "Why do you say that? Do you know any Jews?" Dietrich testily responds. The incident dramatizes Bonhoeffer's natural inclination to champion Germany's Jews and foreshadows his inevitable collision with Nazi anti-Jewish policies. Dietrich's affinity for things Jewish is underscored by Giardina when he falls in love with a Jewess named Elisabeth Hildebrandt.[21]

In subsequent passages of *Saints and Villains*, Bonhoeffer's sympathy for Jews is repeatedly confirmed. His parishioners describe him as "obsessed with the Jewish Question"; he wanders through Berlin's Jewish district in search of Elisabeth, whom he later helps escape from Germany; he pleads with his coconspirators to do something for the Jews (until his brother-in-law reminds him that "the saving of Jews is not your assignment"); he daydreams of pulling a trainload of Jews to freedom; and Schindler-like, he bribes an SS official in an effort to save Elisabeth's husband from deportation. Then, in the book's final scene, while in transit to his own execution site, Bonhoeffer passes a caravan of Jews on a death march "from Auschwitz and Treblinka," watching "as the scarecrow men, women, and children make their painful way, driven by armed guards like draft horses ready to die in the traces." "'The absent ones,' Dietrich says. And thinks he is better off on the road with them." Artificial though this scene is, in highlighting Dietrich's longing to identify and suffer with Jewish victims of the Third Reich, it is faithful to the Bonhoeffer Giardina has portrayed in the previous 450 pages.[22]

Mary Glazener's *The Cup of Wrath* accentuates Bonhoeffer's response to anti-Jewish persecution through references to documented history (such as Bonhoeffer's opposition to his church's adoption of the Aryan clause, his reaction to *Kristallnacht*, and his role in "Operation-7"), as well as fabricated episodes in which Bonhoeffer comes to the aid of vulnerable Jewish men. In one such scene, Dietrich and his cousin are walking the streets of Berlin when two SA men forcibly remove a Jew from an "Aryan only" bench. As the Brown Shirts prepare to give the offending "non-Aryan" a thrashing, Bonhoeffer moves into action and pretends the man is a friend he is late in meeting. With tears in his eyes, the Jew responds, "Thank you. Thank you very much. Those men—there's no telling . . ."[23]

Each of these American authors highlights Bonhoeffer's camaraderie with and empathy for threatened Jews, sentiments they believe launched him on a path of political resistance. They reassure us that, at least with regard to the issue of anti-Semitism, Bonhoeffer's heart and mind were in the right place from the beginning. Thus, despite scholars' insistence on exploring the anti-Jewish themes in Bonhoeffer's writings and Yad Vashem's refusal to recognize Bonhoeffer as a "righteous gentile," images of the pastor-theologian as someone who risked his life to protect Jews have become an enduring feature of Bonhoeffer's American reception.

As we will see, this portrait of Bonhoeffer as "righteous gentile" endures in part because Americans who become convinced that their culture or government has become Nazi-like are instinctively drawn to Bonhoeffer's anti-Nazi credentials. And nothing says "anti-Nazi" like a robust and sacrificial defense of German Jews.

Moral Hero

As awareness of Bonhoeffer's story pervades American society, his legacy is more likely to be construed in ecumenical, interfaith, and even nonreligious terms. The commanding image in Bonhoeffer's portrait as nonsectarian "moral hero" is the opponent of Nazism whose unwavering commitment to human dignity places him in prison for "his beliefs."

A key aspect of this universalizing portrait is Bonhoeffer's expansive spirituality. In *The Cost of Moral Leadership*, the first book-length study of Bonhoeffer's spirituality, authors Geffrey B. Kelly and F. Burton Nelson carefully illumine the contours of the theologian's religious experience while remaining sensitive to the concerns of spiritual seekers. For readers likely to think of themselves as more spiritual than religious, Kelly and Nelson emphasize that Bonhoeffer never equated "religion with all its institutional structures and laws" with faith as God's gift, and even had a habit of annoying the German ecclesiastical establishment.[24]

Remarkably, this depiction of Bonhoeffer's spiritual life by two devout Christians is strikingly similar to the sketch drawn by the agnostic psychiatrist Robert Coles, who has explored Bonhoeffer's moral legacy in two books—*Dietrich Bonhoeffer* (part of Orbis Books' Spiritual Masters) and *Lives of Moral Leadership: Men and Women Who Have Made a Difference.* In the former study the psychiatrist claims that the essence of Bonhoeffer's spiritual legacy is not in his words or books but "in the way he spent his time on this earth." Bonhoeffer's "spiritual gift to us," in other words, is "his life." Similarly, in *Lives of Moral Leadership* Coles depicts Bonhoeffer as a "compelling moral and spiritual leader" whose life became an "extended moral vigil."[25]

Efforts to present Bonhoeffer as a moral hero have often implied that he transcended a parochial background to shed religious exclusivism. For instance, James W. Fowler's *Stages of Faith*, the seminal work in the field of "faith development," presents Bonhoeffer as an example of the highest of six stages, which he calls "universalizing faith." Universalizers, according to Fowler, "create zones of liberation from the social, political, economic and ideological shackles we place

. . . on human futurity" and "are often experienced as subversive of . . . structures (including religious structures)." In addition to Bonhoeffer, Fowler's candidates for stage-six faith are Gandhi, Martin Luther King Jr., Mother Teresa, Dag Hammarskjöld, Abraham Heschel, and Thomas Merton.[26]

In more popular venues, Bonhoeffer's universal appeal is illuminated by portraying him as someone who by clinging to a "core set of beliefs" became a voice of clarity amid "the moral confusion of our time." Even scholars who are quite aware of Bonhoeffer's theological commitments have emphasized the universal dimensions of his legacy. In *What Freedom? The Persistent Challenge of Dietrich Bonhoeffer*, Keith W. Clements eloquently expresses Bonhoeffer's attraction "at the simply human level." The German pastor-theologian's story, Clements writes, "is a deeply stirring saga, whose appeal will not be confined to the Christian, or to those who look to him as a theological resource. One so socially privileged, so culturally rich, so gifted intellectually, who has every opportunity to enjoy what he has and to exploit it for his own fulfillment, yet who chooses to live without privileges, accepting risks and making ventures for justice at a time when so many compromised themselves—there is a universal appeal in this."

Clements concludes that because Bonhoeffer belongs "not first to church history or to the Christian camp but to the human race," he stands among those who represent "the further possibilities of the human spirit."[27] These "further possibilities" have drawn attention even from notorious atheists. In *God Is Not Great: How Religion Poisons Everything* (2009), Christopher Hitchens claims Bonhoeffer for humanity by arguing that in resisting the Nazis he "acted in accordance only with the dictates of conscience." This was all that was left to him, according to Hitchens, since by the end of his life Bonhoeffer's faith had "mutated into an admirable but nebulous humanism." Anyone with even a cursory knowledge of Bonhoeffer knows this interpretation is implausible. But it highlights the persistent attraction of the pastor-theologian's legacy in a post-Christian world, even among archenemies of religious faith.[28]

A new chapter in the story of Bonhoeffer's reception as a universal moral hero was recently written by Nancy Koehn, a historian at Harvard Business School, in her book *Forged in Crisis: The Power of Courageous Leadership in Turbulent Times* (2017). Dedicated to exploring "ordinary people doing extraordinary things," Koehn offers in-depth studies of five consummate leaders—Abraham Lincoln, Frederick Douglass, Dietrich Bonhoeffer, scientist Rachel Carson, and explorer Ernest Shackleton. Maintaining that these leaders were made, not born, Koehn claims that leadership development is a self-conscious project undertaken by men and women who "intentionally choose to make something better of who they were."[29]

Koehn devotes about eighty pages to narrating Bonhoeffer's "leadership journey" and deducing its lessons. Although she reveals an impressive grasp of the political and theological contexts in which Bonhoeffer lived and worked, her intended audience is interested less in twentieth-century theology than in contemporary world problems. As she recites the crucial junctures in Bonhoeffer's adult life, Koehn draws lessons for these would-be leaders, writing that Bonhoeffer's decision to return to Germany in 1939 teaches us that "no matter the mission—whether it be fighting injustice, starting a company, or teaching a classroom of fifth graders—leaders have to put a stake in the ground acknowledging what they're doing and why."[30]

Koehn locates a key to Bonhoeffer's talent for leadership in his personal habits. Like others in her study, Bonhoeffer used time alone "to detach himself from a particular moment and survey the larger scene from different angles." Just so, contemporary leaders must rely on self-discipline to direct their attention and energy "toward what really matters." Following a description of Bonhoeffer's role as director of the illegal seminary at Finkenwalde, Koehn notes that "the ability to develop and sustain an effective community is a critical skill for today's leaders." People followed Bonhoeffer, she writes, in part because of "his ability to listen well and take others seriously on their own terms."[31]

Koehn also notes that despite a period of depression precipitated by his arrest and imprisonment, Bonhoeffer's resolution to embrace life, come what may, highlights the importance of "manag[ing] one's emotions during times of turbulence." In some ways, Koehn concludes, Bonhoeffer's life contains leadership lessons without parallel:

> Of the five people in this book, no one else so clearly exemplifies the power of Mahatma Gandhi's riveting claim "My life is my message." Bonhoeffer's leadership—of those who knew him during his life and the millions of people who have encountered that life after it ended—has consisted of much more than his external achievements. It has been felt in how he made his way throughout the world: the mission he undertook, the choices he made, the courage he summoned, and the respect that he accorded himself, others, and goodness in the midst of moral ambivalence and inversion.[32]

For our purposes, the importance of *Forged in Crisis* lies not in any specific observations on Bonhoeffer's leadership style but in Koehn's remarkable ability to shape descriptions of Bonhoeffer's life and thought without relying on religious or theological language. What those wishing to "craft lives of purpose, dignity and impact" should expect to find in Bonhoeffer, according to Koehn, is not a faithful witness to the Christ who suffers in a broken world but someone who is able to find "goodness in the midst of moral ambivalence."[33]

Like other attempts to universalize Bonhoeffer's legacy, Koehn seeks to broaden his appeal through the language of sacrifice, morality, spirituality, and mature faith, idioms ideal for communicating a humanistic message that eschews sectarian concerns.

EACH OF THE PORTRAITS of Bonhoeffer explored in this chapter prepares us to understand how the German pastor-theologian has figured in American public discourse since 9/11 (the subject of part 2). In the critical patriot we see the tendency of interpreters to view Bonhoeffer as an internal critic of an unpopular government. In the righteous gentile we encounter the propensity to view Bonhoeffer as a man of principle willing to risk his life to defend the innocent, as well as the inclination to ignore inconvenient aspects of his legacy. In the moral hero we catch a glimpse of Bonhoeffer's appeal across and beyond traditional religious boundaries. In the following chapter we turn to a portrait of Bonhoeffer that is crucial to understanding his American reception—his enduring popularity among evangelicals.

CHAPTER THREE

Gradual Embrace: The Evangelical Bonhoeffer before Metaxas

THE EMERGENCE OF THE POPULIST Bonhoeffer during the Bush and Obama years, to which we will turn shortly, is rooted in long-standing American portrayals of the pastor-theologian, including the critical patriot, the righteous gentile, and the moral hero. More important than any of these for understanding the battle for Bonhoeffer in the twenty-first century, however, is the evangelical Bonhoeffer, which developed gradually beginning in the 1970s before receiving a tremendous boon with the publication of Eric Metaxas's 2010 biography, *Bonhoeffer: Pastor, Martyr, Prophet, Spy.*

Early Reservations

In an overview of Bonhoeffer's reception among evangelicals, Timothy Larsen describes the current environment as one of "euphoric Bonhoeffer-mania." But such an assessment makes it easy to forget that the evangelical romance with Bonhoeffer was hardly love at first sight. Early relationship deal-breakers ranged from Bonhoeffer's smoking habit to concerns about his prison theology. As a result, until recently evangelical attitudes have alternated between absolute rejection and cautious embrace, with the default position something akin to wary appreciation.[1]

Larsen identifies the earliest evangelical engagement with Bonhoeffer in 1960, when Anglican bishop Stephen C. Neill wrote about

"Dietrich Bonhoeffer and worldly Christianity" in his book *Brothers of the Faith.* "Far from being embarrassed or perplexed by the controversial passages in the Letters," Larsen writes, Neill "quotes them with relish." But the tone set by Neill would not be adopted in other early evangelical assessments of Bonhoeffer's theology. More typical was Leon Morris, whose book *The Abolition of Religion: A Study in Religionless Christianity* was published by InterVarsity Press in 1964. Morris expressed appreciation for some of Bonhoeffer's writings but was less than enthusiastic about the theological musings in his prison letters. The concept of "religionless Christianity," for instance, left him "perplexed and perturbed" because Morris assumed Bonhoeffer was calling for an abandonment of corporate worship and other distinctive Christian practices.[2]

This evangelical concern with Bonhoeffer's prison letters reflects the use to which they were being put during the 1960s by secularizing theologians like James A. T. Robinson, William Hamilton, and Paul van Buren. As concepts such as "Christian atheism" and the "death of God" came to be associated with Bonhoeffer, an understandable ambivalence toward his theology took root among American evangelicals. This ambivalence was reflected in the pages of magazines like *Christianity Today* and *Moody Monthly*, which during the mid-1960s published articles on Bonhoeffer's theology with titles like "Religionless Christianity: Is It a New Form of Gnosticism?" and "The Old 'New Worldliness,'" which expressed the concern that the acceptance of "worldliness" meant ignoring Christ's call to holy living.[3]

Despite these lingering concerns, popular appreciation of Bonhoeffer's brave stance against Nazism steadily grew among American Christians, including evangelicals. Awareness of this phenomenon has led some evangelical scholars to remind their coreligionists of the dangers of an uncritical embrace of Bonhoeffer. For instance, as Bonhoeffer's evangelical star was just beginning to rise in 1972, Cornelius Van Til argued that, despite his personal bravery, Bonhoeffer's theology was unorthodox and did not honor Christ. Although such warnings have done little to dampen enthusiasm for Bonhoeffer among the ranks of American evangelicals, they continue to be sounded. In fact, Van Til's thoroughgoing rejection of Bonhoeffer's evangelical credentials was reiterated twenty-five years later by historian Richard Weikart, who in *The Myth of Dietrich Bonhoeffer: Is His Theology Evangelical?* (1997) assailed evangelicals' "uncritical endorsement" of Bonhoeffer by attempting to demonstrate the fundamental incompatibility of his thought with Christian orthodoxy.[4]

Among the problems cited by Weikart is Bonhoeffer's view of Scripture. Although nothing about Bonhoeffer appeals to evangelicals like his emphasis on scriptural authority, Weikart claims that many are unaware that Bonhoeffer accepted the validity of "liberal biblical criticism" and even welcomed the works of Rudolf Bultmann. According to Weikart, Bonhoeffer also was deeply influenced by liberal and neo-orthodox theology and never completely forsook Barthianism. Neither did he undergo the sort of personal conversion familiar to evangelicals, according to Weikart. And although conservative Christians delight in the pro-life stance Bonhoeffer espoused in *Ethics*, Weikart reminds them that his positions on euthanasia, abortion, and suicide "must be seen as concrete commands for the present situation, not as objective norms that can be applied universally."[5]

According to Weikart, because Bonhoeffer's distance from contemporary evangelicalism is a matter of theological substance rather than style, evangelicals' assumption that Bonhoeffer shared their deepest commitments is a dangerous misconception. For this reason he does not recommend Bonhoeffer's books even for edification, since his theology shares "elements of deception common in the main currents of twentieth-century theology."[6]

Bonhoeffer's Triumph in the Evangelical Heart

Despite some traces of lingering opposition, by the end of the 1990s Bonhoeffer had become almost universally admired by American evangelicals. Larsen claims, in fact, that today Bonhoeffer is for evangelicals the most widely cited and respected theologian, not only of the twentieth century, but since the period of the Reformation. While this point is arguable, there is certainly evidence to support it.

For instance, at the end of the 1990s the editors of *Christian History* magazine (published by Christianity Today, Inc.) asked readers and historians to list the five most influential Christians of the twentieth century, as well as the five Christians who had been most influential for them. When the results were published in the magazine's winter 2000 edition, Bonhoeffer ranked tenth among both historians and general readers on the "most influential" list, and fifth on each of the most "personally influential" lists. Bonhoeffer was not only the highest ranked theologian, but was among just a handful of figures who finished in the top ten in all four categories. The others—Billy Graham, C. S. Lewis, Mother Teresa, Martin Luther King Jr., and Francis Schaeffer—are all evangelists, activists, or apologists.[7]

A further indication of Bonhoeffer's high stature among American evangelicals is his regular appearance in the sorts of "inspirational" literature marketed to conservative Christians. For instance, Bonhoeffer is featured in several biography series distributed by evangelical publishers, including *Dietrich Bonhoeffer: The Life and Martyrdom of a Great Man Who Counted the Cost of Discipleship* in Bethany House's Men of Faith series, *Dietrich Bonhoeffer: Opponent of the Nazi Regime* in Barbour's Heroes of the Faith series, and *Dietrich Bonhoeffer: In the Midst of Wickedness* in Youth with a Mission's Christian Heroes: Then & Now series.[8]

In 1991 *Christian History* devoted an entire issue to Bonhoeffer. And in 1997 Focus on the Family Radio Theatre produced *Bonhoeffer: The Cost of Freedom*. Shaped to appeal to the political and religious sensibilities of the evangelical community, this Peabody Award–winning drama communicates Bonhoeffer's significance in a peculiar American idiom: "Faith. Freedom. Individual liberties. We often take them for granted . . . until they're taken away from us," reads the play's promotional literature.[9]

In the early 1990s Bonhoeffer also found a home in the genre of "Christian fiction" when Michael Phillips included him in *The Eleventh Hour*, the first volume in his Secret of the Rose series. Phillips stated that he had made Bonhoeffer a character in his novel in order "to honor him and give him what I consider his rightful stature in the history of European evangelicalism in this century." A second work of Christian fiction in which Bonhoeffer plays a role arrived in 2008 with Suzanne Woods Fisher's *Copper Fire*.[10]

How does one explain Bonhoeffer's remarkable popularity and influence among American evangelicals? Larsen suggests that part of the answer is evangelicals' tendency to view Bonhoeffer as a clergyman (as opposed to a theologian), noting that when evangelical leaders refer to Bonhoeffer, "pastor" is often the descriptor of choice. According to Larsen, evangelicals are likely to respect those engaged in "the work of the ministry" over professional theologians who presumably have "little awareness of or concern for what their [theories'] effect might be on the church and the faithful." As an evangelical biographer puts it, Bonhoeffer "did not just talk about theology; he lived it."[11]

A similar observation comes from Mark DeVine, who notes how Bonhoeffer's approach to the Bible resonates with American evangelicals. Eschewing the "pretentious, unbelieving, and eventually abortive higher-critical abuse of the biblical text," DeVine writes, Bonhoeffer saw the Bible as God's word to individual Christians and thus the engine of personal discipleship. DeVine argues that although Bonhoeffer was not himself an evangelical, in his submission to the Scriptures he seems very familiar to those who are. "While liberal theologians debated the question of what it means that the Bible is the word of God," DeVine concludes, "Dietrich Bonhoeffer acted on this simple but genuine conviction."[12]

Another explanation for evangelicals' admiration of Bonhoeffer takes into account his identity as "martyr," a term that acknowledges his willingness to die rather than forsake his faith. Even his fiercest evangelical opponents, Larsen writes, are impressed by Bonhoeffer's willingness to endure "the cost of discipleship." This phrase, of course, indicates the special place in the evangelical mind occupied by *The Cost of Discipleship*, whose English title resonates with the evangelical notion that Christianity without active "discipleship" is tepid and ineffectual, a safe haven for those Bonhoeffer calls "pseudo-Christians."[13]

Its honored place in the annals of evangelical literature was confirmed when the book, often referred to by evangelicals simply as *Cost*, was named one of the ten "best devotional books of all time" by the *Christian Reader* and placed second behind C. S. Lewis's *Mere Christianity* on *Christianity Today*'s list of "100 books that had a significant effect on Christians in the twentieth century." Evangelically themed study guides to accompany *The Cost of Discipleship* are published as part of InterVarsity's Christian Classics Bible Studies and Holman's Shepherd's Notes on Christian Classics.[14]

A further point of connection for evangelicals is Bonhoeffer's "conversion," the deeply felt experience of personal reintegration he underwent sometime in the early 1930s. This experience assumes great importance in evangelical accounts of Bonhoeffer's life, with some biographers describing a "conversion experience . . . as deep as St. Augustine's or Charles Wesley's." When interpreted as the transition from "nominal" Christianity to a personal faith rooted in inner experience, Bonhoeffer's "great liberation" reminds evangelicals that, then as now, becoming a theologian doesn't necessitate one being a Christian.[15]

Not to be overlooked are the devotional and homiletical qualities of much of Bonhoeffer's writing, which resonate with evangelical piety and are accentuated in the increasingly popular "gift" editions of his sermons, poems, and reflections on Scripture. Finally, Bonhoeffer's description of Christian community and the practices that sustain it in *Life Together* has led many evangelicals to regard this book as one of the "classics of modern Christian literature." As Richard Weikart observes, "Just as *The Cost of Discipleship* has stirred the interest of evangelicals concerned with spiritual impoverishment of individual Christians . . . *Life Together* has appealed to those concerned with the spiritual destitution of the church as a community."[16]

Whatever the reasons for Bonhoeffer's enduring appeal among American evangelicals, portrayals arising from the evangelical world have naturally imagined him as reflecting evangelical sensibilities and concerns. But this does not mean conservative Christians are in agreement on Bonhoeffer's significance for American evangelical life.

A Multifaceted Bonhoeffer

In fact, it is misleading to speak of *the* evangelical Bonhoeffer, as images of the pastor-theologian embraced by those calling themselves evangelicals are no more monolithic than American evangelicalism itself. Thus it will be helpful to explore in more detail some of the ways

Bonhoeffer functions among evangelicals—as Christian hero, culture warrior, ecclesiological guide, and privileged critic.

Bonhoeffer the Christian Hero

The most prevalent and broadly influential evangelical constructions of Bonhoeffer are transmitted in narrations of his heroic life. These come in two varieties—contributions to the previously noted book series honoring heroes of the faith (in which Bonhoeffer is often the only modern theologian) and works of "Christian fiction."

Books in the second category represent a distinctively evangelical contribution to Bonhoeffer's American reception. Michael Phillips's *The Eleventh Hour* (1993), discussed in detail in the previous chapter, places the historical Bonhoeffer in an evangelical narrative where he plays the hero's mentor and soul mate. This casting reflects Phillips's conviction "that the saga of brave and committed evangelical believers in Germany during the Second World War cannot in an accurate way be told without the large, looming presence of Dietrich Bonhoeffer playing a pivotal role."[17]

In Suzanne Woods Fisher's *Copper Fire* (2008), a book probably best described as an evangelical romance novel, the main character is a half-Jewish German woman named Annika who volunteers to work as a courier for the anti-Nazi resistance after her father is murdered. Annika's link to the German resistance is her "friend and mentor" Dietrich Bonhoeffer, who, when members of their resistance cell are in danger, helps Annika emigrate by transporting her to the Swiss border. Bonhoeffer has arranged refuge for Annika with Robert Gordon, an Arizona pastor he befriended when both were students at Union Theological Seminary in New York.

Annika eventually falls in love with Gordon, marries him, and takes on an American identity. But she must return to Germany to retrieve Elisabeth, her Jewish cousin who has survived Dachau. As Annika devotes herself to rehabilitating Elisabeth and tracking a Nazi war criminal, Gordon gathers information for a book on Bonhoeffer's life, most of it transmitted through Annika, who has maintained a correspondence with Dietrich's sister Sabine Leibholz. Since Bonhoeffer is responsible for bringing the book's heroine together with her husband, he naturally is the subject of many of their conversations. In both these examples of Christian-themed historical fiction, Bonhoeffer serves as the main character's spiritual inspiration, no doubt reflecting the role he plays in the lives of many American evangelicals.[18]

These works share with evangelical biographies of Bonhoeffer a presentation of the pastor-theologian in unmistakably heroic tones. Bonhoeffer's heroism is reflected not only in his words and actions but also in his rugged good looks and physical prowess. According to one biographer, Bonhoeffer "was large boned, muscular, and blond," with "strong looking shoulders and hands, and . . . steel blue determination in his eyes." Another tells us that he "had a muscular build . . . liked athletics . . . [and] enjoyed exercising in the bracing cold."[19]

Bonhoeffer the Culture Warrior

Another way Bonhoeffer has functioned among American evangelicals is as a soldier in the "culture war" that heated up in the 1990s. This is when evangelical leaders such as Charles Colson and James Dobson began to invoke Bonhoeffer as a model of risky discipleship at a time when some Christians were questioning the wisdom of active cultural engagement. Watching America move in what they regarded as a godless direction during the Clinton years, evangelicals like Colson and Dobson appealed to Bonhoeffer as a warning against cultural accommodation and a model for "taking back" American society.

For Colson, Bonhoeffer's emphasis on "costly grace" could remind "true Christians" that obedience to God requires a willingness to swim against the cultural mainstream. After the bitterly fought 2000 presidential election, Colson wondered how Christians might fare under a government "whose policies we sharply disagree with—even one whose positions we find morally offensive." Citing Bonhoeffer, he responded that while political leaders must be respected and prayed for, there are times when Christians are called to oppose unjust regimes. In fact, Colson declared, "civil disobedience must be chosen whenever civil magistrates frustrate our ability to obey God."[20]

The evangelical leader who has most consistently cited Bonhoeffer as a model for Christian cultural engagement is also arguably the most influential—James C. Dobson, founder and president of Focus on the Family. In a series of articles published between 1999 and 2002, Dobson offered Bonhoeffer's life as a case study in Christian activism. For instance, in a *Christianity Today* piece titled "The New Cost of Discipleship," Dobson addressed the claim that Christians waste their time and energy opposing things like abortion, homosexual marriage, pornography, and the assault on "traditional values." Citing Bonhoeffer's "failed activism," Dobson asked: "Since when did being outnumbered and underpowered justify silence in response to evil?" Instead of taking a stand against the Nazi regime and paying with his life, should Bonhoeffer have accommodated Hitler's henchmen just because he had no chance of winning?[21]

In the May 2000 edition of his *Focus on the Family Newsletter*, Dobson revisited the dark night of twentieth-century German history in search of lessons for the American present. Following a long quote from Bonhoeffer's *Ethics*, written "before he was hanged, naked, from a piano wire in 1945" (a description that would seem to apply to everything Bonhoeffer wrote), Dobson updated Bonhoeffer's famous confession of guilt on behalf of the German church: "Thirty-nine million babies have been killed by abortionists since 1973, to which many of our church leaders remained passive." Assessing the church's culpability in this tragedy, Dobson again echoed Bonhoeffer: "By her own silence, [the church] has rendered herself guilty because of her unwillingness to suffer for what she knows is right." With Bonhoeffer's example before his readers, Dobson reminded them that "the battle to save our culture" was not over.[22]

Bonhoeffer the Internal Critic

While Colson, Dobson, and others have been inspired by Bonhoeffer to assert Christian influence in the larger culture, spokesmen for the so-called evangelical Left have staked their own claim on Bonhoeffer's legacy, often in extended critiques of the American church and its cultural accommodations.

Among the authors to position Bonhoeffer as an internal critic of American evangelicalism are David P. Gushee and Glen Stassen, both of whom left Southern Baptist Seminary in the wake of that institution's hard turn to the right. Writing in *Sojourners* in 1994, Stassen, Gushee, and Michael Westmoreland-White offered Bonhoeffer's "incarnational discipleship" as a model of engaged evangelicalism for the 1990s. Blending Bonhoeffer's voice with those of Martin Luther King Jr. and Christian rescuers of Jews during the Holocaust, the authors offered a penetrating critique of American evangelicalism. In the process, they accused Southern Baptists and other evangelicals of a litany of sins, including reducing Jesus to "a personal savior and a name to be praised, without discipleship," becoming "addicted to secular ideologies of greed, self-indulgence, polite racism, patriarchal authoritarianism, militarism, and just plain apathy without compassion," confusing loyalty to the Bible with "an authoritarian ideology imported from secular politics," doing too little to combat racism, and construing patriotism "as uncritical allegiance to the nation and the government."[23]

In a *Christianity Today* essay commemorating the fiftieth anniversary of Bonhoeffer's death in 1995, Gushee further fleshed out what he saw as the German theologian's relevance for contemporary evangelicalism by focusing on one of its most "besetting sins"—the tendency to acculturate itself to the "American way of life." "How frequently we have confused being Christian with being American, loving nation with loving God," Gushee wrote. "How often we have mixed unjust and oppressive cultural norms like racism and indifference to injustice into this distasteful stew, calling it Christian." As part of his Bonhoeffer-inspired dissent against the default positions in evangelical social ethics, Gushee asked readers to consider with whom Bonhoeffer was calling them to stand in solidarity. Could it be immigrants? The unborn? Poor mothers and their children? Prisoners? With this list Gushee sought to unsettle the conscience of evangelical Christians, reminding them of Bonhoeffer's message that authentic Christianity can lead one "into principled opposition to nation and culture—even to a gallows, or a cross."[24]

Jim Wallis is another progressive evangelical who has sought to foreground the societal aspects of Bonhoeffer's legacy in ways likely to disturb traditionalists. In "When I First Met Bonhoeffer," Wallis tells of discovering the German pastor-theologian while a young seminarian and a veteran of the student protest movements of the 1960s. It was the pastor-theologian's merging of the political and personal, Wallis writes, that initially attracted him to Bonhoeffer, and that attracts him still. Fresh from a secular movement "that had lost its way," Wallis found in Bonhoeffer "a deep connection between spirituality and moral leadership, religion and public life, faith and politics." Although Wallis acknowledges that this Bonhoeffer may sound a bit like a liberation theologian, he reminds readers that "the liberal habit of diminishing the divinity of Christ, or dismissing his incarnation, cross and resurrection had no appeal for Bonhoeffer."[25]

Charles Marsh is another scholar who reveals Bonhoeffer's potential as a "faithful critic" of American evangelicalism's naive patriotism. Marsh's book *Wayward Christian Soldiers*, written in 2007 as the Bush era wound down and the Iraq War lingered, was a jeremiad against conservative Christian elites who, "in exchange for political access and power, ransacked the faith and trivialized its convictions." According to Marsh, when evangelical leaders claim that "Providence" has insured the victory of a Republican presidential candidate and aver that "our God is pro-war," the movement has lost its way, seduced by "the piety of cosmic entitlement." In condemning evangelicals' easy accommodation to war and inattention to its horrible consequences, Marsh employs Bonhoeffer's axiom that "he who does not cry out for the Jew may not sing Gregorian chants" to lament the fate of Iraqi children: "How I wish our dear brother Billy [Graham] would say 'Only he who cries out for the Iraqi child may sing "Just As I am."'"[26]

Since the 1970s, the Bonhoeffer of progressive evangelicals has been institutionalized in the Jesus People USA Evangelical Covenant Church, an intentional community in uptown Chicago. In a recent review of literature on Bonhoeffer in the church's *Cornerstone* magazine, Chris Rice notes that during the period of the community's founding, Bonhoeffer's *Cost of Discipleship* was "required reading" at Jesus People USA. "As we understand it," Rice explains, "*Discipleship* wrestles Christianity away [from] the idolatry of Christian nationalism. But beyond that, it returns faith to its original allegiance—Jesus Christ himself. In Bonhoeffer's unflinching reading of the Sermon on the Mount we find the Christ who means what he says."[27]

Socially progressive evangelicals like Gushee, Stassen, Wallis, Marsh, and Rice have fashioned an evangelical Bonhoeffer whose function is to remind Christians that their primary loyalty is to God, not to church or nation. This Bonhoeffer does not hesitate to condemn American culture but saves his most stinging criticisms for the way evangelical Christians have allowed its values to shape them. The damning evidence cited by these internal critics ranges from idolatrous Christian nationalism to easy accommodation to war to the conflation of Christianity with the American way of life. Their solution is to remind evangelicals that authentic faith may lead Christians into "principled opposition to nation and culture."

Bonhoeffer the Ecclesiological Guide

Another group of evangelicals with a keen interest in Bonhoeffer identify with the "emerging church" movement. Although emergents defy traditional labels, the movement has deep roots in evangelicalism, is studied by scholars at flagship evangelical institutions such as Fuller Theological Seminary, and is the subject of books published by evangelical presses like Zondervan, InterVarsity, and Baker.

According to Andrew D. Rowell, the emerging church movement is drawn to Bonhoeffer primarily for his emphasis on church renewal. Responding to a changing cultural situation they believe is in some ways analogous to Bonhoeffer's own, emergents have concluded that Christian practices must be rethought for a postmodern, post-Christian age. Among the emergent themes informed by Bonhoeffer's ecclesiology, according to Rowell, are intense fellowship in local communities, a commitment to justice based on the church's existence "for others," and a desire to recover ancient spiritual disciplines.[28]

The most substantial engagement with Bonhoeffer's theology on behalf of the emerging church movement is Ray S. Anderson's *An Emergent Theology for Emerging Churches.* Anderson looks to the ecclesiology outlined in Bonhoeffer's *Communio Sanctorum*, where the budding theologian sets forth the "basic axiom" that "Christ exists as community." Like Rowell, Anderson adopts Bonhoeffer's credo that the church must exist for others: because Christ exists for me as the neighbor, he writes, "the reality of God in Christ is not an abstract concept but the concrete reality of the other person, whether Christian or not, who makes the same demand on me as does Christ."[29]

On the crucial question of the church's relationship to the world, Anderson again looks to Bonhoeffer for guidance. In *Ethics*, a text cited most often by evangelicals in connection with Bonhoeffer's condemnation of abortion, Anderson discovers a church that "does not possess Christ for itself but finds Christ in the world." Again referring to *Ethics*, Anderson defines the church's mission in incarnational terms: through God's taking on flesh, "all men are taken up, enclosed and borne within the body of Christ, and this is just what the congregation of the faithful are to make known to the world by their words and by their lives."[30]

Finally, Anderson asks whether there is theological relevance for the emerging church movement in the concept of "religionlessness" developed in Bonhoeffer's prison letters. In his day, when religion had become irrelevant, Anderson writes, Bonhoeffer spoke of Christ as the incarnation of God "without using religious language and without presenting Christ to the world as a religious person." In this way the gospel of salvation, reconciliation, and hope could be proclaimed "even if religion no longer was viewed by the world as either true or relevant."[31]

The distinctive nature of emergents' appropriation of Bonhoeffer is perhaps most evident in the texts they cite. Perennial evangelical favorites like *Discipleship* and *Life Together* are rarely mentioned, while *Communio Sanctorum*, *Ethics*, and *Letters and Papers from Prison* are mined for insights on renewing the church in a postmodern world.

TWO IMPORTANT POINTS EMERGE from this overview of the evangelical Bonhoeffer, points that should be kept in mind as we move forward to consider the populist Bonhoeffer that has emerged in the twenty-first century. One is that although it developed gradually over several decades, evangelical enthusiasm for Bonhoeffer is hardly new. Despite real concerns about his theology among conservative scholars during the 1960s and '70s, evangelicals steadily warmed to Bonhoeffer, and by the 1990s were invoking him as a Christian hero, a culture warrior, a critical patriot, and a guide for ecclesiological renewal. The literature associated with each of these evangelical portraits of Bonhoeffer is substantial.

The second point is that, with few exceptions, appropriations of Bonhoeffer by American evangelicals are reasonably argued and text based. They vary in quality, of course, and inevitably emphasize aspects of Bonhoeffer's life and thought likely to appeal to conservative Christians. But at their best they maintain a respect for Bonhoeffer's cultural distance from American evangelicalism, and do not suggest that he is properly understood only from an evangelical perspective.

As Charles Horne wrote in 1966, even though conservative Christians find *The Cost of Discipleship* appealing, they "must not be deceived into thinking that [Bonhoeffer] writes as a fundamentalist" (a term that would soon be replaced by "evangelical" for Christians like Horne). While Richard Weikart's thoroughgoing criticisms of Bonhoeffer represent a minority position within the evangelical community, they remind us that there has always been within American evangelicalism a determination to take Bonhoeffer's theology seriously, as well as an unwillingness to ignore aspects of his legacy considered incompatible with evangelical commitments. As we will see, all this would change with Eric Metaxas.[32]

PART TWO

Bonhoeffer and Homegrown Hitlers

CHAPTER FOUR

Bonhoeffer, Bush, and the "War on Terror"

IN THE WAKE OF THE TERROR ATTACKS of September 11, 2001, public discourse in America shifted, temporarily at least, away from domestic issues and toward questions of international security. In response, Bonhoeffer's name was less likely to appear in considerations of matters such as abortion and more likely to be invoked in discussions of the urgent project of defending Western civilization. Thus Bonhoeffer's role in American life was transformed in the months and years during which the "war on terror" remained central to Americans' political concerns. This new role reflected not only the novel threats occupying the American imagination but also increased cultural awareness of Bonhoeffer's life and thought, as well as the Internet's growth as a forum for communication and debate. The results were an enlargement of Bonhoeffer's presence in the public forum where opinions are aired and debated, as well as a greater urgency to connect Bonhoeffer's legacy to domestic and international affairs. Attempts to bring Bonhoeffer to bear in discussions of America's response to the war on terror represent an important chapter in the story of his American reception, as well as helpful background for understanding the populist Bonhoeffer's appeal.

Hawk or Dove?

Despite 9/11's initial unifying effect on the American public, by the time of the invasion of Iraq in March 2003 American politics had come to reflect the polarization characteristic of our own time. Sincere and well-informed Americans came down on opposite sides of disputes over whether 9/11 justified a military response, and members of both groups were able to make credible claims on Bonhoeffer's legacy.

Although Bonhoeffer had been held up as an antiwar icon in the 1970s and a critic of Cold War bellicosity during the 1980s, prior to 9/11 there were few thoughtful attempts to utilize the German pastor-theologian or his thought to support a hawkish political agenda. But as the war on terror was proclaimed in the long shadow of the assault on the Twin Towers, Americans began to identify Bonhoeffer's conspiracy against Hitler's life as a precedent for resorting to violence in situations of political extremity.

The first to try to harness Bonhoeffer in responding to international terrorism may have been George W. Bush, who, nine months after 9/11, addressed the German Reichstag to thank that country's legislators for their support in combating terrorism. Bush noted that as freedom-loving people faced a "new totalitarian threat" so reminiscent of twentieth-century fascism, they could find inspiration in the "stand against Nazi rule" taken by Bonhoeffer, who "gave witness to the Gospel of life, and paid the cost of his discipleship." As military action in Iraq began to look more and more likely, others relied on Bonhoeffer to bolster their position on the impending conflict.[1]

Bonhoeffer's role in the debate over the war on terror's moral status was assessed by Robert O. Smith in a 2005 article titled "Bonhoeffer, Bloggers, and Bush: Uses of a 'Protestant Saint' in the Fog of War." As the march toward military action in Iraq gathered momentum in early 2003, Smith observed, "references to Bonhoeffer became *de rigueur* in religiously informed discourse regarding U.S. foreign policy." The invasion that began in March only heightened Bonhoeffer's role in discussions of the conflict, so that by November 2005 Smith counted more than one hundred discrete online references to Bonhoeffer related to the war on terror, many explicitly supportive of Bush administration policies.[2]

Responding to widespread reliance on Bonhoeffer to justify political violence, theological ethicist Walter Wink in 2002 warned readers of "the Bonhoeffer assumption"—the supposition that the German pastor-theologian's decision to "join the death squad against Hitler" could be used to rationalize military action in the present. American thinkers who read Bonhoeffer this way, Wink argued, "overlook his clear statement that he does not regard this as a justifiable action—that it's a sin—and that he throws himself on the mercy of God." Bonhoeffer's actions were emphatically not, Wink wrote, "a legitimization of war."[3]

Nevertheless, many commentators were impressed by Bonhoeffer's movement from "pacifism" to violent resistance under the pressure of totalitarian repression. Among these was Richard Land, president of the Southern Baptist Convention's Ethics and Religious Liberty Commission, who in January 2003 reminded readers that although Bonhoeffer had once been a pacifist, he eventually "joined the resistance, including their plot to assassinate Hitler in 1944." To clarify Bonhoeffer's relevance for the situation at hand, Land invoked Martin Luther King Jr., who purportedly said that "if your opponent has a conscience, then follow Gandhi. But if your enemy has no conscience, like Hitler, then follow Bonhoeffer." According to Land, both men understood that when an enemy "has no conscience, then violence may be permissible and necessary." Since Saddam Hussein was undoubtedly conscienceless, Land suggested that Americans had a "moral imperative" to oppose him with force.[4]

But not everyone was convinced by this reading of Bonhoeffer's bearing on the international situation. A reader responding to Land's claims pointed out that the analogy with Germany was flawed because Bonhoeffer did not put Hitler into power, while the US government had provided Saddam with funds to buy weapons "and were more than happy to call him an ally when he used those weapons against our enemies (and the Kurds within his own country)." The commenter, who went by the screen name "hamlet2002," concluded that, unlike Bonhoeffer, Americans must admit their "own sin" in this matter: "We are not liberators. At best, we are using quick and easy way [*sic*] to mop up a huge mess of our own making . . . and murdering innocent civilians to do it."[5]

The same month (February 2003) a blogger writing in support of a US invasion of Iraq alluded to Bonhoeffer's 1933 essay "The Church and the Jewish Question" and its suggestion that the church may be called "to drive a spoke into the wheel" of state power, claiming that it was time for the United States to "throw itself into the spokes of the wheel in Iraq." In a mirror image of this argument, Jonathan Wilson-Hartgrove cited "The Church and the Jewish Question" to argue that those who follow Christ must be willing to "jam a spoke in the wheel" of the American government. A blogger who had spent time in Iraq following the first Gulf War wrote that his experience watching the Iraqi people "being oppressed and beaten" had profoundly challenged his pacifism. As he explained, "I arrived in Iraq a pacifist Christian and left as a Bonhoeffer Christian," that is, one who had come to believe there are "worse things than the use of force. Like the brutality of Saddam."[6]

Professional Scholars Weigh In

Many guardians of Bonhoeffer's legacy were uncomfortable with the German theologian being portrayed as a moral ally in George W. Bush's war on terror. In a 2003 commentary in the online version of the *Baptist Standard*, Al Staggs, whose one-man portrayal of Bonhoeffer's last days in *A View from the Underside: The Legacy of Dietrich Bonhoeffer* had toured the country for twenty years, declared that the patriotic demonstrations being staged in American churches in the run-up to the Iraq invasion were "no less disturbing" than the swastika-draped sanctuaries that were emblems of Christian enthusiasm for the Nazi revolution. According to Staggs, Bonhoeffer believed no nation could claim ultimate allegiance for Christians, who were obligated "to impede the immoral and unjust actions of the government."

Staggs went on to insist that if America invaded Iraq, Iraqi civilians would be victims to the same degree the Poles had been in 1939, and that millions of Americans who did not speak out against a preemptive strike would become "bystanders." "Bonhoeffer would say that all of these people," wrote Staggs, "moral as they may appear, are nonetheless complicit in the guilt of the senseless and needless deaths of innocent people in Iraq, not to mention the lives of our own troops." While not directly comparing George W. Bush with Hitler, Staggs called similarities between the unqualified nationalism of Christians in Nazi Germany and contemporary America "abundantly clear." Bonhoeffer's legacy, Staggs concluded, should remind Americans of their responsibility to "do everything possible to prevent this attack on an independent nation that poses no immediate threat to us."[7]

Geffrey B. Kelly and F. Burton Nelson are well-known interpreters of Bonhoeffer who in the wake of 9/11 emphasized his relevance for thinking about Christian discipleship. Writing in 2003, Kelly and Nelson observed that while many Americans assumed that the German pastor-theologian would have supported US antiterror military engagements against the "Hitler-like tyrant" Saddam Hussein, if they were to examine Bonhoeffer's writings more carefully, "they might find a withering condemnation of any political system, including that of the United States, that engages in ideological, domineering, manipulative attitudes toward vulnerable peoples and nations."[8]

Because Bonhoeffer was being cited so regularly as the drumbeat of war grew louder, journalists began to seek out Bonhoeffer scholars for their insights. For example, the January 18, 2003, edition of the *Washington Post* quoted Victoria Barnett's statement that, "if Bonhoeffer were an Iraqi he would be part of a dissident movement opposing the Hussein regime. At the same time, because he was a pacifist, he would seek a peaceful solution to the conflict." In response, a blogger asked whether, if Bonhoeffer were convinced there was no alternative to keeping weapons of mass destruction out of Saddam Hussein's hands, he "might have supported such action . . . even while believing it was a sin."[9]

As war commenced, debate on American involvement in Iraq occupied the thoughts of public intellectuals, some of whom sought Bonhoeffer's help in sorting out the options for responsible action. One of these was Jean Bethke Elshtain, the University of Chicago political theorist who had been concerned with Bonhoeffer's thought for at least a decade. Exploring the traditional concept of "just war," Elshtain invoked both Hitler and Bonhoeffer in arguing that the war on terror qualified as just by classical standards. In May 2003, Elshtain asked with regard to the suffering of Iraqis if Americans were going to provide them with "iodine and Band-Aids" or whether it might be necessary, as Bonhoeffer put it, to "put a spoke in the wheel."[10]

In an interview with *Books and Culture* in September, Elshtain referred to Bonhoeffer's concept of "free responsibility" in maintaining that he represented a middle way in the divisive ethical debate over the justice of American military involvement in Iraq. Then, in an interview published in 2005, Elshtain stated that because Islamism was a "totalizing ideology" on par with Stalinism and Nazism, one had to take it just as seriously, and spoke approvingly of Bonhoeffer's decision to leave the "sanctuary of private virtuousness" and risk "dirty hands" in order to act responsibly in the world.[11]

Stanley Hauerwas is another high-profile thinker who weighed in on Bonhoeffer's significance for an American nation at war. In a 2004 book titled *Performing the Faith: Bonhoeffer and the Practice of Nonviolence*, Hauerwas claimed that Americans needed to be informed by Bonhoeffer's "understanding of why no regime, including democratic regimes, can hope to be just without also being truthful." Although *Performing the Faith* made few references to the Bush administration or its policies in Iraq, the political significance of Hauerwas's interest in Bonhoeffer became clear toward the book's end, where he opined that "much that has been said after September 11, 2001 has been false," including President Bush's announcement of the "war on terror." Feeling compelled to say *something* in the wake of 9/11, Hauerwas claimed, Bush settled on "we are at war," "magic words" that became for Americans a normalizing discourse that "ironically . . . makes us feel safe." Bonhoeffer, however, can help Christians refuse to accept the lies that made "war" the only imaginable response to 9/11.[12]

Hauerwas was not the only Christian pacifist to find inspiration in Bonhoeffer's legacy as America was waging war in Iraq. In August 2005, after a federal judge ordered the Christian peacemaking group Voices in the Wilderness to pay a $20,000 fine for taking medicine into Iraq in violation of US economic sanctions, the organization issued a statement that concluded with a reference to Bonhoeffer,

> who asked of himself and his co-conspirators in resistance to Hitler, whether they were yet of any use. We too live in times of unspeakable peril and violence. We too live in times when questioning and resisting our government is the one path remaining to act for justice. We too have struggled and seen untold numbers of innocent people die at our government's hand. We too answer as Bonhoeffer did, that yes, indeed, our acts and fidelity to our brothers and sisters throughout the

> world are not only of use, but of absolute necessity. We invite all to join us in a conspiracy of life to end our country's war against the Iraqi people.[13]

Exploring Bonhoeffer's legacy from a different perspective was Southern Baptist theologian Mark DeVine, author of *Bonhoeffer Speaks Today: Following Jesus at All Costs* (2005). In addressing Bonhoeffer's relevance for interpreting the ongoing conflict in Iraq, DeVine reflected a view of Bonhoeffer's significance for the war on terror held among a wide swath of evangelical Christians. While "we cannot say for certain how Bonhoeffer would assess the overthrow of Saddam Hussein or efforts to stop Al Quaida," DeVine wrote, without question the United States was confronting "urgent matters of human atrocity" similar in heinousness to those perpetrated by the Nazis. He concluded that "those calling for restraint, patience, and understanding while innocents die" cannot claim Bonhoeffer as their guide:

> What does the legacy of Bonhoeffer's life and work have to say in the face of the targeting of innocents, the maintenance of rape rooms, torture chambers, and mass graves? I would suggest that the recognition of responsibility in such circumstances should lead to resistance and active opposition to the perpetrators of these crimes. Certainly, Bonhoeffer's designation of the Nazi regime as evil diverges from sanguine liberal assessments of human nature and the seemingly inexhaustible patience for discussion and pursuit of mutual understanding, or at best, the leveling of economic sanctions while thousands die and millions live in servile fear of the torture and execution of their loved ones and themselves.[14]

Bush Becomes Hitler . . . Sort Of

In 2001 Michael Van Dyke wrote prophetically that "Dietrich Bonhoeffer's life can serve as a model for twenty-first century Christians who are faced with the prospect of newly emerging paganisms and overweening rulers." Although Van Dyke's perspective was that of an evangelical Christian concerned that Al Gore might follow Bill Clinton into the White House, his words actually portended the role Bonhoeffer would assume in combating the "overweening ruler" who defeated him.[15]

As we have seen, between 9/11 and the invasion of Iraq in March 2003, Bonhoeffer was mainly called on to illuminate the morality of using violence to stop a conscienceless tyrant. But as the war dragged on and the costs and casualties mounted, an alternative version of Bonhoeffer's significance began to emerge. In this construal, the German pastor-theologian's importance lay not in helping Americans weigh the use of military force in neutralizing a foreign dictator, but in inspiring internal resistance to a repressive regime.

When, within a few months of the commencement of the Iraq conflict, there were rumblings of Christian resistance to Bush's war on terror, Bonhoeffer was naturally called on for guidance. Among the first to appeal to his legacy was Baptist seminary professor David Alan Black, who in July 2003 invoked Bonhoeffer and the Barmen Declaration of 1934 to decry America's "growing totalitarian mentality." Things had come to the point, Black wrote, that the American church would do well "to consider the steps taken by the Confessing Church in Germany in calling Christians to repentance during the dark days of Hitler's Third Reich." Asking whether Americans were in a similar situation, Black was unequivocal:

> The indications that we may be on our way to a totalitarian society concern mainly our doctrine of national security. With the United States engaged in the military occupation of Iraq, our president emphatically insists that the necessity of a war against that sovereign nation was based on a real and imminent threat against the United States of America, despite compelling evidence to the contrary. We are told that in the interest of national security we must all be willing to sacrifice our personal freedoms in the name of the Patriot Act and other measures that reduce the Bill of Rights to a worthless scrap of paper. In the name of security we are told that a government must not let its people know too much or they will be in danger of losing their influence in the world.

When government leaders ask us in the name of God to "trust and obey [them] in life and in death," Black maintained, we must follow the example of the Barmenites by saying no, "because we have already said yes to the one Word of God whom we are obligated to trust and obey in life and in death."[16]

By 2006, Bonhoeffer was being cited regularly in critiques of Bush administration policies. In a *National Catholic Reporter* article published a month before the centennial of Bonhoeffer's birth in February, Raymond A. Schroth revisited the theologian's legacy with the domestic political situation firmly in mind. Reflecting the shift in the way Bonhoeffer's connection to American politics was being understood during Bush's second term, Schroth contended that Bonhoeffer's importance for "the mess we are in today" lay not in supposed similarities between Hitler and Saddam Hussein but in the totalitarian features of Bush's America. According to Schroth, the oppressive traits of the American government had become so obvious that viewers of the 2003 documentary film *Bonhoeffer* couldn't help noticing that "the Gestapo taps citizens' phone lines, tortures its prisoners and slaps suspects into jail without lawyers or trials for years. Hitler describes himself as a prophet: He is the savior who will rescue his people from an insidious worldwide menace. . . . And to watch first Hitler surrounded by men in uniform goose-stepping and 'Heiling' and then to see our own Field Marshall Bush in his military leather jacket propped up against a photo-staged background of cheering GIs is creepy indeed."[17]

According to Schroth, Bonhoeffer was not a reliable guide on the question of the moral and practical value of political violence. In fact, he argued, assassination not only violates the teaching of Jesus but is counterproductive, since "for us to kill Saddam Hussein or any world leader is a moral invitation to our enemies to do the same to us." For this reason, Schroth argued, Americans in search of guidance from Bonhoeffer must find it in his courage rather than in his ethical judgment.[18]

The following month—February 2006—another author sought to relate Bonhoeffer's legacy to the "mess" in America. This time it was Larry Rasmussen, retired professor of theology at Union Theological Seminary in New York and author of a classic study of Bonhoeffer's ethic of resistance. Rasmussen's article in *Sojourners* began with the suggestion that Americans might be flirting with homegrown totalitarianism. Like Schroth, Rasmussen introduced this claim with a reference to Martin Doblemeier's *Bonhoeffer*, which by 2006 had been seen by thousands of Americans. Rasmussen described a public viewing of the film after which a man who described himself as a Holocaust survivor stood up and said, "I can tell you what year this is; it's 1932."

The man's comment led Rasmussen to recall a 2004 speech by Fritz Stern, in which the German historian drew distinct parallels between contemporary America and 1930s Germany. Stern's message was that the rise of National Socialism was neither inevitable nor a function of the mesmerizing power of a single charismatic individual. Too often overlooked, he noted, was the role of conservative intellectuals, financed by corporate interests, who "denounced liberalism as the greatest, most invidious threat, and attacked it for its tolerance, rationality, and cosmopolitan culture." Furthermore, many Protestant clergy shared these conservative elites' rabid nationalism, their disdain for the Weimar period's "loose morals," and their hostility to the liberal-secular state.

When Rasmussen asked what lessons Bonhoeffer may have "for our time," his focus was not on the theologian's decision to enter the German resistance but on his reaction to the fateful events of 1933 as Hitler took steps to consolidate power. By the time of Hitler's appointment to the office of chancellor, Rasmussen noted, Bonhoeffer already sensed the crises that would follow from German Protestantism's "deep enculturation" and its "long-standing ideological and institutional alignment with the state."

Given this strong tradition of "culture Protestantism," Bonhoeffer's blueprint for the church as outlined in his essay "The Church and the Jewish Question" was radical indeed. There he emphasized that, should the government fail to fulfill its mandate to maintain law and order, the church had a duty not only to care for the state's victims but perhaps to risk a direct intervention. Sadly, this was not the path taken by German Protestants, even those in the Confessing Church. According to Rasmussen, when the "confessors" failed to intervene on behalf of Jews beyond its own membership—not to mention gays and lesbians, the euthanized, Roma and Sinti, and imprisoned socialists and communists—"in that moment it forfeited being church."

What are the lessons for the American church in Bonhoeffer's early response to Nazism? Rasmussen asked. First, German Protestantism's cultural captivity made it "unable to take the measure of civic loyalties and faith community loyalties when these conflicted." Second, "amidst crisis and war," even the resisting church had to discover new ways to render faith publicly visible in resistance, community, and institution building. Finally, the German churches were not able to create a genuine movement in sufficient time to counter the growing power of right-wing populism.

Although Rasmussen emphasized that "Germany is not the United States and the 1930s are not the present," he argued that careful attention should be paid to scholars—and Holocaust survivors—who perceive parallels. Without mentioning President Bush or Iraq, Rasmussen's conclusion contained sober counsel for the American church: "Resist the beginnings of compromises that dull the moral senses and take their ease in a life of cheap grace. Resist the beginnings that give evil, willed blindness, and civic passivity a foothold. Don't let the right eye wink at complicity or the left hand abet it. Resist becoming unwitting accomplices to an errant leader. Resist all the places in your own soul that give way. A discerning spirituality is as vital as the right politics and indispensable to it."[19]

Charles Marsh is another Bonhoeffer scholar who revisited the theologian's legacy in the midst of the protracted conflict in Iraq. In *Wayward Christian Soldiers*, published in 2007 as the "immoral and catastrophic war in Iraq" was becoming less and less popular in America, Marsh used modern German history to illumine what he saw as evangelicalism's deep-seated corruption. He likened prominent evangelicals' support for the invasion of Iraq to the German war delirium of 1914, when German Christians confused "the will of the nation with the will of God." Marsh even inverted the standard evangelical reading of history—according to which conservative Christians identify with the victims of Hitler—by insisting that American evangelicals must ask themselves whether they could have resisted the lure of the Aryan Christ. While dismissing political comparisons between Hitler's Germany and Bush's America, Marsh claimed that acknowledging theological parallels between the two "idolatrous churches" could contribute to "an honest and healthy self-examination of our work and witness."[20]

It is important to note how carefully Rasmussen and Marsh, both trusted interpreters of Bonhoeffer, addressed the lessons of the pastor-theologian's life and thought for contemporary Americans without engaging in facile associations of the "Bush is Hitler" variety. As we will see in the following chapter, in the age of Obama few writers would be so careful.[21]

MANY FACTORS CONTRIBUTED to Bonhoeffer's prominence in discussions of post-9/11 American foreign policy. In addition to the Iraq War and the growth of online venues for political discussion, there were the grassroots success of Martin Doblmeier's documentary treatment of Bonhoeffer's life and the centennial of his birth. These trends came together in February 2006 when the Public Broadcasting System recognized the Bonhoeffer centennial with a nationwide telecast of Doblmeier's film.

The confluence of ongoing military conflict and increased attention to Bonhoeffer's story made it difficult to consider his legacy without considering the Iraq War, and vice versa. For instance, in a 2004 episode of the American Public Media radio program *Speaking of Faith* on which Doblmeier was a guest, many listeners connected Bonhoeffer with America's war on terror. Naturally, comments ranged widely, with some remarking on "the fascist leanings of our current government" and others comparing Bonhoeffer to Osama bin Laden and the 9/11 terrorists. Around the same time, a Yahoo online discussion group called "Bonhoeffer's Cell" heated up when someone commented that Bush and Hitler shared much in common, including "their illegitimate use of Christianity to support their war and political agendas," and that Bonhoeffer would have opposed the American president were he alive. When some members became angry and threatened to leave the group, the moderator was forced to intervene.[22]

This overview of Bonhoeffer's ubiquity in American political discourse in the years after 9/11 points us toward several conclusions.

First, as Americans considered the morality of an unprovoked attack on a sovereign nation, it was comforting to recall Bonhoeffer's decision to join the anti-Hitler resistance. As Ben Domenech, a Bush political appointee and cofounder of RedState.org, opined in mid-2003, Bonhoeffer's choice to resort to violence was "fundamentally righteous." It not only made him a hero but allowed him to oppose "the greatest tragedy in the history of modern man."[23]

Second, once Bonhoeffer had been employed to justify American military action in Iraq, he began to show up in the rhetoric of Christian hawks whenever they perceived American interests were at stake. In August 2005, for example, Pat Robertson turned to Bonhoeffer to defend his controversial suggestion that the United States assassinate Venezuelan president Hugo Chavez. In a press release, Robertson noted that "the brilliant Protestant theologian Dietrich Bonhoeffer" had said that someone watching a madman driving a car into a group of innocent bystanders is obligated to try to wrestle the steering wheel out of his hands. This was the reasoning behind Bonhoeffer's decision to plot against Hitler's life, Robertson explained, and his "example deserves our respect and consideration today." In May 2006, when the question of the hour was whether to launch a preemptive strike on Iran, naturally Bonhoeffer entered that discussion as well.[24]

Third, as the Iraq War dragged on, it became increasingly apparent that the Bonhoeffer card could be played on both sides of the political table, as it were. In January 2006, for instance, when a commenter on *Beliefnet* made an implicit comparison between Bonhoeffer and anti-war protestor Cindy Sheehan, another commenter complained that "Bonhoeffer was executed by the Nazis for his witness, while Ms. Sheehan gets tons of admiring publicity." Four days later, a new post claimed that Bonhoeffer would look at what was going on in Washington, understand Sheehan's sense of urgency, and "adore" her.[25]

Finally, domestic resistance to the war in Iraq gave rise to a phrase that, though it would not become popular for another eight years, hinted at the use to which Bonhoeffer could be put in times of crisis. In 2007, Voices for Creative Nonviolence (formerly Voices in the Wilderness), which led delegations to Iraq and challenged economic sanctions imposed by the United States and the United Nations, invoked the phrase "Bonhoeffer moment" as a rallying cry to encourage resistance against American military involvement in Iraq and Afghanistan. Voices member Jeff Leys, who was facing legal consequences for an act of "nonviolent civil disobedience" at the US Military Entrance Processing Command, wrote that "the Bonhoeffer Moment of nonviolent civil resistance and disobedience to the world war being waged by the United States is clearly at hand. . . . It is time for us to learn lessons from the German resistance to Hitler, to the Nazi regime and to the war waged by the German nation-state. We must engage the Long Resistance to this current world war, using every nonviolent means to bring about its end."[26]

As these words were spoken, the American public was actually losing interest in the "world war" and entering a contentious campaign season. As we will see in the next chapter, the proclivity for viewing Bonhoeffer's legacy through the lens of one's political orientation would only intensify with the election of Barack Obama.

CHAPTER FIVE

Bonhoeffer, Obama, and the "Culture of Death"

As we saw in the previous chapter, the impulse to interpret the American political scene in the light of Dietrich Bonhoeffer's life and thought gained considerable momentum in the wake of the terrorist attacks of September 11, 2001. Particularly between 2002 and 2006, Americans sought the pastor-theologian's guidance in sorting through the options for responding to 9/11 and preventing future attacks. Scholars, bloggers, and online commenters argued not only about whether preemptive military action was theoretically just, but also whether Bonhoeffer's decision to resort to violence against Hitler could be appropriated to support it.

Despite divergent views of how to approach terrorists and the states that harbor them—not to mention how Bonhoeffer's response to Hitler might inform this approach—nearly everyone agreed that the terrorists were the "bad guys" and that the closest thing to a fascist threat facing the United States came from foreign actors like Saddam Hussein and Osama bin Laden. Liberals occasionally invoked Nazi Germany in criticisms of George W. Bush's penchant for solving problems with military force and suspending civil rights during "wartime." But in this regard he was treated no differently than Richard Nixon and Lyndon Johnson, both of whom had been "Hitlerized" for their support of the Vietnam War.[1]

However, as the war in Iraq dragged on and more and more Americans concluded that the invasion had been a mistake, echoes of Nazi Germany began to be detected in the Bush administration's misleading claims about Saddam's "weapons of mass destruction," in the president's military posturing, in the government's treatment of "enemy combatants," in Patriot Act–enabled surveillance on American citizens, and in "idolatrous churches" enthusiastic for war and unable to resist the allure of empire. Still, Americans who heard these echoes were generally careful to emphasize that, as Larry Rasmussen put it in 2006, "Germany is not the United States and the 1930s are not the present."

With the election of Barack Obama in 2008, however, not only the object but also the tone of these complaints shifted. Despite continued US military engagement in Iraq and Afghanistan, during the Obama years invocations of Nazi Germany—and of Bonhoeffer—would be connected almost exclusively with domestic issues. Such rhetoric was not unprecedented. Critics of Bush-era domestic policies had occasionally raised the specter of "Germany in the '30s"—for instance, in attacks on the supposedly "totalitarian mind-set" of public schools. But after 2008 such fleeting accusations were replaced by a steady barrage of charges that Obama's domestic commitments represented a threat to American democracy that might plunge the country into a dark night of fascist oppression.[2]

Obama's ethnic "otherness" cannot be removed from this equation, of course. Regardless of how one felt about George W. Bush or his policies, he was a member of a prominent American family who in his more thoughtful moments had the nation's best interests at heart. But to many on the right, Barack Obama was at best a pseudo-American who was committed to destroying the nation they loved. Eventually, hysterical claims about Obama—that he was a noncitizen, a secret Muslim, perhaps even the antichrist—became a regular feature of anti-Obama discourse among alienated conservatives.[3]

Long-standing insults designed to paint liberal elites with a Nazi brush—"feminazi," "gay gestapo," "jackbooted government thug"—remained staples of conservative commentary. But during the Obama years these hackneyed phrases were accompanied by a steady stream of explicit references to the president's presumably Hitler-like characteristics. Some of the efforts to paint Obama in Hitlerian tones were quite spectacular. In 2013, for instance, a video billboard in Kendallville, Indiana, depicted the president with a toothbrush mustache and called for his impeachment. "He has earned his mustache," a spokesman for the group responsible for the billboard said. "It's not a gas chamber but it's an economic policy. It's the same effect. If you're dead, you're dead."[4]

By Obama's second term attempts to Hitlerize the president and his signature policies became so ubiquitous one could encounter them not only while listening to the radio on the way to work but also while watching C-Span. Speaking on the floor of the US Senate in 2013, for instance, Ted Cruz told fellow lawmakers that funding the Affordable Care Act would be akin to appeasing Hitler. "Look," Cruz said, "we saw in Britain, Neville Chamberlain, who told the British people, 'Accept the Nazis. Yes, they'll dominate the continent of Europe, but that's not our problem. Let's appease them [since] . . . we can't possibly stand against them.'" Of those who argued that Obamacare could not be defunded, Cruz complained that if it were the 1940s, "we would have listened to them."[5]

Attempts to link Obama and *Der Führer* became so common by 2014 that they were being catalogued in leading newsmagazines. Among Obama's Hitlerian features, according to the politicians and pundits cited in these stories, were his vague references to "change" during the 2008 election campaign, his "blitzkrieg" attack on the American economy, his "socialist" health-care agenda, his order that "National Park Service thugs" close federal monuments during a government shutdown, his encouragement of envy against the "1 percent" (with one critic comparing Obama's antipathy toward "successful Americans" with Hitler's toward "Jews and Gypsies"), his decision to hold BP financially accountable for the 2010 Gulf oil spill, his role in "nationalizing" troubled banks after the financial collapse, his consideration of executive action on gun safety, and his plan to tax the income of venture capitalists. Although these news articles had a summative character, they made no claim to be exhaustive.[6]

This multilayered portrait of Obama as an American Hitler dedicated to the destruction of the nation's institutions and values, as ridiculous as it may appear in retrospect, is crucial for understanding the role Bonhoeffer would come to play in conservative reaction to his administration. But it is also important to consider two longstanding features of American Christian rhetoric—appropriation of the German Church Struggle by Christians in conflict with their denominations' stances on sexuality, and comparisons between state-sanctioned abortion and the Nazi Final Solution.

Appropriating the German Church Struggle

American Christians have long been drawn to an epic version of the German Church Struggle, the contest between the Confessing Church (*Bekennende Kirche*) and German Christians (*Deutsche Christen*) for control of the German Evangelical Church during the early years of Nazi rule. In this heroic account of the church struggle, anti-Nazi and pro-Nazi Christians fought for the soul of German Protestantism, with members of the Confessing Church demanding a decisive rejection of National Socialism and a robust defense of German Jews. Although this representation of German church history has not withstood scholarly scrutiny, it continues to be embraced in some American church circles.

For example, in 1996 Chuck Colson invoked the Confessing Church and its campaign against pro-Nazi Protestants to rally American Christians in the pro-life cause. Addressing a recent legislative setback for antiabortion forces in a Supreme Court decision that silenced antiabortion activists, Colson drew a direct link between beleaguered pro-lifers and the "confessing" minority in Nazi Germany. He noted that when the Confessing Church was born at the Confessing Synod of Barmen in May 1934, organizers found it necessary to declare independence from both the German state and a co-opted Protestant church, an act that "led to the formation of the Confessing Church under the leadership of Niemöller and Bonhoeffer." If present trends continue, Colson wrote, members of the pro-life movement may discover that they are "closer to Barmen than to the triumph of the Religious Right."[7]

Later in the 1990s this version of the "church's confession against Hitler" was widely embraced by conservative Protestants in mainline American denominations that were moving to embrace homosexual persons and ordain openly gay clergy. In reaction to these proposed changes, denominational affinity groups referring to themselves as "confessing movements" arose within the Presbyterian Church (USA), United Methodist Church, and United Church of Christ. Such lay-clergy associations organized traditionalists in these denominations and mobilized them in support of traditional sexual mores.

In appealing to the legacy of the Confessing Church, these groups implied that American Christians faced a "confessional situation" analogous to that precipitated by the German Evangelical Church's efforts to adopt the racist "Aryan paragraph" in 1933. That is, these "confessing" movements implied that in resisting changes to their denominations' sexuality standards, they were claiming the mantle of the *Bekennende Kirche*'s principled stand against the Nazi-compromised Protestant majority. Naturally, many congregations aligning themselves with these "confessing" groups staked a symbolic claim to the Barmen Declaration, which they regarded as a univocal statement of the Confessing Church's anti-Nazi stance.[8]

Mainline critics of these groups pointed out how poorly sexuality debates in North American churches conformed to the situation of Protestant "confessors" living under a totalitarian regime. Furthermore, as Princeton Seminary's William Stacy Johnson noted in 2001, use of the name "Confessing Church" by opponents of sexual equality was ironic, since the term "stood for people risking their lives for the conviction that the gospel of grace extends to everyone." But these grassroots movements proved fairly impervious to criticism from theological elites, who were often viewed as responsible for the churches' drift away from their theological moorings.[9]

While confessing movement spokespersons rarely made explicit references to church struggles in Germany or South Africa, their moral stature was enhanced by their association with Christians who, it was believed, had boldly protested the church's cultural captivity in their own time. As mainline denominations steadily liberalized their views of sexuality, many "confessing" congregations split or disaffiliated from their church bodies, robbing Confessing Church movements of their identity as faithful remnants fighting for the souls of their denominations. But their affinity for the symbols of anti-Nazi resistance illumines how profoundly the German Church Struggle's putative heroes have energized the American religious imagination.

Revisiting the American Holocaust

American "confessing" movements helped conservative Protestants claim the legacy of the anti-Hitler resistance against ecclesiastical opponents who were believed to have compromised the gospel in an era of loosening cultural mores. Another rhetorical strategy popularized in the 1990s—the association of state-sanctioned abortion with the Nazi Final Solution—went further, suggesting not only that Christians should oppose their liberal coreligionists for control of their denominations, but that they were obligated to actively resist murderous cultural institutions.

Christian attempts to link abortion with the Holocaust are not new, and they did not begin with American Protestants. According to a recent study, the connection can be traced to a 1951 statement by Pope Pius XII, after which it became a favorite of Catholic commentators. But American Protestant pro-lifers took up the analogy with a vengeance in the 1990s, as they likened abortion of "defenseless children" to Hitler's assault on Jews, and passivity before this "American holocaust" to the German public's accommodation to Nazism. Based on his courageous opposition to the persecution of German Jews, Bonhoeffer became both symbol and guide for pro-life Christians who wished to emulate his defense of the innocent.[10]

In 1995 Erwin Lutzer proclaimed that in the midst of America's "silent 'holocaust' in which five thousand tiny victims lose their lives every day," Bonhoeffer calls Christians to action. In 2000 Bonhoeffer was identified as an exemplar of opposition to abortion by Focus on the Family's James Dobson. "What if today were 1943," Dobson asked rhetorically, "and you were in Nazi Germany and knew that Hitler and his henchmen were killing Jews and Poles and Gypsies and homosexuals and the mentally handicapped, among other 'undesirables'?" "I thank God," he concluded, "that Dietrich Bonhoeffer did not shrink in timidity when he saw unmitigated wickedness being perpetrated by the Nazis."[11]

As these examples suggest, in the 1990s referring to abortion as a "silent" holocaust became a standard rhetorical strategy among American pro-lifers, with Bonhoeffer and the Confessing Church reminding Christians of their obligation to oppose state-sanctioned "murder" in

America. Naturally, more radical activists took the abortion-Holocaust analogy to its logical conclusion, calling clinics "abortion chambers" and "death camps" and collecting information on abortion providers in "Nuremberg files." A website maintained by Missionaries to the Unborn paired photos of aborted fetuses with scenes from Nazi camps under headings such as "body parts," "experimentation," "killers," "final solution," "waste management," and "trophies."[12]

For some, these vivid parallels called for violent resistance, including assaults on abortion providers. And they inevitably brought to mind the example of Bonhoeffer, who concluded that the immensity of the Nazis' crimes obliged him to work for Hitler's elimination. Predictably, the German pastor-theologian became something of a patron saint among radical antiabortion activists. John Brockhoeft, for instance, who in 1994 was serving time in federal prison for firebombing an abortion clinic, reminded readers of his prison blog that the "ordained Lutheran minister" was an example of "absolute, Christian commitment to the cause of innocent human life." Based on "the perfect parallel" between abortion and the Nazis' slaughter of Jews, Brockhoeft wrote, he and others in the radical antiabortion movement regarded Bonhoeffer as a hero.[13]

This claim on Bonhoeffer by those responsible for or supportive of vigilante actions against abortion providers forced moderate pro-lifers to reconsider Bonhoeffer's role in the antiabortion cause. In response, some activists complained that while groups like Christian Action Coalition and Operation Rescue had once highlighted Bonhoeffer's statements on the evil of abortion and the justifiability of civil disobedience, attempts to stop abortion by attacking providers had led to a noticeable decrease in pro-life leaders' willingness to refer to Bonhoeffer.

In essence, the supposed analogy between abortion and the Holocaust became a victim of its own success. If abortion really was a "silent Holocaust," then people of faith were called not just to protest it but to end it by any means necessary. Those committed to heeding this call perceived in Bonhoeffer a willingness to sacrifice his own safety to oppose the Nazi Holocaust, and heard in his story of resistance a direct question: What are *you* doing to arrest this ongoing assault on innocent life? Moderate pro-lifers consistently condemned vigilante violence, but if abortion was as evil as they declared it to be, it was difficult to dismiss claims that Bonhoeffer was the ideal model of faith-based resistance, or that conscientious Christians should "jam a spoke in the wheel" of this deadly industry.

Updating the Nazi Analogy

Chastened by this problem, Christians seeking to play the Nazi card in the twenty-first century have expanded their focus beyond abortion to encompass other domestic issues, particularly religious freedom, the defense of marriage, and the spread of "liberalism." Clues as to how the Nazi specter would be raised during the age of Obama were to be found in "The Manhattan Declaration: A Call of Christian Conscience," which was released just ten months after the 2008 election.

According to declaration coauthor Timothy George, the Manhattan Declaration was a "statement of Christian conscience affirming the sanctity of human life from conception to natural death, the dignity of marriage as a lifelong covenantal union between one man and one woman, and religious freedom for all persons." In other words, the declaration addressed the threats perceived by traditionalist Christians who continued to lament the legality of abortion but sensed that American culture was drifting steadily away from them on several fronts.[14]

The Manhattan Declaration was focused on "Life," "Marriage," and "Religious Liberty," but a portentous subtheme was its emphasis on Christians' duty to oppose oppressive states. Indeed, the declaration's first sentence identified "resisting tyranny" as a vital element of the Christian tradition. In this spirit, the preamble reminded readers of the cultural struggles waged by Christians through the ages—against the Roman Empire, slavery, the divine right of kings, and human trafficking, and in support of women's suffrage and black civil rights.[15]

The Manhattan Declaration hinted that American Christians might be required to adopt an oppositional posture vis-à-vis their government as churches confronted "the instruments of coercion to compel people of faith to compromise their deepest convictions."

Although specific mention was made of the Obama administration's views on abortion, the declaration's broader target was what it termed America's "culture of death," which it claimed threatened life's beginning in "embryo-research" and "therapeutic cloning" and its end in the promotion of assisted suicide and voluntary euthanasia. On the matter of religious liberty, the declaration emphasized the right to worship God according to the dictates of one's conscience and "to express freely and publically [one's] deeply held religious convictions." Restrictions on freedom of conscience, the declaration claimed, lead inevitably to "soft despotism" and the disintegration of civil society that is "a prelude to tyranny."[16]

The Manhattan Declaration reminded readers that through the centuries Christianity had taught that civil disobedience "is not only permitted, but sometimes required." Martin Luther King Jr.'s "Letter from Birmingham Jail" was cited favorably in this connection, as was his "willingness to go to jail, rather than comply with legal injustice." Given these references to MLK's program of nonviolent direct action, it is not surprising that the declaration ended on a note of defiance. "We will not comply with any edict that purports to compel our institutions" in any antilife act, the authors wrote, "nor will we bend to any rule purporting to force us to bless immoral sexual partnerships." Furthermore, "no power on earth will intimidate us into silence or acquiescence."[17]

The Manhattan Declaration's only explicit reference to Nazi Germany appeared in connection with the contemporary practice of assisted suicide, which it linked to Nazi "eugenic notions" such as "life unworthy of life." References to the German Church Struggle were more subtle, but evident to anyone familiar with the literature of the period. For instance, echoes of the Barmen Declaration were discernible in the Manhattan Declaration's reference to the God who "has laid total claim on our lives," as well as its reminder that "those who have been entrusted with temporal power . . . fulfill the first responsibility of government." Even clearer was an allusion to Bonhoeffer's *Discipleship*, written in the midst of the German Church Struggle: "Christians today," the declaration claimed, "are called to proclaim the gospel of costly grace."[18]

At the unveiling of the Manhattan Declaration in 2009, Eric Metaxas, whose work is more fully explored in the following chapter, explicitly associated the document with the legacy of Barmen. "The situation that compelled Bonhoeffer and the other Confessing Church leaders to draft the Barmen Declaration in the 1930's," Metaxas declared, "is not so terribly different from the current situation." Passing over the inconvenient facts that Bonhoeffer was neither a participant at the Barmen Synod nor involved in drafting its declaration, Metaxas invoked the theologian's reputation as a defender of Nazi victims in order to link the Obama administration with Hitler's persecution of the churches, something he would do with increasing frequency in the months and years ahead.[19]

Connections between the Manhattan Declaration and the German Church Struggle were explored more fully in the spring 2011 issue of *Beeson*, an official publication of Beeson Divinity School, whose dean, Timothy George, was a declaration coauthor. In "A Tale of Two Declarations," George noted the significance of the Manhattan Declaration's appearance roughly seventy-five years after the Barmen Synod of 1934 and revealed that early drafts of the document had cited the Barmen Declaration as precedent and inspiration. References to the Confessing Church's iconic statement were deleted from the declaration's final form, George revealed, when it was judged that "the plight of the church in North America today was not analogous to the repression Jews, Christians and many others experienced in Hitler's Germany."[20]

George's note of caution was gainsaid, however, by the message communicated on the magazine's cover, which announced the issue's theme—"Revisiting the Manhattan Declaration"—over a picture of Bonhoeffer's face and the words "Confessing Christ in Nazi Germany." Furthermore, George's article was followed by a long excerpt from Metaxas's recently published biography of Bonhoeffer and an endorsement of Metaxas's own judgment on Barmen's relevance for interpreting the Manhattan Declaration. According to Metaxas, "Bonhoeffer faced a church that had bowed its knee to the reigning culture, [and] we are facing that today as well."[21] Including these words in an epigraph for his article, George ignored Metaxas's loose grasp of the historical details surrounding the Barmen Declaration's publication and judged that he had correctly discerned the "underlying similarity" between the two statements.

For his part, George noted that the Barmen and Manhattan declarations both appeal to the authority of Scripture and both warn that Christian faith can be distorted by accommodation to prevailing ideological and political convictions and the assumption that some areas of life do not belong to Jesus Christ (both points clearly echoing the language of the Barmen Declaration). Finally, George asserted that both declarations recognize what Bonhoeffer famously called "the cost of discipleship." In her own contribution to the discussion, *Beeson* editor Betsy Childs followed Metaxas in linking the Manhattan Declaration directly with Bonhoeffer's legacy. "What began in Germany as a battle over issues became a battle that cost lives," she wrote, "and Bonhoeffer willingly laid his down."[22]

The Manhattan Declaration was the first high-profile effort by American Christian leaders to resist what it anticipated would be the Obama administration's assault on pro-life sensibilities and religious liberty protections. The declaration's intentional resonance with the events and documents of the German Church Struggle, as well as its advocates' efforts to associate it with the life and work of Dietrich Bonhoeffer, previewed the role both would play in conservative Christians' opposition to government decisions and policies during Obama's presidency.

The Metaxas Factor

The parallels between Obama's America and Hitler's Germany implied in the Manhattan Declaration were made explicit by Eric Metaxas with the publication of *Bonhoeffer: Pastor, Martyr, Prophet, Spy* in 2010. The book itself, which is the subject of the following chapter, offered some clumsy analogies designed to narrow the cultural distance between Nazi Germany and twenty-first-century America. These included likening the debate among "the neo-orthodox Barthians and the historical-critical liberals" to contemporary disagreements between "strict Darwinian evolutionists and advocates of so-called Intelligent Design," and explaining that a Swedish bishop regarded Bonhoeffer "as an Episcopal bishop might today regard an evangelical."[23]

But in interviews associated with the book's publication, Metaxas had a great deal more to say about the "spectacular parallels" between Nazi Germany in 1933 and the United States in 2010, repeatedly comparing Bonhoeffer's struggle against fascism with the fight to protect American freedoms from government encroachment. Metaxas repeatedly noted that he hadn't wanted to write his Bonhoeffer book—that in fact it was "agony"—but that he had felt called to do so, in part to illuminate the similarities he saw between his own era and Bonhoeffer's. One of these parallels, according to Metaxas, was the role of liberalism in corrupting the church. On Glenn Beck's television show in August 2010, Metaxas explained that the German churches had failed to resist Nazism because they were under the influence of "theological liberalism." When Beck noted that this was "in many ways, what we have here now," Metaxas responded, "absolutely, the parallels to the US are stunning."[24]

Another connection purported by Metaxas was America's ongoing protection of abortion rights. Speaking at the 2012 National Prayer Breakfast in Washington and surrounded by President Obama, Vice President Biden, and former Speaker of the House Nancy Pelosi, Metaxas linked abortion to both slavery and Nazism. After carefully describing the inhumane treatment of Africans and European Jews by those claiming to be Christians, Metaxas asserted that contemporary Americans' acceptance of abortion made them no better than the Germans of Hitler's time. "Whom do we say is not fully human today?" Metaxas asked in a clear reference to the unborn.[25]

In statements related to the publication of *Bonhoeffer*, Metaxas also claimed parallels between government threats to religious freedom under Hitler and Obama. In an interview published in *Harper's*, Metaxas said the question facing Germans in the 1930s was the very one facing Americans today: "When do state concerns begin encroaching on the authority of the church to a point where the church needs to shout 'halt'?" If the church is healthy, he answered, "it will check the unbridled growth of the state and will protect its own members—and others, too—from illegitimate state power."[26]

In a 2010 statement to the Catholic News Agency, Metaxas added specificity to his charge of government infringement on the church's rights. Just as the Third Reich had bullied the German church, he alleged, the US government was bullying the church on the issues of sexuality, abortion, euthanasia, and stem-cell research. Under these conditions, Metaxas concluded, we would do well to take our lead from Bonhoeffer. Addressing the 2013 meeting of the Conservative Political Action Committee (CPAC), Metaxas reiterated Bonhoeffer's role in guiding the American defense of religious freedom. "It's because of Bonhoeffer that I find myself thinking about the issue of Religious Freedom," he said. "Many people have said they see disturbing parallels between what was happening in Germany in the Thirties and America today on that issue. I'm very sorry to agree."[27]

Encouraged by such statements, sympathetic reviewers of *Bonhoeffer* offered their own opinions on the Hitlerian features of Obama's America. On the Fox News website, for instance, Lauren Green noted the wave of enthusiasm that had carried Barack Obama into office, suggesting that Bonhoeffer's legacy for Americans involved "the untold dangers of idolizing politicians as messianic figures. Not just in the 1930s and '40s, but today as well." Her thought was completed by a blogger who responded, "That's Obama and his followers he [Bonhoeffer] was warning us about."[28]

SUPPOSED PARALLELS between Germany under Adolf Hitler and America under Barack Obama, noted with varying degrees of subtlety by Eric Metaxas and the authors of the Manhattan Declaration, extended a rhetorical tradition of couching Christian resistance to American domestic policies in images of the German Church Struggle. After 2008, this tradition was adjusted to account for the violent excesses of pro-life activists, perceived threats to religious freedom from the Obama administration and the Supreme Court, and the growing cultural acceptance of homosexuality and same-sex marriage. After looking more closely at the role of Eric Metaxas in shaping a portrait of Bonhoeffer fit for battle with American liberalism, we will explore how the populist Bonhoeffer was positioned to resist the normalization of same-sex marriage and pave the way for the Trump revolution.

CHAPTER SIX

The Metaxas Phenomenon

As we saw in an earlier chapter, since the 1970s American evangelicals have been drawn to Bonhoeffer in growing numbers and with increasing intensity. As evangelical portraits of Bonhoeffer have multiplied, only infrequently have they attracted serious attention from mainstream Bonhoeffer scholars. But when Eric Metaxas shook the literary world in 2010 with his hugely successful *Bonhoeffer: Pastor, Martyr, Prophet, Spy*, members of the Bonhoeffer guild were forced to take notice.

A Bonhoeffer Biography for the Age of Obama

Bonhoeffer won the Evangelical Christian Booksellers Association's Christian Book Award for Non-Fiction and the Becket Fund's Canterbury Prize for Religious Freedom. More importantly, in 2011 the book spent two months atop the *New York Times*'s best-seller list for e-book nonfiction. The book not only achieved impressive commercial success; it also propelled its author into the national spotlight. *Bonhoeffer: Pastor, Martyr, Prophet, Spy* earned Metaxas regular guest appearances on nationally syndicated radio and television shows and led some to call him "the next Chuck Colson."[1]

I first heard Eric Metaxas's name while in Florida visiting my parents in 2009. From their bedroom I heard a summons to "come quick"; there was, my mother shouted excitedly, "a Bonhoeffer guy on Huckabee." Since none of the "Bonhoeffer guys" with whom I was familiar would be caught dead on Mike Huckabee's show on the Fox News Channel, my curiosity was piqued. I walked into my parents' room and beheld, sitting across from the jovial former Arkansas governor, a youngish, well-dressed gentleman in horn-rimmed glasses. I quickly ascertained that this evangelicalese-speaking author had a passion for Bonhoeffer and a talent for self-promotion. But I had no idea how deeply he would influence Bonhoeffer's American reception in the months and years ahead.

Game-Changer

In several ways Metaxas's biography represented a milestone in the history of Bonhoeffer's American reception. First, *Bonhoeffer* garnered significantly more media attention than previous attempts to present Bonhoeffer in evangelical dress. Second, Metaxas was more aggressive—and more hyperbolic—than previous authors in portraying Bonhoeffer as an opponent of "liberalism" in the religious and social spheres. As Metaxas put it in a subsequent book titled *Seven Men and the Secret of Their Greatness*, although Bonhoeffer respected and was able to learn from them, he was definitely "not a theological liberal." Third, the popular acclaim garnered by the book led to an unprecedented scholarly backlash, first from Bonhoeffer scholars and then from evangelical opinion makers, some of whom began to consider whether the evangelical love affair with Bonhoeffer masked some fundamental incompatibilities.[2]

Finally, far more than previous biographies of Bonhoeffer, Metaxas's portrait reflected the concerns of the time and place in which it was written. In the book, but particularly in postpublication comments and interviews, Metaxas claimed that Bonhoeffer was relevant to twenty-first-century American readers because he struggled against the very forces with which they were concerned. Tapping into widespread conservative opposition to the presidency of Barack Obama, Metaxas helped turn Bonhoeffer into a culture warrior for Americans determined to resist the encroachment of secular liberalism. It will behoove us to review in turn these distinctive aspects of *Bonhoeffer: Pastor, Martyr, Prophet, Spy* and its reception.

A Closer Look

The flurry of media interest that greeted Metaxas's *Bonhoeffer* was unlike anything ever witnessed by those who track the theologian's American reception. This attention, in turn, produced an unprecedented response from scholars who previously had paid scant notice to appropriations of Bonhoeffer's life aimed at "popular" audiences. *Bonhoeffer: Pastor, Prophet, Martyr, Spy* was not a Focus on the Family radio drama, a mass-market "Christian romance," or a website comparing Bonhoeffer with antiabortion activists. It was a full-blown biography by a Yale-educated author whose previous book on William Wilberforce had also been a *New York Times* best seller.

Bonhoeffer demanded attention in another way: no other biographer had been so dismissive of the scholarly consensus on Bonhoeffer's life and legacy reached over the previous half century. The book's bibliography listed a few standard works, but Metaxas indicated that he viewed Bonhoeffer's scholarly reception as "a terrific misunderstanding." This grand misapprehension had "lamentably washed backward over his earlier thinking and writing," Metaxas claimed, and led "many *outre* theological fashions" to claim Bonhoeffer as their own, or, worse, make him something he was not in a "sincerely believed hoax." Although Metaxas was referring primarily to appropriations of Bonhoeffer's theology by 1960s death-of-God theologians, his words could be reasonably interpreted as a summary dismissal of all interpretations of the pastor-theologian that had preceded his own.[3]

Metaxas's comments in media interviews encouraged this construal, as he complained that Bonhoeffer had suffered from decades of misinterpretation by "liberals." When asked by an interviewer for *Christianity Today* whether he would describe Bonhoeffer as an evangelical, Metaxas's answer was unequivocal. "Bonhoeffer is more like a theologically conservative evangelical than anything else," he said, adding, "he was as orthodox as Saint Paul or Isaiah, from his teen years all the way to his last day on earth." This fact needed to be emphasized, Metaxas explained, because theological liberals had "made Bonhoeffer in their own image."[4]

The theme of willful misrepresentation was further developed in an interview for *National Review* with Kathryn Jean Lopez, who began by asking Metaxas how Bonhoeffer had become "an atheist hero." "It's sheer lunacy," Metaxas responded, that this "ultra-devout Christian" had come to be celebrated by the likes of Christopher Hitchens and Bishop Spong. It's "as if the Tea Party were to hail Stalin and Bernie Sanders as their ideological icons." Such misunderstandings, Metaxas explained, were rooted in long-standing myths that would be "once and for all exploded" in his book.[5]

Among these misguided myths were that Bonhoeffer was an advocate of "income-redistributionist social justice" and a pacifist—an idea perpetuated by members of "the Sixties anti-war movement" who seemed to believe that, had he lived, Bonhoeffer would have been "the third person in bed with John and Yoko." But the most insidious distortion of Bonhoeffer's legacy, according to Metaxas, was the idea that during his imprisonment he had "drifted away from orthodox Christianity toward some kind of 'post-Christian humanism.'"[6]

Informed by these comments, reviewers began to present this grand plot to distort Bonhoeffer's legacy as the book's central theme. Among the first to do so was Joseph Loconte of the *Wall Street Journal*, who applauded what he called the biography's "theological sophistication" and wrote that until Metaxas had arrived on the scene to set the record straight, this "orthodox Christian" had been misinterpreted by those who argued that Bonhoeffer "favored social action over theology."[7]

By the middle of 2011, Metaxas was taking his myth-busting message to the television airwaves on the Fox News Channel. Sitting before a portable blackboard on which a time line of Bonhoeffer's life was scrawled in white chalk, Metaxas explained to Glenn Beck's audience that for fifty years Bonhoeffer's legacy had been effectively "hijacked by the hard left—really by agnostics and atheists."[8]

"Fifty Years" of Misappropriation

This claim that Bonhoeffer had suffered from a half century of interpretive distortion implied that virtually everything written about Bonhoeffer since the 1960s had been tainted by the influence of radical secularizing theologians like William Hamilton, Thomas Altizer, and Paul van Buren. As Metaxas put it in his interview with *National Review*, "the secular Left has since the 1950s hailed Bonhoeffer as an apostle of the so-called 'God is Dead' movement."[9]

But this charge is inaccurate on two counts. First, Bonhoeffer's role as "an apostle" of radical theology had been exceedingly short-lived because the death-of-God movement itself vanished by the late 1960s. Second, that Bonhoeffer's portrayal as a "Christian atheist" was badly misguided is something on which nearly all scholars have come to agree. Beginning in the mid-1960s, in fact, interpreters like Eberhard Bethge and Paul Lehmann convincingly argued that the death-of-Goders were badly misconstruing Bonhoeffer's theological legacy. "Seldom has an author, living or dead," Lehmann wrote in 1966, "been so misrepresented by his commentators and translators." The secularizing theologians' inability to fairly interpret Bonhoeffer or appreciate his theological concerns has been a virtually settled matter in Bonhoeffer scholarship ever since.[10]

Yet Metaxas seizes on misuse of Bonhoeffer by one of the briefest theological movements of the twentieth century to cast suspicion on Bonhoeffer scholarship in its entirety. He does so by conflating mainstream Bonhoeffer scholars with "agnostics and atheists" in careless phrases like "liberal 'God is dead' theologians." The irony is that the portrait of Bonhoeffer developed by death-of-God theologians is generally viewed by scholars as a cautionary tale about interpreters who, like Metaxas, look into Bonhoeffer's face only to behold their own reflections.[11]

Metaxas's effort to lump an entire field of theological inquiry into the category of leftist wish-fulfillment naturally impoverishes his perspective on Bonhoeffer. One place this poverty becomes evident is his treatment of the prison letters. For instance, in assessing the seminal concept of "religionless Christianity" (which Bonhoeffer explored in letters to Eberhard Bethge in the spring and summer of 1944) Metaxas writes that what Bonhoeffer meant by "religion" was "the ersatz and abbreviated Christianity that he spent his life working against." But recent scholarship has shown that Bonhoeffer's understanding of "religion" shifted considerably over time as he engaged the thought of Karl Barth, Wilhelm Dilthey, and William James, among others. Furthermore, it is clear that Bonhoeffer's critique of religion in the prison letters was not a condemnation of less-than-authentic Christianity but a recognition that the cultural ethos that had previously determined the form of Christianity's message was undergoing irrevocable change.[12]

Similarly, Metaxas's assertion that Bonhoeffer's prison musings are "simply an extension of his previous theology" ignores the complexity of the continuity question in Bonhoeffer studies. While it is true that there are important points of consistency between Bonhoeffer's early and late theological writings, Metaxas's claim that Bonhoeffer's thought "never [underwent] any kind of significant theological change" is a simplistic and misleading summary of his intellectual development. Finally, Metaxas's categorical statement that Bonhoeffer "was not a pacifist" ignores decades of scholarship regarding the theologian's developing views of war and peace.[13]

Scholarly Backlash

When popular acclaim for *Bonhoeffer: Pastor, Martyr, Prophet, Spy* threatened to eclipse the results of a generation of scholarship behind a cloud of distortions and exageration, Metaxas naturally found himself on the radar of professional Bonhoeffer scholars. Their reaction was almost unequivocally negative.

Leading Bonhoeffer experts, all conspicuously absent from lists of the book's endorsers, offered assessments of *Bonhoeffer: Pastor, Martyr, Prophet, Spy* that ranged from highly critical to scathing. Writing in *Sojourners*, Nancy Lukens called the biography "stunningly flawed" and noted "glaring factual errors, distortions, and omissions." In the *Christian Century*, Clifford Green characterized the book as "simplistic" and "polarizing." And in the *Association of Contemporary Church Historians Quarterly*, Victoria Barnett employed the adjectives "silly," "bizarre," and "clueless" before concluding that the book was "badly flawed." Together, these reviews constituted a stinging rebuttal to Metaxas's publisher's claim that his "groundbreaking" book represented "the definitive Bonhoeffer biography for the 21st century."[14]

These reviewers pointed out numerous factual errors, including misspellings and "missing, incomplete and garbled sources," and noted Metaxas's sparse references to the recently published critical editions of Bonhoeffer's writings in the Dietrich Bonhoeffer Works in English series. More troublingly, they argued that Metaxas's weak grasp of German history showed he had failed to engage in the background research required to present a reliable portrait of Bonhoeffer and his times. On almost every topic crucial to grasping Bonhoeffer's context, these reviewers concluded, *Bonhoeffer* oversimplified and misinformed.[15]

If readers did not seem to notice or care about these things, it was in part because Metaxas summarized matters of scholarly complexity with formulations that were clever, though rarely clarifying. For instance, Metaxas summed up Nazism's relationship to Christianity, a complicated topic about which a great deal has been written in recent years, with the simplistic claims that the "anti-Christian" Nazis "pretend[ed] to be Christians" and that "Hitler had no religion other than himself."[16]

Evangelical Reservations

The popular enthusiasm that lifted *Bonhoeffer: Pastor, Martyr, Prophet, Spy* to the top of the *New York Times* best-seller list proved a mixed blessing. The book's immense success attracted unprecedented negative attention from mainstream scholars, which in turn led some evangelical opinion makers to publicly express reservations about the portrait of Bonhoeffer constructed by Metaxas. Already in June 2010, in fact, *Books and Culture* sounded a note of caution regarding the Metaxas phenomenon. "Unsurprisingly," reviewer Andy Rowell wrote, "Eric Metaxas gives us a Bonhoeffer who looks a lot like an American evangelical—an extraordinarily courageous American evangelical. Bonhoeffer grows up in a family with privilege, travels abroad, gets advanced degrees, teaches Sunday school, daily reads his Bible and prays, is dismissive of American liberal theology, breaks with the institutional church, is not a complete pacifist, and is concerned about abortion." While this picture of Bonhoeffer is not inaccurate, Rowell wrote, it could induce "cognitive dissonance" for readers who are aware of the differences between the ways Bonhoeffer and American evangelicals speak of matters such as evangelism and biblical interpretation.[17]

This dissonance was explored more thoroughly by Richard Weikart in a review titled "Metaxas's Counterfeit Bonhoeffer: An Evangelical Critique." Weikart argued that while Metaxas had "serve[d] up a Bonhoeffer suited to the evangelical taste," his claim that Bonhoeffer was as "orthodox as the Apostle Paul" could only be attributed to a lack of familiarity with the German theologian's thought. "Metaxas does not seem to know," Weikart wrote, that Bonhoeffer had doubts about the virgin birth, rejected the notion of verbal inspiration, warned against viewing claims of Christ's resurrection as ontological statements, and rejected apologetics as misguided. Furthermore, contrary to Metaxas's picture of Bonhoeffer as a model of devotional piety, by his own admission Bonhoeffer was less faithful in the "daily discipline of scriptural meditation and prayer" than Metaxas suggests.[18]

"How did Metaxas get it so wrong?" Weikart asked. In part, his insufficient grounding in the fields of history, theology, and philosophy caused him to get "in over his head." Weikart even doubted whether Metaxas had read much of Bonhoeffer's own writings, some of which, he noted, "contain ideas that would cause most evangelicals to cringe (or worse)." Citing "bona fide Bonhoeffer scholar[s]" such as Victoria Barnett and Clifford Green, Weikart concluded his review by lamenting that despite the preponderance of evidence for the pastor-theologian's complexity, evangelicals might actually prefer Metaxas's counterfeit Bonhoeffer.[19]

With time, more and more evangelical opinion makers have chosen to embrace a more complex Bonhoeffer than that offered by Metaxas. In May 2010, popular evangelical blogger Tim Challies sang the praises of Metaxas's book, which, he said, had become one of his favorite biographies. In early 2011, however, after encountering reviews by Weikert and Green, Challies offered a more sober assessment of *Bonhoeffer*. Although initially reluctant to acknowledge what these authors were saying about the book, he was eventually inclined to accept "the weight of scholarship and experience" they brought to the critical task. They may well be right, Challies concluded, that Bonhoeffer "was simply too unorthodox to appeal to the likes of me." While Metaxas's book remained among Challies's favorites, he was forced to acknowledge that "we evangelicals may just prefer a safe and friendly character over an accurate one."[20]

At about the same time, evangelical blogger Carl Trueman interpreted the Metaxas phenomenon as evidence of a "general tendency in American evangelical circles to claim anybody who is helpful or admirable as an evangelical of some sort." It is evangelicals' equivalent, he suggested, of Karl Rahner's notion of "anonymous Christians." "I can understand the need to make our heroes like us," Trueman wrote, but "would be very surprised if we can make [Bonhoeffer] 'one of us' without fundamentally twisting his life and thought."[21]

In late 2012, Michael Hayes launched a blog called *Bonhoeffer and Evangelicals*, partially in response to the popularity of *Bonhoeffer: Pastor, Martyr, Prophet, Spy*. Hayes's verdict on the book was that Metaxas was "a good story teller but quite inept in theology, dismissing Bonhoeffer's mature thought without understanding it at all." While Hayes maintained that Bonhoeffer shared the "foundations of our faith—especially a trust in Scripture as the Word of God and a deep devotion to Jesus Christ," he conceded that Bonhoeffer matured in his thinking in ways evangelicals have been reluctant to explore.[22]

In early 2011, growing doubts concerning Metaxas's portrait of Bonhoeffer had reached the pages of *Christianity Today*, American evangelicalism's leading magazine. Jason B. Hood charged Metaxas with missing the fact that Bonhoeffer was actually "a liberal with some evangelical sympathies or leanings" and wondered if the book's "passion had outrun [its] theological sophistication." Hood echoed Bonhoeffer scholar Nancy Lukens in his claim that Metaxas's book suffered from being agenda-driven.[23]

The Metaxas Agenda

Are Lukens and Hood correct in concluding that Eric Metaxas's biography of Bonhoeffer is driven by a theological or political agenda? Or are the book's misrepresentations the inevitable consequence of a nontheologian trying to write about one of the most thoroughly researched figures in modern theology, aided by a publisher chiefly interested in appealing to the sensibilities of evangelical readers? While Metaxas's inexperience has certainly affected the book's reliability, there is much evidence that his biography of Bonhoeffer is driven by a conscious and multifaceted agenda.

One aspect of this agenda is easier to recognize when we consider *Bonhoeffer* alongside Metaxas's best-selling biography of William Wilberforce, published in 2007. Just as *Amazing Grace: William Wilberforce and the Heroic Campaign to End Slavery* found readers anxious to embrace an evangelical Christian who steadfastly opposed the Atlantic slave trade, *Bonhoeffer* tapped into Christians' need to be assured that there was, as the book's promotional copy put it, "a profoundly orthodox Christian theologian whose faith led him to boldly confront the greatest evil of the 20th century." In a 2013 interview, Metaxas succinctly described the role these two men play in his apologetic project: "Wilberforce, because of his faith, stood up for African slaves. Bonhoeffer, because of his faith, stood up for Jews. That's Christianity to me."[24]

Of course, stories of Christians who "stood up" for the oppressed have the important function of demonstrating that at crucial moments when the line between good and evil was clearly illuminated, Christians could be found on the right side of history. From Metaxas's perspective, it is also vital that these up-standers be orthodox Christians with evangelical sensibilities. Portraying Wilberforce in this way was relatively easy given his close identification with British evangelicalism. But translating Bonhoeffer's life and thought into an Anglo-American evangelical idiom was not so simple. What was required was nothing short of a transformation of Bonhoeffer's image in the American mind. As Metaxas told *Harper's*, "because Bonhoeffer has been so consistently portrayed as a theological liberal, it's important for us to see the other side, and I hope I've shown that in my book."[25]

Among the obstacles to making Bonhoeffer evangelical-friendly are his clear intellectual debt to arch-liberals like Adolf von Harnack and the neo-orthodox giant Karl Barth, his affinity for thinkers like Edmund Husserl and Rudolf Bultmann, and the prison letters in which he appears to welcome a secular, postreligious world. Precisely because these letters are the sources for concepts such as "world come of age" and "religionless Christianity" that have long vexed evangelical interpreters, Metaxas is adamant that Bonhoeffer's imprisonment did not lead him to relinquish any of his fundamental convictions. As Metaxas told an interviewer, the notion that the theological ruminations in these letters indicate a drifting away from orthodox Christianity is an invention of "the secular Left."[26]

Maintaining an evangelical-friendly portrait of Bonhoeffer also required Metaxas to draw very selectively from his writings. For instance, although Metaxas quotes from Bonhoeffer's magnum opus *Ethics* only four times, one of these passages is the pro-life proof text in which abortion is called "a violation of the right to live which God has bestowed upon this nascent life." The effort to appeal to evangelical sensibilities is more subtly evidenced when Metaxas writes that Bonhoeffer sought not only to teach his students but also to "'disciple' them in the true life of the Christian." "Disciple" is not a word Bonhoeffer would have employed as a transitive verb, of course; but this usage resonates pleasantly with the ethos of American evangelicalism.[27]

A second dimension of the agenda driving Metaxas's *Bonhoeffer* is the author's need to recast Christianity's dismal record of complicity in Nazi anti-Semitism by portraying Bonhoeffer as a "righteous gentile" who died "giving his life for the Jews." Unfortunately, Metaxas's efforts to depict Bonhoeffer and other Confessing Church leaders as staunch opponents of Nazi Jew-hatred lead him to distort the historical record, for instance in his claim that the Barmen Declaration "repudiated antisemitism." In truth, Barmen's failure to address the "Jewish Question" is so widely acknowledged that a standard resource on the Holocaust concedes that the declaration did "not mention Jews or express the slightest critique of Nazi antisemitism . . . so that Nazis could sign the document in good conscience." Metaxas's depiction of the Barmen Declaration as condemning anti-Semitism is more than a factual error; it is a by-product of his effort to portray Bonhoeffer and other Confessing Church leaders as unflinching advocates of Jewish rights under Hitler.[28]

The same agenda is evident in Metaxas's analysis of "The Church and the Jewish Question," the essay from April 1933 in which Bonhoeffer responded to German Christian efforts to introduce the "Aryan Paragraph" in Protestant churches. Metaxas simply ignores the essay's well-documented anti-Jewish dimensions, presumably because they do not conform to his profile of Bonhoeffer as a "righteous gentile vs. the Third Reich." As we have seen, Bonhoeffer's description of the Jews as a "witness people" destined to suffer for their rejection of Christ is so well known that it has been cited by Yad Vashem in refusing to honor him as one of the "righteous among the nations," despite his documented involvement in an effort to rescue German Jews. Metaxas also ignores Bonhoeffer's warnings in "The Church and the Jewish Question" and other writings about re-creating "modern Jewish Christianity" in the church. Metaxas simply refuses to allow these uncomfortable dimensions of Bonhoeffer's theological legacy to mar his portrait of a philo-Semite whose theology was as pro-Jewish as his sacrificial actions.

A third aspect of Metaxas's agenda that drives his portrayal of Bonhoeffer is his aspiration to link forces and institutions in contemporary America with the fascist ideology Bonhoeffer gave his life to resist. As we saw in the previous chapter, in interviews promoting *Bonhoeffer* Metaxas frequently likened the theologian's struggle against German fascism to the fight to defend American liberties from government encroachment, particularly freedom to dissent from the state's positions on sexuality, abortion, euthanasia, and stem-cell research. Metaxas has also noted "spectacular parallels" between liberalism's role in corrupting churches in Nazi Germany and contemporary America, as well as both cultures' assaults on "innocent life."

This dimension of Metaxas's agenda is so strong that it is responsible for one of the book's more glaring errors—the statement that Hitler was "democratically elected." As this claim is demonstrably false, it undoubtedly reflects poorly on Metaxas's knowledge of the period he is describing, not to mention the competence of his editors. But this mistake is best understood as a reflection of that part of Metaxas's authorial agenda that compels him to point out parallels between Bonhoeffer's time and our own. In this case, he does so by reminding readers that democracies do in fact elect fascist leaders. As Metaxas puts it elsewhere in the book, it was "Hitler's election to office [that] destroyed the office."[29]

Metaxas was not the only Christian conservative claiming that the Obama administration was showing signs of totalitarian intent. In fact, Frederick Clarkson has noted that in 2009 this sort of rhetoric became increasingly prominent on the Christian Right. "We have heard predictions of civil war, revolution and martyrdom," Clarkson writes, as well as "calls for political assassinations and secessionist civil war from White Southern Christian Nationalists." Metaxas's warnings were less apocalyptic, of course, but given his stature as a best-selling author, they were much more influential.[30]

Metaxas's Bonhoeffer in Context

To fully appreciate how novel is Metaxas's portrait of Bonhoeffer, we must view it not only in the context of the pastor-theologian's American reception but also in light of evangelical assessments of his legacy over time. As we saw in an earlier chapter, these assessments have run the gamut from serious engagements with Bonhoeffer's theology, to "heroes of the faith" biographies, to novelistic works of Christian fiction, to projects for church renewal, to cultural commentaries on issues as diverse as abortion and poverty. Even evangelical interpreters who are knowledgeable of his theology disagree on questions such as the degree of continuity in Bonhoeffer's thought, the extent to which it is informed by theological "liberalism," and whether his familiar pious language obscures unorthodox theological commitments.

Yet the majority of evangelical readings of Bonhoeffer acknowledge that his cultural context, intellectual training, and personal concerns were vastly different from those of contemporary Americans. Timothy Larsen says as much when he notes that "it is not standard for evangelicals to claim that Bonhoeffer was himself an evangelical" and uses their reception of Saint Augustine to illustrate the point. "Evangelicals like and admire Augustine's life, thought and writings," Larsen writes, "but they do not pretend that he was an evangelical in the contemporary American sense of that term."[31]

But this is, in effect, what Metaxas has done, and why his portrayal of Bonhoeffer strays so far from the trajectory set by the serious evangelical interpreters that preceded him. In fact, Metaxas's attempt to make Bonhoeffer's theological orthodoxy axiomatic represents a significant retreat from the increasing care with which evangelical theologians have engaged Bonhoeffer as a conversation partner over the last half century. In this sense Metaxas does a disservice to evangelical, and all other, interpreters of Bonhoeffer by reinforcing a notion against which most of them have long fought—that Bonhoeffer's writings are a sort of Rorschach test onto which one can project contemporary interests and needs.

IN AN INTERVIEW TO PROMOTE his Bonhoeffer book, Eric Metaxas predicted that once he revealed "the real story of who [Bonhoeffer] was, of his extreme courage, and of his profound Christian faith," the German theologian would become much better known. This is one thing Metaxas got absolutely right. *Bonhoeffer: Pastor, Martyr, Prophet, Spy*—and the media attention it has generated—has probably made Bonhoeffer more popular in America than he has ever been. And despite the book's flaws, the consequences of its popularity are not all negative, for they include discussion among evangelicals about how comfortable conservative Protestants should be with Bonhoeffer, as well as direct engagement between Bonhoeffer scholars and popular assessments of his life and thought.[32]

But, as we will see, Metaxas's biography of Bonhoeffer has made his role in American political discussions less nuanced, more strident, and less deferential to scholarly expertise. Most interpreters prior to Metaxas acknowledged that Bonhoeffer was a complex figure who could be read in different ways, and few argued that opposing views were a result of conscious efforts to "hijack" his legacy. That is, before Metaxas the battle for Bonhoeffer was a generally nonviolent enterprise in which interpretive schemes were advanced, contested, and subsequently revised. Metaxas, however, has helped transform Bonhoeffer interpretation into a zero-sum, winner-take-all contest. The results are explored in the following chapters.

PART THREE

Triumph of the Populist Bonhoeffer

CHAPTER SEVEN

Kairos: "A Bonhoeffer Moment in America"

THE PHRASE "Bonhoeffer moment" emerged as a rallying cry for the Christian Right rather unintentionally. Toward the end of his keynote address at the 2012 National Prayer Breakfast, Eric Metaxas proclaimed: "The grace of the living God . . . is the only thing that can bring Left and Right together to do the right thing. So can we humble ourselves enough . . . to ask Him in a real prayer to show Himself to us, to lead us to do what is right? Can we do that for the country, for the world? This is a Bonhoeffer moment. If we will humbly ask God, cry out . . . 'Lord lead us!'"[1]

The concept of the "Bonhoeffer moment" did not immediately catch on. But three years later—in March 2015—the expression would enter the public lexicon as Christian activists anxiously awaited the decision of the US Supreme Court in *Obergefell v. Hodges*, which would determine the constitutionality of state laws banning same-sex marriage. Many evangelical Christians perceived the moment as a sort of *kairos*—the New Testament term for a time pregnant with meaning and opportunity. An endorsement of traditional marriage by the Supreme Court would be an important victory for conservatives in the culture war. An unfavorable decision in *Obergefell*, however, could transform America's moral environment as no legal decision had done since *Roe v. Wade*.

On March 10, thirty or so Christian leaders participated in an hour-long conference call in which the implications of the impending Supreme Court decision were discussed and possible responses considered. The main participants were Rick Scarborough, president of Vision America Action; James Dobson, founder of Focus on the Family; and Mat Staver, founder of Liberty Counsel. In his opening remarks, Scarborough expressed widespread concern about the ruling soon expected from the Supreme Court. "We believe," he said,

> that the majority of the Court will rule in favor of elevating what we have always taught to be a sinful lifestyle to the stature of a civil right—forcing us to choose between their ruling and our religious convictions that are based on Scripture. This ruling will conflict with our deeply held conviction and religious belief. With the current administration there is every reason to believe that the Executive Branch will use the full weight of the Federal justice system to enforce this. We must be prepared for that possibility. We have all known that this day would likely come and Christians would be put at odds with the culture and the courts. I believe we are there. We are approaching a Bonhoeffer moment in America.[2]

The next speaker was Staver, who confirmed that this was a critical juncture in American history: "The photographer out in New Mexico, the baker in Oregon, [the] Washington florist . . . they are all facing the same thing. We either all stand together or we hang separately. This is indeed a Bonhoeffer moment." Others participants on the call repeated the slogan, which was soon picked up by journalists and bloggers.

While the phrase "Bonhoeffer moment" remained undefined, it resonated among Christians who believed their right to exercise religious freedom was under threat from many directions. If one knew where to look, the signs were everywhere—growing cultural acceptance of homosexuality and the opening of mainline Christian denominations to gay marriage; the US Supreme Court decision in *Burwell v. Hobby Lobby Stores* (2014) that determined closely held for-profit corporations could be exempted from certain regulations if their owners objected on religious grounds; the likelihood that Hillary Clinton would follow Barack Obama into the White House; and the ongoing "war on Christmas." These developments contributed to the perception that America's foundations as a Christian nation were under attack and generated deep anxiety among evangelicals as they awaited the Supreme Court's decision in *Obergefell v. Hodges*.

The conference call on which evangelical leaders strategized about how to prepare for their Bonhoeffer moment gave rise to a widely circulated marriage pledge that echoed with notes of resistance. Titled "We Pledge in Solidarity to Defend Marriage and the Family and Society Founded upon Them" and signed by top conservative leaders, the pledge delivered a sharp warning: "Make no mistake about our resolve. While there are many things we can endure, redefining marriage is so fundamental to the natural order and the common good that this is the line we must draw and one we cannot and will not cross." For the time being, such vague threats of resistance would find traction mainly in the blogosphere.[3]

Among those who resonated with the tone of this "marriage pledge" was blogger Larry Tomczak, who, after recounting a disturbing series of recent departures from traditional cultural standards related to "natural marriage and sexual purity," concluded that America was indeed facing a "Dietrich Bonhoeffer Moment." Tomczak counseled his readers to prepare themselves for the sort of risks faced by the German pastor-theologian, who "chose civil disobedience and disobeyed Nazi law" in order to assist threatened Jews. Tomczak cited biblical figures Moses, Daniel, Esther, Peter, and John as examples of faithful men and women who knew that "when man-made laws are contrary to divine laws," they must be disobeyed. "Brace yourself," he advised, "and prepare to face new challenges requiring risk-taking as the new normal in an increasingly secular society."[4]

Tomczak's drafting of Bonhoeffer to fight in the war against same-sex marriage drew a careful rebuttal from blogger Bob Seidensticker. Responding to the claim that the Supreme Court was about to "impose" homosexual marriage on the states, Seidensticker countered with a reminder of what had actually been at stake for Bonhoeffer: "You want an imposition? . . . [Bonhoeffer] was hanged in Flossenbürg concentration camp just weeks before the end of the war for working with the Resistance. *That's* an imposition." Was Tomczak really equating speaking out against same-sex marriage with Bonhoeffer's history of "standing up to the Nazis, protecting Jews . . . working to overthrow Hitler, and getting executed"? Seidensticker asked.[5]

In late April the pending "Bonhoeffer moment" was proclaimed in public for the first time. The herald was Rev. Ron Johnson Jr., executive director of the Indiana Pastors Alliance, the venue, a statehouse rally in support of Indiana's Religious Freedom and Restoration Act. (The measure had passed in March but was subsequently amended following a tidal wave of corporate pushback.) Johnson accused Governor Mike Pence and other state leaders of failing to "stand for biblical truth" and caving in to pressure from business, media, and gay rights groups. For a few days, Johnson's invocation of Bonhoeffer became the subject of editorials and letters in the *Indianapolis Star*. Among the responses was the observation that since homosexuals were among those persecuted under Nazi rule, Bonhoeffer surely would not have promoted legislation that allowed anti-gay discrimination.[6]

The Southern Baptists Have Their Bonhoeffer Moment

By early May, monitors of the Christian Right were beginning to notice and respond to Bonhoeffer's burgeoning role in the rhetoric employed by the forces of anti-marriage equality. An article in *LGBTQ Nation* observed that Bonhoeffer was "increasingly invoked by Christian Right leaders as they compare the situation in the United States to Nazi Germany and cast him . . . as a role model for Christian Right resistance." This article did not mention the phrase "Bonhoeffer moment." But the expression was about to become much better known.[7]

On June 15, in an address to five thousand assembled "messengers" to the Southern Baptist Convention's (SBC) annual plenary gathering, convention president Rev. Ronnie Floyd used the phrase "Bonhoeffer moment" in a stinging indictment of the Supreme Court and the nation's moral decline. Floyd warned that the impending Court announcement could alter "not only our nation's belief and practice of traditional and biblical marriage," but also its commitment to religious liberty. "This could be a watershed moment in our history," he cautioned, "possibly changing the trajectory of our nation unlike anything we've seen since" *Roe v. Wade*. Floyd directed a challenge to American Christians beyond the SBC, emphasizing that a "Bonhoeffer moment" precipitated by the Supreme Court would affect "every pastor in the United States who believes the Word of God." Floyd warned that while some evangelicals might bow down to "the deception of the inclusiveness of same-sex marriage, we will not bow down, nor will we be silent."[8]

Because the SBC is America's largest Protestant denomination with about 16 million members, its annual convention regularly makes national news. Floyd's speech, however, brought the gathering unprecedented attention, and reaction continued to percolate until the end of June. Floyd's references to Bonhoeffer were reported not only in conservative religious publications like *Charisma* and *Christianity Today* but also by mainstream news outlets from Fox News to MSNBC. The same day as Floyd's SBC speech, commentator Todd Starnes cited his Bonhoeffer reference in an opinion piece for *Fox News Online* and predicted that Floyd would soon suffer attacks from "intolerant bullies and the radical speech police."[9]

By that evening Floyd's speech was the subject of multiple news reports, including a segment on MSNBC's *Rachel Maddow Show*. After playing a clip of Floyd's speech, Maddow did her best to clarify the Bonhoeffer allusion for her progressive audience: "What he's referencing, of course, is the German Lutheran pastor who was part of a plot to kill Hitler during World War II," she explained. Maddow then paraphrased Floyd's argument with characteristic wit: "So the head of the Southern Baptists today [was] saying: American pastors are going to be having an 'assassinate Hitler moment' if the Supreme Court says that gay people can get married."[10]

Two days later, writing on the *Huffington Post*'s religion blog, Jeffrey Small called Floyd's invocation of Bonhoeffer to oppose marriage equality a "bold act of misappropriation." Small noted that using the pastor-theologian to justify bigotry was "especially egregious" considering his historical context, which Small clumsily described as "a Nazi prison where he was held captive and then executed for opposing Hitler's brutal treatment of the Jews." Shifting analogies, Small predicted that when the debate over LGBT rights and same-sex marriage has ended, opponents of equal rights will be judged as "backwards as those who supported segregation." It is no coincidence, he concluded, that those who wish to deny equal protection for sexual minorities today are often the same groups who opposed black civil rights a generation ago.[11]

Reactions in the blogosphere to Floyd's Bonhoeffer references echoed Small's, with added outrage. One blogger called the SBC a "hate group" and interpreted Floyd's Bonhoeffer allusion this way: "Who's this Bonhoeffer guy? Oh, just a German Lutheran pastor and conspirator in various anti-Nazi resistance efforts, including plots to assassinate Hitler. So the SBC is now engaged in 'spiritual warfare' . . . and every pastor is facing a 'Bonhoeffer moment,' so . . . they should start plotting to assassinate someone? Presumably a crazed dictator? We don't actually have one of those handy right now in America, but I bet the SBC can think of some leader who deserves to die. (Hint: the black guy. He's talking about the black guy)."[12]

At the end of June, in a post provocatively titled "No, You Are Not the Bonhoeffer in This Moment," Alyson Miers challenged Floyd's claim to Bonhoeffer's legacy and warned of the consequences of opposing inevitable cultural shifts. "Fifty years from now," she wrote, echoing Small, "opponents of gay rights—emphatically including civil marriage—will be the ones that we struggle to explain to our disbelieving, horrified grandchildren." As others had done, Miers reminded readers of the irony that gays and lesbians were among the groups targeted by the Hitler regime. Stressing Bonhoeffer's unpopular solidarity with innocent minorities, Miers concluded that "if Ronnie Floyd had lived in Germany at that time, he wouldn't have sympathized with Bonhoeffer."[13]

In a post on the *Patheos* blog, Chuck Queen called Floyd's proclamation of a Bonhoeffer moment "crazy" and reminded readers that Bonhoeffer had "opposed Hitler by forming the Confessing Church" and paying "the ultimate price for his opposition with his life." Queen went on to assert that although he himself had encountered opposition for his public support of same-sex marriage and LGBT inclusion, he did not regard himself as a victim of persecution, and neither should those with opposing views. "For Floyd to draw upon Bonhoeffer here," Queen concluded, "is a disservice and dishonor to Bonhoeffer's good name."[14]

As the battle for Bonhoeffer raged on in early 2015, a post at the *Red State* blog titled "This Generation's Bonhoeffer Is among Us . . . Tragically" imagined a pastor who has been asked to officiate at the wedding of two women. He tells the congregation that while he can acknowledge their entry into a legally binding contract, he cannot pronounce them "married in the eyes of God" since, despite the recent decision of the US Supreme Court, "he cannot celebrate something that is an affront to almost all of my congregants, and an abomination before the Lord my God, Jesus Christ." The women sue the pastor and, after he is indicted for violating "the Schumer Hate Speech Act" of 2017, his neck is broken by the US marshals sent to arrest him by President Clinton.[15]

In the midst of these fierce debates over same-sex marriage, religious freedom, and the role of Bonhoeffer in guiding American Christians' theological and political commitments, the Supreme Court decision in *Obergefell v. Hodges* came down on June 26. Now that the decision conservatives had feared was a reality, the threatened Bonhoeffer moment seemed to have arrived. Before reviewing the shape it took, however, we need to look more closely at the moment's genealogy.

Backgrounds of the Bonhoeffer Moment

What contributed to the decision to invoke Dietrich Bonhoeffer at such a critical juncture in evangelicals' engagement with American culture? In addition to the "confessing" movement in American Protestantism discussed in a previous chapter, two phenomena help illuminate the proclamation of a "Bonhoeffer moment" in 2015: the history of conservative reactions to landmark US Supreme Court decisions and Eric Metaxas's role in portraying Bonhoeffer as a model for evangelical activism.

Resistance to US Supreme Court Decisions

Evangelicals' declaration that they would defend "traditional marriage" regardless of the decision handed down in *Obergefell v. Hodges* was not the first time American Christians had vowed to resist a decision of the Supreme Court. The example most often cited by evangelicals themselves is *Roe v. Wade* (1973), which determined that a woman's decision to seek an abortion was protected under the Constitution's guarantee of the right to privacy. But in the run-up to *Obergefell*, evangelicals began to invoke older Supreme Court decisions that came to be regarded as such miscarriages of justice that they were subsequently overturned. They pointed, for instance, to *Dred Scott v. John F. A. Sandford* (1857), which declared that the enslaved African American plaintiff could not sue for his freedom since he was not an American citizen, and *Buck v. Bell* (1927), which upheld a state law permitting compulsory sterilization of the intellectually disabled.

The marriage pledge circulated in March 2015 explicitly mentioned these cases as examples of the Supreme Court's failure to execute justice at critical moments in American history. According to the pledge's authors, the Court was "wrong when it denied Dred Scott his rights and said, 'blacks are inferior human beings,'" and wrong when it upheld Virginia's eugenics law in *Buck v. Bell*. With these cases in mind, signers of the pledge promised to regard any court decision that normalized same-sex marriage "the same way history views" these decisions.[16]

However, a much clearer historical precedent for evangelical reactions to the Court's decision in *Obergefell* is the firestorm that greeted *Brown v. Topeka Board of Education* (1954), in which state laws establishing "separate but equal" schools for black and white students were judged unconstitutional. The parallel is compelling not only because conservatives' visceral response to *Brown* signaled their strategy of "massive resistance" to the civil rights movement, but because the decision was interpreted by many as an attempt to overturn a divinely sanctioned order. While some Christian denominations—notably including the Southern Baptist Convention—initially supported *Brown*, before long southern Christians of nearly every stripe were decrying the decision as legislative overreach, not to mention a violation of God's will revealed in Scripture. As Jerry Falwell put it in a 1958 sermon condemning *Brown*, "when God has drawn a line of distinction, we should not attempt to cross that line." In fact, much evangelical Christian reaction to *Brown* could be summed up in words from the 2015 marriage pledge: "Our highest respect for the rule of law requires that we not respect an unjust law that directly conflicts with higher law."[17]

Given that the results of the civil rights movement are almost universally endorsed by Americans today, resistance to *Brown* is not a historical analogue opponents of same-sex marriage wish to acknowledge. For this reason, conservative critics of *Obergefell* have not only ignored this history of opposition to civil rights but actually compared their own struggles against government oppression to those of African Americans. To this end they have regularly invoked the "incorrect and . . . tragic" decision in *Dred Scott v. Sandford* and the writings of Martin Luther King Jr. and other emblems of the civil rights movement.

In fact, in the months before the *Obergefell* decision, "Selma" became a symbolic touchstone for Christians who were demanding that the federal government acknowledge their "rights." As Rick Scarborough noted during the conference call on which the "Bonhoeffer moment" was first proclaimed, it was significant that Christian advocates of traditional marriage were taking their stand very near the fiftieth anniversary of the 1965 Selma-to-Montgomery march. "The timing of this conference call in coordination with the anniversary of the stand on the bridge in Selma is remarkable," Scarborough opined. "Things do not change if no one stands up and takes the brunt."[18]

There is a twofold irony in these attempts to draw parallels between resistance to same-sex marriage and advocacy for black civil rights. First, many Americans regard the quest for gay equality as parallel with—even an extension of—the American civil rights movement. Second, conservative Christians of the sort now invoking Bonhoeffer moments were generally opponents of the black liberation struggle when the movement's results were still in doubt. Awareness of this uncomfortable fact may be behind evangelical efforts to belatedly locate themselves on the right side of American history by laying claim to iconic figures and events of the civil rights movement. Yet evangelical indifference and antagonism toward the long civil rights movement in America suggest that a better parallel for their efforts may lie in the massive resistance to social change mounted by their parents and grandparents in the 1950s and '60s.

This is a point Jeffrey Small emphasized in his response to Southern Baptist Convention president Ronnie Floyd. "The angry opposition of the SBC toward granting gay couples the same rights as heterosexual couples," Small wrote, "echoes back to an earlier troubling time in church history in which southern Baptists fought against equal rights for another oppressed minority group in this country: blacks." Noting that it took 150 years before the SBC issued a formal apology for its support of segregation, Small wondered whether the SBC's "new agenda of exclusionism and discrimination" would require a similar confession of guilt in the future.[19]

The Metaxas Factor

It would be foolish to assert a cause-and-effect relationship between a book and a political movement that emerges five years after its publication. But one should not underestimate the role of Eric Metaxas in shaping the rhetorical environment in which the Bonhoeffer moment became intelligible to evangelicals in 2015.

Metaxas did not invent the evangelical Bonhoeffer, of course, but, as we have seen, his 2010 book *Bonhoeffer: Pastor, Martyr, Prophet, Spy* pushed evangelical familiarity and comfort with Bonhoeffer to a new level while stifling reasoned debate about the pastor-theologian's legacy. Since in promoting his Bonhoeffer biography Metaxas had repeatedly emphasized the "spectacular parallels" between contemporary America and Germany in the 1930s, it is not surprising that as conservative resistance to Obama was peaking during his second term, Metaxas continued to voice the view that Nazi Germany comprised a warning for America.

While being interviewed on American Family Radio (AFR) in May 2015, for instance, Metaxas restated his claim that God was using Bonhoeffer's story to awaken people to the "frightening" analogues between assaults on religious liberty in Nazi Germany and those in present-day America. "I really believe the story of Bonhoeffer is the gift of God to the American church today," Metaxas told AFR's Tim Wildmon. "We all need to . . . understand . . . what happened to Germany, a Christian nation, [and] what can we learn from that."

Metaxas added that America was "at a tipping point." "If the church does not wake up right now," he warned, "it is game over, we've been neutralized, just like in Germany; that's exactly what happened to the church, they woke up and it was too late."[20]

By repeating such claims in print and over the airwaves, Metaxas succeeded in establishing Bonhoeffer as a trustworthy model for American evangelicals who were increasingly disaffected from their federal government. And Metaxas's outlets for shaping this portrait of Bonhoeffer had only increased between 2010 and 2015. In fact, by the time the phrase "Bonhoeffer moment" was coined by evangelical leaders, Metaxas had become a bona fide public intellectual with a nationally syndicated radio show.

While Metaxas's influence is impossible to quantify, it surely helps explain why the phrase "Bonhoeffer moment" received so little clarification from the Christian leaders who employed it. Since American evangelicals are not known for lionizing academically trained Continental theologians, one might expect them to offer some rationale for making one of them a paradigm of Christian political action. Yet in proclaiming the Bonhoeffer moment, neither Rick Scarborough, Mat Staver, Ronnie Floyd, nor anyone else made an effort to explain the phrase by referring to Bonhoeffer's life, theology, or historical milieu. This is particularly striking in the case of Floyd, who invoked Bonhoeffer before several thousand Southern Baptist laypersons.

The best explanation for the failure of evangelical leaders to offer any elaboration of the Bonhoeffer moment is the most obvious one—elaboration was unnecessary because these leaders shared with their audiences an intuitive understanding of the expression. By developing and disseminating a portrait of Bonhoeffer as an evangelical culture warrior who refused to bow before the Nazis, Metaxas did more than anyone to create this common understanding. In fact, it is likely that by 2015 Metaxas's portrait of Bonhoeffer had become so ubiquitous among evangelicals that it was nearly impossible for them to hear the phrase "Bonhoeffer moment" without it coming to mind.

The Bonhoeffer Moment Arrives . . . Sort Of

While the evangelical leaders who proclaimed 2015's Bonhoeffer moment remained vague about what it meant or what exactly it had to do with Bonhoeffer, they did hint that it would involve antigovernment resistance. "We are not going to bow, we are not going to bend, and if necessary we will burn," announced Rick Scarborough. "We either all stand together or we hang separately," offered Mat Staver. "We will not bow down, nor will we be silent," proclaimed Ronnie Floyd.

So at the end of June, when the Supreme Court emphatically crossed the line evangelical leaders had drawn in the sand, many were anxious to learn what form the Bonhoeffer moment would assume. No one could have predicted that the symbol of principled resistance to *Obergefell*—the Bonhoeffer in the "Bonhoeffer moment"—would be a middle-aged county clerk in Morehead, Kentucky, named Kim Davis. It was ironic that Davis was a lifelong Democrat; it was inconvenient that she had a complicated marital history; and it was downright embarrassing that she belonged to an anti-Trinitarian Pentecostal sect. However, Davis's brief stint in jail for refusing to grant marriage licenses to same-sex couples credited the claim that she was a victim of government persecution, a personification of what Mike Huckabee called the "criminalization of Christianity."[21]

As Davis's legal saga played out during the fall of 2015, evangelical leaders did their best to make her over as the face of Christian resistance to government overreach. While it strained the imagination to compare Dietrich Bonhoeffer with this thrice-divorced rural Kentuckian, Mat Staver did his best when he nominated her for *Time*'s Person of the Year. As the "first Christian in America jailed as a result of the Supreme Court decision," Staver wrote, Davis "joins a long list of people who were imprisoned for their conscience," including Martin Luther King Jr., Jan Hus, John Bunyan, and, of course, Dietrich Bonhoeffer.[22]

Bo Wagner, a Baptist minister in Mooresville, North Carolina, went further, interpreting Davis's five-day incarceration through the lens of King's "Letter from Birmingham Jail," the early Christians' refusal to obey prohibitions on preaching in Jesus's name, and the faithful men and women throughout history who had decided to "obey God rather than men." Not surprisingly, this great cloud of witnesses featured Bonhoeffer, the "preacher and martyr of World War II Germany" who, Wagner wrote, "decried the follower mentality of Christians who obeyed the authorities who were slaughtering Jews all around them."[23]

A Different Sort of Bonhoeffer Moment

In one of many ironies associated with Bonhoeffer's American reception, at the very moment the German pastor-theologian was being used to rally American Christians against normalizing same-sex love, Bonhoeffer scholars were exploring the homoerotic undertones in the theologian's relationship with his closest male friend.

In *Strange Glory: A Life of Dietrich Bonhoeffer* (2014), Charles Marsh argued that Bonhoeffer's relationship with Eberhard Bethge had been quite unusual. Not only had they shared a bedroom at Dietrich's parents' house and celebrated "anniversaries" in their own relationship, but they "kept a joint bank account, signed Christmas cards from 'Dietrich and Eberhard,' fussed over gifts they gave together, planned elaborate vacations, and endured numerous quarrels." Marsh emphasized that the men's relationship had remained chaste, that although Bonhoeffer was "smitten" with his younger friend, his love had gone unrequited and unconsummated. But as Bonhoeffer sought "an ever-deepening intimacy" Bethge could not reciprocate, the men's friendship naturally became "ambiguous and confusing." Marsh's nuanced conclusion was that the relationship "strained toward the achievement of a romantic love, one ever chaste but complete in its complex aspirations."[24]

In a 2016 book titled *The Doubled Life of Dietrich Bonhoeffer*, Diane Reynolds took Marsh's suggestions further. Based on Dietrich's strong identification with the main character in George Santayana's *The Last Puritan*, his obsessive concern to be with Bethge in the years after Finkenwalde, and other aspects of their "entwined lives," Reynolds maintained that Bonhoeffer was "in love" with

Bethge, and even detected a "nascent queer theology" in some of his writings.[25]

Marsh and Reynolds gave careful articulation to suspicions that had lingered for years in the Bonhoeffer guild: that the relationship between Dietrich and Eberhard was deeper and more emotionally fraught than that between most heterosexual men in most times and places. To this point, the idea that Bonhoeffer might have been gay has not been embraced by most scholars. But the fact that it was articulated at precisely the cultural moment at which Bonhoeffer was being used to rally resistance to "the gay agenda" is compelling evidence of the growing disconnect between scholarly study of Bonhoeffer's life and popular use of his legacy.[26]

THOSE CLAIMING in 2015 that America faced a Bonhoeffer moment implied that Christians were facing threats analogous to those Bonhoeffer confronted after the rise of Hitler and warned that they would react in analogous ways. By linking the Bonhoeffer moment to a willingness to "stand together or . . . hang separately," evangelical leaders suggested that the time for speaking had past. However, just which actions of the Nazi state were comparable to the legalization of same-sex marriage was never made clear.

Presumably, if the Bonhoeffer moment implied the possibility of martyrdom, American conservatives believed they were facing the sort of conditions that had driven Bonhoeffer to join the anti-Hitler resistance in 1939. This is when he concluded that full-blown opposition to the German government had become his only effective moral option. War was imminent; thousands had been placed in extralegal "protective custody" or murdered outright; free speech and open debate had been almost totally suppressed; hundreds of thousands of Jews had been forced to emigrate and the rest appeared to be in mortal danger. Subterfuge, conspiracy, and even violence, Bonhoeffer reluctantly determined, were now the only avenues for exercising Christian responsibility.

Most observers surely had difficulty comparing the situation of American Christians who would have to tolerate same-sex marriage with that facing Germans on the eve of World War II. And yet 2015's

"Bonhoeffer moment" was not a rhetorical ploy. The expression captured the imagination of American evangelicals precisely because it reflected how seriously they regarded the cultural shifts taking place around them. And it warned Americans, or should have, about how they would approach the 2016 presidential election.

CHAPTER EIGHT

Surprise: Bonhoeffer Gets Trumped

By the end of 2015, the "Bonhoeffer moment" that had been confidently proclaimed only a few months earlier evaporated in a cloud of ridicule and parody. Despite repeated attempts to link Kim Davis's stand against the state of Kentucky with Dietrich Bonhoeffer's heroic anti-Nazi resistance, the phrase "Bonhoeffer moment" appears not to have been uttered in public after the Supreme Court's decision in *Obergefell* was announced in June. The court had called the bluffs of Christian leaders, and it appeared they had no response. Apparently, they had overplayed their hand.

But as the crisis surrounding *Obergefell* faded from the headlines, American conservatives found new opportunities to invoke Bonhoeffer in the raging culture war. In August 2015, a year after the police shooting of Michael Brown in Ferguson, Missouri, and the subsequent launch of the Black Lives Matter movement, television personality Glenn Beck held an "All Lives Matter" march and rally in Birmingham, Alabama. Addressing a crowd of about twenty thousand, Beck held up a purple triangle of the sort used to label incarcerated Jehovah's Witnesses in Nazi Germany and announced, "The Germans were good at categorizing people. They made categories for everyone. But this one was particularly dangerous. Dietrich Bonhoeffer wore a purple triangle."[1]

It was tempting to conclude that Beck had become caught up in the moment when he carelessly merged Bonhoeffer's fate with the Nazis' persecution of Jehovah's Witnesses. But Beck's reference to Christians wearing purple triangles was neither unintentional nor new. At Liberty University in 2014, for instance, Beck had claimed that being forced to wear the purple triangle in a Nazi concentration camp meant "you were a Bible scholar." In both cases Beck seems to have taken the German term for Jehovah's Witnesses (*Bibelforscher*, or "Bible student") as a Nazi description of anyone they regarded as a student of the Bible. Although this error was uniquely Beck's, it pretty well summed up the decontextualized role Bonhoeffer had come to play in American political discourse in mid-2015.[2]

Against such attention-grabbing, though sadly misinformed, appeals to Bonhoeffer, more thoughtful assessments of his relevance struggled for recognition. The same month that Beck was lumping Bonhoeffer together with Jehovah's Witnesses, Lael Arrington wrote despairingly of Americans' weariness with the political class and advocated a "Bonhoeffer alternative to doublespeak and cunning." Citing a paragraph from Bonhoeffer's "After Ten Years," Arrington claimed that although comparisons of the current American political and cultural climate to that of Nazi Germany were automatically dismissed, "we have to form our own opinions" as we read the words of "brave, thoughtful people" such as Bonhoeffer.[3]

In September the blog of the International Bonhoeffer Society's Bonhoeffer Center sought to reframe the previous months' framing of the American "Bonhoeffer moment." "Perhaps a 'Bonhoeffer Moment' as the acceptance of guilt is the type of moment the church currently needs," wrote the author, one that "brings the Church to her knees in humble repentance before her God." But efforts to set the conversation about Bonhoeffer and America on solid historical ground would have to navigate crosscurrents of conflicting assumptions that were about to merge with a tidal wave of election season rhetoric.[4]

The Trump Factor

To this point, Bonhoeffer's name had not been invoked in support of any particular member of the large bevy of candidates vying to replace Barack Obama in the White House. But in an insightful article in the *New York Times* in September 2015, Molly Worthen indirectly linked Bonhoeffer with the candidacy of Donald Trump, perhaps for the first time. In "Donald Trump and the Rise of the Moral Minority," Worthen did not mention the "Bonhoeffer moment" controversy that had unfolded a few months earlier. But she did observe Trump's high poll numbers among evangelicals, as well as an internal rift between evangelicals calling for culture war and those claiming that "Christians must adjust to life as a minority in American Babylon."

Worthen noted that Trump's vow to "make America great again" was resonating with evangelical voters in the old Christian Right mold who felt the country slipping from their grip. Others, however, were taking the loss of cultural capital in stride, concluding that evangelicals should reject Christian nationalism and embrace their role as "a new moral minority." These evangelical leaders, including never-Trumpers like Russell Moore, president of the Ethics and Religious Liberty Commission of the Southern Baptist Convention, tended to emphasize "witness" over power, Worthen wrote. Their goal was to persuade fellow evangelicals that "the Gospel thrives when being a Christian is a difficult, countercultural position."

Identifying historical models for this new breed of "countercultural warriors," Worthen drew attention to a "selective genealogy" that omitted anyone who had once used "the language of martyrdom and resistance to defend white supremacy" and included William Wilberforce and Dietrich Bonhoeffer. Noting that he had written biographies of both men, Worthen interviewed Eric Metaxas, who informed her that Bonhoeffer's story was relevant for Americans in 2015 because Christians in Germany did not understand that "sirens need to go off" when the state interferes in the freedom of religion.

Worthen doubted that the policies of Nazi Germany could be compared to, say, the Obama administration's contraception mandate. But Metaxas insisted that the window was closing on evangelicals' "God-given freedoms." In response to Metaxas's call for Christians "to be a loud, humble, bold, gracious, winsome voice," Worthen quipped that "winsome" was not the first word that comes to mind when one thinks of Donald Trump, whose tirades, she noted, are more reminiscent of George Wallace than William Wilberforce.[5]

Worthen got a lot right in this piece. Trump's popularity among evangelicals in late 2015 was certainly a harbinger of things to come.

And the rift she identified within evangelicalism between "power" and "witness," as she put it, carried real explanatory value. Worthen also saw that advocates of a "moral minority" might reach a political dead end, since "on the campaign trail, anger and xenophobia play better than repentance and grace." What Worthen could not have seen, however, is the role Metaxas, whom she upheld as a model of evangelical "winsomeness" combining "glossy sophistication and orthodoxy," would play in the Trump revolution.

Bonhoeffer and the 2016 Campaign

As if to signify that Bonhoeffer would play an outsized role in American public discourse during 2016, on January 1 Marian Wright Edelman wrote in her "Child Watch" column on the Children's Defense Fund website that the United States had reached an inflection point "as wars and terrorism abroad are echoed in violence, suspicion, and fear at home." Referring to the recently launched "We Are Better Than This" campaign that called on politicians and the media to "stop the spread of hate and division" and citing a litany of existential threats facing American children, Wright wrote: "Dietrich Bonhoeffer, the great German Protestant theologian who died opposing Hitler's holocaust, believed that the test of the morality of a society is how it treats its children. We flunk Bonhoeffer's test every hour of every day in America as we let the violence of guns and the violence of poverty relentlessly stalk and sap countless child lives."[6]

In April 2016 there was another broad-based expression of concern at the alarming rhetoric that had become a defining feature of the 2016 election cycle. Titled "Called to Resist Bigotry: A Statement of Faithful Obedience" and signed by over fifty Christian leaders, the statement concluded that "the ascendancy of a demagogic candidate and his message, with the angry constituency he is fueling, is a threat to both the values of our faith and the health of our democracy." Invoking the very misattribution Eric Metaxas had helped popularize, "Called to Resist Bigotry" claimed that the "German pastor and theologian" once wrote that "silence in the face of evil is itself evil: God will not hold us guiltless. Not to speak is to speak. Not to act is to act." In a *Huffington Post* piece commenting on the statement and its significance, Jim Wallis repeated the "silence" quote and noted that Bonhoeffer's writings were "experiencing a renewal among many Christians, especially younger ones."[7]

In the early months of 2016, Bonhoeffer was occasionally cited in attacks on particular presidential candidates. In an April assault on Bernie Sanders published on the *Front Page* website, for example, Jack Kerwick leveled charges against the candidate that appear quite ironic given the results of the general election. Sanders's popularity should not be a surprise, Kerwick wrote, since in the era of "political correctness" the way one treats one's family, friends, neighbors, and colleagues has lost all moral significance. According to Kerwick, Sanders believed that moral virtue could be equated with support for an activist national government that confiscates and redistributes citizens' legitimately acquired resources. To add an air of theological legitimacy to his attack on Sanders, Kerwick cited Bonhoeffer's *Discipleship*, which he mistakenly described as being written "in the late 1930's, while [he] sat in a prison cell." The "cheap grace" Bonhoeffer described in that book, Kerwick claimed, is akin to political correctness and Bernie Sanders's morality.[8]

By early May, as it became clear that Hillary Clinton and Donald Trump would face off in the general election, the salient question for evangelical voters who leaned Republican was whether they could ignore Trump's moral failings and shift their support from outspoken Christian candidates like Mike Huckabee, Ted Cruz, and Ben Carson. Aware that some bewildered evangelicals were considering sitting out the election altogether, Eric Metaxas reshaped his favorite Bonhoeffer "quote" about speaking and acting into a moral imperative to vote. "As Bonhoeffer said 'Not to cast a vote for the two majors IS to cast a vote for one of them.'– Ethics, pp. 265–6," Metaxas wrote in a May 22 tweet.

Metaxas's weaponizing of the silence quote, and its growing ubiquity in the public sphere, made many curious about where exactly it could be found in Bonhoeffer's writings. Metaxas's reference to "Ethics, pp. 265–6" provided a starting point for researching the question, but when it turned out that the words were not there or anywhere else in *Ethics*, an effort to locate their source began in earnest. Taking the lead was blogger Warren Throckmorton, who concluded that the quote was not to be found anywhere in the Bonhoeffer corpus. The words "Not to speak is to speak. Not to act is to act" probably had their source in a 1971 book by Robert K. Hudnut, Throckmorton found. From there they made their way into the "Heroes" exhibit of a Philadelphia museum and eventually to Metaxas's Bonhoeffer biography. Although Throckmorton's findings were published in mid-2016, they did nothing to diminish the phony quote's association with Bonhoeffer in the run-up to the election.[9]

In June Metaxas expressed his conviction that Christians not only *could* vote for Trump but *must* do so. Despite "all of his foibles, peccadilloes, and metaphorical warts," Metaxas reasoned, Trump was "nonetheless the last best hope of keeping America from sliding into oblivion, the tank, the abyss, the dustbin of history." Interviewed by the *Daily Caller* at the Republican National Convention in July, Metaxas expanded on this warning with the declaration that Hillary Clinton's appointees would so tilt the Supreme Court against religious liberty and toward judicial tyranny that should she be elected, Americans would not get a second chance "to keep the republic."[10]

In the same interview, Metaxas charged that Democrats favored illegal immigration so that the country could never "demographically elect somebody who is a constitutionalist again" and articulated the implications of failing to vote in the upcoming election: "We have an obligation to say that 'if I don't vote, I understand that I am allowing Hillary Clinton to become the president if I don't vote for Donald Trump.'" Those who love America, he continued, sometimes have to hold their noses and "vote for the person who is going to do the least damage or who is going to pull you back from the brink. I am genuinely convinced that means voting for Trump."[11]

In a September interview with *Decision*, the magazine of the Billy Graham Evangelistic Association, Metaxas reiterated that anyone considering not voting in the election simply did not appreciate what was at stake. "It's all hands on deck. God forbid we should sit this one out," he warned. When asked why he referred to the present as a "Bonhoeffer moment," Metaxas proceeded carefully. He acknowledged that the upcoming election presented "a deeply unpalatable choice" for many voters, but stressed the consequences of failing to take responsibility when so much hung in the balance. "So many in Bonhoeffer's day couldn't be bothered with politics, but God raised up Bonhoeffer to blow the trumpet and call God's people to stand up to injustice," Metaxas noted. The question today is whether God's people will "step aside or will stand in the breach" and demonstrate that they care about those "suffering as a result of our government's policies."[12]

In August antiabortion activist Janet Porter announced that she too would be voting for Trump, citing his promises to appoint pro-life Supreme Court justices, restore religious liberty (specifically by removing the Johnson Amendment, a provision in the US tax code that prohibits nonprofit organizations from endorsing or opposing political candidates), and build a wall on the country's southern border. "With Trump," Porter wrote, "we'll get free speech for pastors, judges who'll protect our religious liberty, and . . . people . . . saying 'Merry Christmas' again." To Christian voters who were thinking of taking a pass in 2016, Porter too had a warning from Bonhoeffer: "You might feel good about yourself sitting out this election, but I can assure you, unborn babies won't." She then cited the bogus Bonhoeffer quote that "Not to speak is to speak. Not to act is to act" and, echoing Metaxas, added, "Not to vote is to vote."[13]

By October, as the election campaign heated up, references to Bonhoeffer appeared with greater frequency among Christians trying to sort out their options. Evangelical seminary professor Wayne Grudem wrote a series of articles advising Christians to support Trump—for his policies, if not for his character—which in turn triggered an "avalanche of repudiation" from Christian never-Trumpers. In response to this controversy, Mark DeVine (also a seminary professor) asked readers of *Red State* to "revisit a few chapters from the extraordinary life of Dietrich Bonhoeffer" by consulting primary documents like *Ethics* and *Letters and Papers from Prison*. DeVine did not counsel Christians to vote for or against Trump, but he did stress the necessity of voting, citing Bonhoeffer's view that "Christian virtue . . . does not shrink back from the moral cesspool that is this world."

"For Bonhoeffer," DeVine wrote, "when the suffering of others is at stake, virtue acts to stop, prevent, or mitigate the suffering . . . even if such service threatens to soil one's ostensibly 'clean hands,' or jeopardizes one's . . . reputation." DeVine also utilized Bonhoeffer's image of jamming a spoke into the wheel of the state in challenging voters to consider which "wheel"—Trump's or Hillary's—was likely to destroy the most innocent lives. "Surely Election Day 2016 beckons each voting age American follower of Jesus Christ to jam his or her own spoke into one of those two wheels," he concluded. While DeVine's counsel appeared evenhanded, it was surely difficult for many evangelicals to imagine a greater threat to "innocent life" than unfettered access to abortion.[14]

As the election approached, Bonhoeffer was being claimed overwhelmingly on the right—but there were significant exceptions. In a June interview on National Public Radio, political commentator David Brooks asserted that Trump's ascendancy had precipitated "a Joe McCarthy moment or a Dietrich Bonhoeffer against Hitler moment." While Brooks claimed he was not comparing Trump to Hitler, he did affirm that the current political moment required "Dietrich Bonhoeffer-type heroism." This was unusually prophetic preelection commentary, but full-throated proclamations of Bonhoeffer's relevance for the anti-Trump resistance were still several months away.[15]

Metaxas Doubles Down

The "October surprise" for Republicans arrived right on schedule. On October 7 the *Washington Post* published video of a conversation between Donald Trump and television host Billy Bush from 2005 that featured Trump making lewd and misogynistic comments. Although these video revelations threatened to derail his surging campaign by undermining Trump's support among evangelicals, within the week Eric Metaxas came to the rescue with a *Wall Street Journal* op-ed piece titled "Should Christians Vote for Trump?" The title suggested that recent events had made this an open question, but from Metaxas's perspective it was not.

Metaxas admitted that Trump's comments were "horrifying" and that many regarded them as a "deal-breaker." But what if, he asked, the other candidate also had deal-breakers? Metaxas mentioned two: that Hillary had "actively enabled sexual predation in her husband," and that she had used her position as secretary of state to funnel hundreds of millions of dollars into her foundation, "much of it from nations that treat women and gay people worse than dogs." The solution to this dilemma of the deal-breakers, Metaxas wrote, was not to flee moral compromise by refusing to choose the lesser of two evils. In fact, not voting—or voting for a third candidate who could not win—was a rationalization designed to assuage one's conscience while the nation suffered.

So what to do? Metaxas noted that both William Wilberforce and Dietrich Bonhoeffer had faced similar difficulties. For instance, in his efforts to end the slave trade, Wilberforce had often worked with parliamentarians he knew to be vile and immoral. As for Bonhoeffer, he too did things that disgusted most Christians of his day, most infamously by supporting a plot to assassinate the head of his government. He was horrified by the plot, Metaxas reminded his readers, but joined it nonetheless because he knew that to stay "morally pure" would allow the murder of millions to continue. Bonhoeffer understood that doing nothing or merely "praying" was not an option. He also knew that God was merciful, and that even if his actions were wrong, God would see his heart and forgive him; thus he knew he must act.

"It's a fact," Metaxas continued, "that if Hillary Clinton is elected, the country's chance to have a Supreme Court that values the Constitution—and the genuine liberty and self-government for which millions have died—is gone." Thus, helping elect her—even by refusing to vote—would make one "responsible for passively electing" a candidate who has championed partial-birth abortion, defended a man who raped a twelve-year-old, contributed to the rise of the Islamic State, and is determined to spread her statist view of America. Metaxas admitted that pulling the lever for a man "many think odious" might be difficult. But he urged readers to think of a vote for Trump not as support for a morally compromised candidate but as a defense of those who would be affected by the election's results. "Not to vote is to vote. God will not hold us guiltless," he concluded.

While Metaxas's advice was clear enough, his argument was confusing. Was Bonhoeffer like Trump because both "did things most Christians of his day were disgusted by"? This analogy asked readers to compare a man who had been caught on tape bragging about committing sexual assault with impunity to a man who had risked his life to defend victims of assault. Or was Bonhoeffer like the voter who was being asked to do something that contradicted his or her values (vote for Trump) because trying to remain "morally pure" by not voting could contribute to a greater evil? Or were Trump and Bonhoeffer linked by their respective battles with fascism, fights that made it impossible for either to remain morally unpolluted?

The fuzzy logic, which was uncharacteristic of Metaxas, revealed his desperation to find an argument that might keep evangelicals in the Trump camp through the election. The result was an impassioned but confusing message to evangelical voters that seemed to boil down to this: "Don't be concerned with Trump's moral flaws. In situations of cultural crisis, one cannot responsibly participate in politics and hope to remain untainted. Understanding this, Bonhoeffer would have voted for Trump. You should too." Just in case voters were not convinced, Metaxas followed up with this tweet on October 16: "Evan McMullin is a good man, but in this election he is a fig-leaf, there to assuage the consciences of religious people. God is not fooled."[16]

Pushback

Reaction to Metaxas's editorial began to be heard almost immediately. On October 17, Jonah Goldberg wrote in *National Review* that an argument that takes the form "don't listen to your conscience because God wants you to vote for Donald Trump" is odd coming from anybody, but "downright bizarre coming from the moral biographer of Wilberforce and Bonhoeffer."[17]

A more robust response to Metaxas's dubious appeal to Bonhoeffer came from Charles Marsh. In a scathing rebuttal published six days after the *Wall Street Journal* piece, Marsh ridiculed Metaxas's over-the-top rhetoric about a "Hitlery" administration and reiterated questions about his credentials as an interpreter of Bonhoeffer. He observed that "over the course of this tumultuous political season" Bonhoeffer's legacy had been frequently invoked "by commentators and operatives across the political spectrum," with Bonhoeffer's story, and that of the Confessing Church, being used to frame the election "in a global and in some cases even metaphysical narrative." However, Marsh opined, when it came to "using Dietrich Bonhoeffer to carry the weight of one's ideological preferences," Metaxas stood alone.

Marsh contended that Metaxas's Bonhoeffer book had been "written with but the slightest familiarity with German theology and history," and that his claim to be saving Bonhoeffer "from the liberals, from the globalists, the humanists, and the pacifists" in order to restore his true identity as a born-again Christian espousing traditional family values was "complete nonsense." In the biography, Marsh continued, "little mistakes cast light on vast tracts of incomprehension," including a "dangerously simplistic portrayal of Nazis as godless liberals and German dissidents as Bible-believing Christians."

Building on his own biography of Bonhoeffer, Marsh observed how poorly Metaxas's portrait of the theologian conformed to the picture illuminated by recent scholarship. First, Marsh wrote, fearful as Metaxas is of "same-sex marriage and other recent LGBT political achievements," he must be embarrassed to realize that Bonhoeffer's letters to his friend Eberhard Bethge reveal his "homoerotic desires." Second, Marsh drew attention to the "prodigiously humanist family" in which Bonhoeffer was raised and how profoundly he was influenced by his time in America, which included "new regions of experience" in Harlem and the Deep South, as well as exposure to the labor movement, poverty, homelessness, crime, and the social mission of the churches. "In these unfamiliar regions, among a nearly forgotten generation of American radicals and reformers," Marsh noted, Bonhoeffer had reexamined his vocation as theologian and pastor.

If we are in a Bonhoeffer moment, Marsh suggested, "it is a moment that confronts us with a different demand: learning to participate in God's created order, to trust in God's promises to bless, linking arms with all those who care about the human condition, asking ourselves how the coming generation shall live. It is learning to struggle along with everyone else, speaking with 'the humility that is appropriate to our limited vision' and our chastened ambitions, taking part in shared human struggle, and bearing witness to the peace that passes all understanding." There is no doubt, Marsh wrote in conclusion, "that honest engagement of Dietrich Bonhoeffer's life and thought moves us a long way from the harrowing worldview of Donald J. Trump."[18]

Another guardian of Bonhoeffer's legacy who was moved to respond to Metaxas's endorsement of Trump was Rob Schenck, evangelical pastor and founder of the Dietrich Bonhoeffer Institute in Washington, DC, whose mission is to apply Bonhoeffer's theological and ethical insights to contemporary social crises. On November 3 Schenck wrote an article in the *Christian Post* expressing his view that Eric Metaxas was "wrong to use Bonhoeffer to support Trump." Schenck acknowledged that Metaxas's Bonhoeffer biography had provided a great service to American evangelicals, but claimed that his recent support of Donald Trump's "troublesome" candidacy threatened to erase the good he had done in "bringing Bonhoeffer into popular Christian culture." Furthermore, Schenck observed that comparing a vote for Trump to the act of assassinating Adolf Hitler was to engage in "dangerous false equivalencies."

In response to Metaxas's claim that Christians must vote for Trump "because the importance of defeating Hillary Clinton rises to the same level of urgency as destroying the Hitler dictatorship," Schenck had this to say: "The suggestion that American Evangelicals face these same conditions (or worse) and, therefore, must risk damnation at least of our consciences, if not of our souls, to ensure a vulgar, opportunistic, reality-show billionaire—whose understanding of the constitutional boundaries of the office he seeks may be perilous at best—is elected, and only to nullify someone we might find equally odious, is a deeply flawed moral argument. It degrades what Bonhoeffer did in the face of true human and global catastrophe and obscures the real moral questions we all must face during this election." Schenck went on to point out that even though Hillary Clinton supported abortion, she would not be able to use the power of the state to compel the practice, as was the case in Nazi Germany. Furthermore, if America were in the dire predicament Metaxas suggested, "Donald Trump would most certainly not be the solution."[19]

PUSHBACK AGAINST Metaxas's October plea for Christians to ignore Trump's glaring moral failures and elect him as president was often fierce and personal. But it was not enough to convince Metaxas to concede any rhetorical ground, nor to keep Trump from winning the election with a larger share of the evangelical vote than any presidential candidate in recent memory.

It would be naive to argue that Eric Metaxas was single-handedly responsible for tilting the 2016 presidential election in Donald Trump's direction. But imagine if Metaxas had used his influence as a trusted evangelical commentator to help Christians consider whether either candidate was the sort of person Bonhoeffer would have endorsed; if, in addition to asking Christian voters to consider the composition of the Supreme Court, Metaxas had used his credibility as an interpreter of Bonhoeffer to warn them about the fatal attraction of populist ethno-nationalism. Imagine that as a result the 81 percent of white, born-again evangelicals who voted for Trump had been diminished by just a couple of percentage points—say, to the roughly 78 percent that had voted Republican in 2004, 2008, and 2012. Eric Metaxas would not have been happy with a Hillary Clinton presidency, but at least he would not have had to share the blame for it.[20]

CHAPTER NINE

Aftermath: A "Bonhoeffer Moment" for Liberals

WHEN THE ENGLISH LANGUAGE Section of the International Bonhoeffer Society convened in San Antonio the weekend before Thanksgiving in 2016, the collective mood was one of shock. Society members had followed the election campaign, as well as the growing role Bonhoeffer had played in it, with a mixture of curiosity and concern and, with varying levels of enthusiasm, had expected Hillary Clinton to become the next president of the United States.

During the campaign, many society members were astonished that Eric Metaxas was using Bonhoeffer to garner votes for Donald Trump. But now that the election was over, they were confronted by a very different kind of Bonhoeffer moment—the election of an ethno-nationalist president. I had considered using my familiarity with Bonhoeffer to warn of a Trump presidency, but the *Huffington Post* religion blog where I generally post online seemed an unsuitable outlet for reaching those who were likely to vote for him. Once Trump had triumphed, however, I felt obligated to say something; so I posted a three-thousand-word Bonhoeffer-inspired response to the election.

The piece, titled "Has the Bonhoeffer Moment Finally Arrived?," appeared a few days after Thanksgiving. I began by identifying myself as a Bonhoeffer scholar "who thinks the German theologian has much to say to us during this unsettling time in our political history." The first thing Bonhoeffer compels us to recognize, I wrote, is that *Trump is not Hitler*. I started there in an effort to distance myself from outrageous claims that with the election of Hillary Clinton America would descend into a fascist nightmare. Turning such arguments back on Trump supporters, though tempting, was not a recipe for clarity. "Claiming that Trump is our Hitler," I reasoned, "may give voice to the outrage and betrayal many of us feel at the recent election results, but it neither does justice to history nor makes thoughtful analysis possible."

Second, I continued, Bonhoeffer reminds us not to be surprised by the enthusiasm with which some Christians are greeting the Trump "revolution." I noted that Mary Solberg's recent translation of documents from the "German Christian" movement in *A Church Undone* compellingly demonstrates how many Protestant Christians responded to Hitler's "seizure of power" in 1933 with giddy enthusiasm. "For many Christians," I noted, "Hitler's quirks and lack of refinement were overshadowed by his promises to restore law and order, reassert the church's cultural relevance, put the country back on par with its international rivals, and generally make Germany 'great again.'"

Because Bonhoeffer saw things differently, I wrote, we like to think that all faithful Christians were as discerning. In truth, however, "Bonhoeffer's early antipathy toward Hitler was regarded with irritation by most Christian leaders in Germany, even among those who opposed the church's nazification." I reminded readers that Bonhoeffer's contemporaries viewed him as an "unreasonable partisan who was too uncompromising in church disputes, too quick to criticize the fledgling Nazi state, and too pessimistic about Germany's auspicious future under Hitler." Remembering these things about Bonhoeffer, I argued, should make us less surprised that so many Christians have become Trump enthusiasts.

Third, I noted, Bonhoeffer helps us see that for American Christians complacency has become a privilege we cannot afford. Bonhoeffer, I pointed out, recognized a threat to the church's very essence in the effort by "German Christians" to align themselves with Nazi ideology by establishing a racist "people's church." He responded with the bold declaration that he could not serve a church in which membership or ordination had become a "racial privilege." This is powerful testimony, I argued, "in the wake of an election whose victor ran on a platform of racial demagoguery [that] appealed to the most racist and xenophobic elements of the American electorate."

As Trump's campaign promises were beginning to instill anxiety and fear in millions of Americans, I wrote, those who do not feel personally threatened must not let their racial (or gender or religious) privilege give rise to complacency. "Will we respond courageously to the prophetic voices among us when President-elect Trump begins to repay the ideological debt owed to those who helped elect him?" I asked. "If he fulfills his promise of creating a registry of American Muslims, will those who claim Bonhoeffer as a guide be among the first to protest—perhaps by being the first in line to register?"

Bonhoeffer scholars, I said, "need to make a careful case that thinking with Bonhoeffer during this fraught time in our political history means embracing our responsibility to those under threat, those who, like the Jewish victims of Nazism Bonhoeffer alluded to in *Ethics*, are the 'weakest and most defenseless brothers of Jesus Christ.'" Finally, I pointed out that Trump is no longer a candidate with odious comments and opinions, but "a president-elect whose policies and appointments have the potential to do real existential harm." I concluded with the words Eric Metaxas had emphasized in his October opinion piece in the *Wall Street Journal*: "God will not hold us guiltless."[1]

The Left Has Its Bonhoeffer Moment

The response to my essay in the *Huffington Post* was remarkable. Within a few days, it had received over eight thousand "likes" on the publication's website. Clearly, many readers shared my concerns and were interested in knowing how Bonhoeffer might guide them in the days and months ahead. Before long, others were looking to the pastor-theologian for help in negotiating America's "new normal."

One blogger recalled Bonhoeffer's ominous radio broadcast of February 1933 in which he warned that popular leaders can easily become "misleaders." When they do, he wrote, "patriotism or statism can become idolatry." Another remarked that "during these especially anxious days," many were turning to Bonhoeffer's writings as "quiet rebukes of the incoming Swaggerer-in-Chief [and] . . . antidotes to the odious bombast that surrounds us." With all the nuance afforded by

Twitter, former Maryland governor Martin O'Malley declared: "Now is not the time for reconciliation. Dietrich Bonhoeffer didn't reconcile with the Nazis. . . . Now we fight."[2]

It was one thing for a Democratic former governor to broach the topic of resistance in a tweet; it was quite another thing for it to become the subject of a *New York Times* op-ed piece by a widely respected moderate Republican. But by mid-February, this is where things stood. In an article titled "How Should One Resist the Trump Administration?" David Brooks reasoned that if "repressive kleptocracy" was the true threat facing the nation, "then Dietrich Bonhoeffer is the model for the resistance." Brooks provided a brief bio of the German pastor-theologian who, he explained, decided it was not enough to bandage victims crushed by the wheel of injustice and that responsible people might be called to jam a spoke in the wheel itself. "If we are in a Bonhoeffer moment," Brooks reasoned, "then aggressive nonviolent action makes sense: marching in the streets, blocking traffic, disrupting town halls, vehement rhetoric to mobilize mass opposition."[3]

Brooks's description of the "Bonhoeffer moment" precipitated by the election reflected the mind-set of many moderate and liberal Christians during the early weeks of the Trump presidency. Concluding that it was time to distinguish themselves from coreligionists who had forfeited their moral authority by supporting Trump, they increasingly looked to Bonhoeffer as an ally. On February 4, Bonhoeffer's birthday, a piece titled "Our Bonhoeffer Moment" appeared in the *Huffington Post*. What the election revealed, author Mark Edington claimed, was that some Christian leaders had cast their lot with Trump "in the hope of renewed influence and proximity to power." This would not have been Bonhoeffer's choice, Edington emphasized, since he understood that, even under totalitarian conditions, his faith obligated him to protect the persecuted and vulnerable.

"To Mr. Trump's skillful manipulations of reality" Edington juxtaposed Bonhoeffer's own words from *Discipleship*: "In this question of truthfulness what matters first and last is that a man's whole being should be exposed, his whole evil laid bare in the sight of God. But sinful men do not like this sort of truthfulness, and they resist it with all their might. That is why they persecute it and crucify it." For

Edington, these words illuminated the stark choice between compliance and truth-telling that might soon face American Christians. "So happy birthday, Dietrich," Edington wrote. "We have not forgotten your example."[4]

The *Englewood Review of Books*, published by a progressive church in Indianapolis, sought to help Christians find their bearings on the new moral landscape of "propaganda (e.g., 'alternative facts') and violence and oppression toward anyone who is not a white heterosexual male." In this environment, the review noted, Americans would do well to return to Bonhoeffer's writings and the "stunning passages" that "shed light on our call to costly discipleship." Among the excerpts cited in the article were one from *Ethics* on "the place of truth [being] usurped by sophistic propaganda" and another from *Letters and Papers from Prison* describing the church's obligation to combat "the vices of hubris, power-worship, envy, and humbug, as the roots of all evil."[5]

The effort to marshal Bonhoeffer's legacy in opposition to Trump received further impetus in a statement released by Bonhoeffer's nephew Christoph von Dohnányi on February 4, Dietrich's birthday. Dohnányi wrote that although Bonhoeffer "learned to love and admire" the United States as a student, "he would be extremely unhappy observing a tendency of religious intolerance in the country he once admired so much for its freedom and acceptance." Dohnányi opined that Bonhoeffer "never could have imagined that this strong, great nation would find itself in the political and ethical crisis it now faces." A nation's heart should never tolerate walls nor turn away those seeking help, he added.[6]

Bonhoeffer Scholars Seize Their Moment

Before the election, most Bonhoeffer scholars quietly lamented Donald Trump's support among evangelical Christians and hoped that preelection polling proved accurate. When it did not, and Trump almost immediately signed an executive order banning travel to and from seven Muslim-majority nations, the English Language Section of the International Bonhoeffer Society (IBS) released a statement that was virtually unprecedented in its forty-five-year history.[7]

The statement announced that society members—who hailed from New Zealand, Australia, South Africa, Canada, the United Kingdom, and the United States—felt called to raise their voices "in support of justice and peace, and in resistance to every form of unjust discrimination and aggressive nationalism." Noting that the United States had "undergone an unusually contentious, bitter, and ugly election that has brought us to an equally contentious, bitter, and ugly beginning of the presidency of Donald J. Trump," the IBS expressed grave concern at the "rise in hateful rhetoric and violence, the deep divisions and distrust in [the] country, and the weakening in respectful public discourse." All of this had contributed, the statement said, to feelings of disempowerment among "the most vulnerable members of our society, including people of color, members of the LGBTQ communities, Muslims, immigrants, refugees, the poor."

The IBS statement reasoned that the best way to understand Bonhoeffer's contemporary message under these circumstances was "not to draw direct political analogies between his time and ours, but to understand the meaning of how he understood his faith and his responsibilities as a citizen in his own times and discern where these words might resonate for us today." The statement then offered a series of references to Bonhoeffer's writings with purported relevance for the present political situation. The list was led by Bonhoeffer's warnings from 1933 that "leaders become 'misleaders' when they are interested only in their own power and neglect their responsibilities to serve those whom they govern," that "when a government persecutes its minorities, it has ceased to govern legitimately," and that the church has an "unconditional obligation toward the victims of any societal order, even if they do not belong to the Christian community."

The statement also drew attention to Bonhoeffer's call for Christians to "speak out for those who cannot speak," his words from *Discipleship* about obedience to Jesus's commands in the Sermon on the Mount, his declaration that "in every moment of distress God will give us as much strength to resist as we need," his claim that "on the basis of their faith and love of neighbor, [individual Christians] are responsible for their own vocation and personal sphere of living, however large or small it is," and his observation that one learns to have faith by taking "seriously no longer one's own sufferings but rather the suffering of God in the world." "In the coming time," the statement concluded, "we will seek to live such a life of witness, not only for the sake of our country, but because our Christian faith calls us to do so."[8]

As 2017 wore on, individual scholars with a professional interest in Bonhoeffer offered their own assessments of his significance for the contemporary political environment. Among them was Reggie L. Williams, who reflected on the connections between white supremacy in Germany and America and noted that Bonhoeffer had opposed fellow Christians who were "enthusiastic about Hitler's efforts to make Germany great again by reviving the splendor of Germany's past." In the current climate, Williams noted, many Christians are energized by the rhetoric of white supremacy and the politics that support it: "One might say that the effort to 'make America great again' has them giving their devotion to a god who resembles the embodied symbol of that national greatness, idealized white humanity, in pursuit of the ideal community, rather than practice concrete service to God by loving their real neighbor. In this climate, following Christ is not popular. Indeed it has never been popular. Not everyone who claims to be a Christian is actually willing to pay the cost of discipleship."[9]

Evangelicals Join the Revolt

As the Trump administration made good on campaign promises to limit Muslim immigration and demonstrated its preference for "alternative facts," dissenting evangelical Christians began to speak out as well. In the February 7 edition of *Christian Today*, for example, Joseph Hartropp asked whether Dietrich Bonhoeffer would have "resisted Donald Trump," a question few evangelicals had contemplated to that point.[10]

Blogger Taylor S. Brown excoriated Eric Metaxas for claiming that conservative Christians had to vote for Trump or risk descending into "socialist, secularist, state-sponsored persecution." Brown called this sort of rhetoric "fear mongering" and denounced Metaxas's postelection defense of "a morally indefensible administration." Metaxas's move "into the realm of idolatry" was "sadly ironic," Brown wrote, for by "selling out to a corrupt, extreme-Right political regime," he had done just the opposite of what Bonhoeffer would do. If this is what evangelical faith now looks like, Brown predicted, non-Christians will want nothing to do with it.[11]

In May evangelical theologian W. Travis McMaken revisited Charles Marsh's biography of Bonhoeffer in light of Trump's first one hundred days in office. One of the passages McMaken read in a new light concerned a letter Bonhoeffer received from his brother Klaus while studying in America. Klaus informed Dietrich that people in Germany were "flirting with fascism," a phrase McMaken found to be a fitting explanation for the results of the recent presidential election. McMaken also pointed to a passage in which Marsh discusses Frank Buchman's naive quest to lead Hitler to Jesus. Quoting Marsh's observation that "Hitler seemed to Buchman a man's man, who by sheer will had concentrated epochal powers at his command," McMaken commented that even today some Christians can look at an authoritarian leader and conclude that a relationship with Christ is the only thing lacking.[12]

Despite these public attacks on Trump by evangelicals, Metaxas continued to defend the president against any and all critics. In an interview with the *Atlantic* at the end of January, Metaxas claimed that his main concern was not Trump's truthfulness but the media's bias against him. Similarly, when asked if he were bothered by the president's executive order on immigration, Metaxas complained about "the outrage" over the order and "the fury at Trump in general."[13]

Having become the face of Christian support for Trump, Metaxas was having to defend himself from all directions, including the evangelical left. The April debate between Metaxas and *Sojourners* founder Jim Wallis on Al Jazeera television revealed just how deeply the 2016 election had divided the broader evangelical community. Asked to assess Trump's first one hundred days in office, Metaxas sought to preempt censure of the president by claiming that in recent decades evangelicals had come to understand that "the Christian faith is about grace and forgiveness, more than it is about . . . morality." Wallis responded that since nonwhite evangelicals had voted overwhelmingly *against* Trump, white evangelicals who voted *for* him revealed that they were more "white" than "evangelical."[14]

Searching for Solid Ground

By summer Bonhoeffer was finding wide resonance among those searching for their moral bearings in Trump's America. Increasingly, he was invoked in dispatches from the anti-Trump resistance, frequently alongside quotations from his writings. In July, MSNBC television host Joe Scarborough's Facebook page featured an extended excerpt from Bonhoeffer's meditation "On Stupidity" from his 1942 essay "After Ten Years":

> Stupidity is a more dangerous enemy of the good than malice. One may protest against evil; it can be exposed and, if need be, prevented by use of force. Evil always carries within itself the germ of its own subversion in that it leaves behind in human beings at least a sense of unease. Against stupidity we are defenseless. Neither protests nor the use of force accomplish anything here; reasons fall on deaf ears; facts that contradict one's prejudgment simply need not be believed—in such moments the stupid person even becomes critical—and when facts are irrefutable they are just pushed aside as inconsequential, as incidental. In all this the stupid person, in contrast to the malicious one, is utterly self-satisfied and, being easily irritated, becomes dangerous by going on the attack.[15]

Scarborough did not directly suggest any connection between Bonhoeffer's words and Donald Trump, his administration, or his supporters. But he didn't have to; by the summer of 2017 Bonhoeffer had become a trusted and familiar weapon in the arsenal of the Trump resistance. For those who felt scandalized by the absurdity of posttruth politics, Bonhoeffer's words about people choosing to ignore "facts that contradict one's prejudgment," "becoming easily irritated," and then "going on the attack" spoke for themselves. Over the next few months, Bonhoeffer's thoughts on stupidity would become the subject of online discussion forums and a *Huffington Post* article lamenting America's "wisdom problem."[16]

Controversy surrounding the Unite the Right rally in Charlottesville, Virginia, on August 11—and President Trump's subsequent comments condemning bigotry "on many sides"—provoked another round of appeals to Bonhoeffer among the ranks of the Trump resistance. This time it was not his reflections on "stupidity" that struck a chord, but his famous (and counterfeit) words on "silence." Interpreting the president's failure to offer a full-throated denunciation of white supremacists as "silence in the face of evil," liberals quickly adopted the Bonhoeffer "quote" that for years had been the property of abortion opponents, and that just a few months earlier had been invoked to stress the importance of voting for Trump.

On August 14 the *Pittsburg (KS) Morning Sun* reported on a rally in that city's Immigrant Park where protestors had expressed solidarity with the Charlottesville victims. Speaking to those gathered of Bonhoeffer's active resistance in Nazi Germany, Frontenac United Methodist Church pastor Annie Ricker said, "In the face of evil, if you are silent your silence is evil, in the face of evil actions, your inaction is itself evil." Four days later, a letter in the *Gloucester (MA) Times* by clergy from the Cape Ann, Massachusetts, area condemned "the acts of hatred" expressed in Charlottesville and concluded by noting that Bonhoeffer, "a clergyman who was executed in 1945 by the Nazis for standing up and speaking out, said, 'Silence in the face of evil is itself evil: God will not hold us guiltless. Not to speak is to speak. Not to act is to act.'"[17]

The next day, a letter to the *Livingston County (NY) News* headed a list of quotes on justice with the ubiquitous dictum about "silence in the face of evil," which the author claimed was "attributed to Dietrich Bonhoeffer." In a letter to the editor of the *Grand Forks (ND) Herald* a few days later, United Church of Christ minister Brad Gibbens described a local interfaith "Solidarity with Charlottesville" rally against fear and hate, concluding with the "silence" aphorism, which he ascribed to "the German minister, theologian, and anti-Nazi dissident, Dietrich Bonhoeffer."[18]

While none of these authors seemed aware of it, in the wake of Charlottesville they had wrested the "silence in the face of evil is evil itself" maxim away from Trump supporters and used it against them. This trend would continue into early 2018, when Bonhoeffer's putative words on "silence" were more likely to be cited in connection with racism than any other subject. As singer-songwriter Sean Russell put it in an opinion piece, "as tiki torches rage openly, the church again is standing by in silence," a fact that would "disgust" Bonhoeffer.[19]

Outrage Becomes Terror

As the calendar turned and America approached the first anniversary of Trump's inauguration, the possibility that his impetuousness and inability to assess consequences might push the country into a nuclear war triggered apocalyptic fears. When a new book indicated that people inside the White House had as little confidence in the president's mental fitness as many outside, fears of a careless, ego-fueled conflagration began to be voiced publicly. Not surprisingly, Bonhoeffer was invoked in the process.

In January 2018 an opinion piece in the *Huffington Post* directly linked Trump, Hitler, and Bonhoeffer in assessing the threat of nuclear conflict. The author was Stephen L. Denlinger, a blogger on faith issues whose decision to write about Trump was precipitated in part by conversations with evangelical friends and neighbors. Denlinger had an unusual perspective on the Trump-Hitler connection, as he lamented that Trump was not *more* like Hitler. At least Hitler planned his war, Denlinger wrote, while "Trump bumbles his way through the day, addicted to cable television, angry at the unfairness of the World."

Denlinger reminded readers that while it is shocking to realize that people "voted for Hitler" (repeating the error that the German chancellor was democratically elected), we must remember that Germans believed he had the right ideas for their desperate moment. He would make Germany "great" again, remove immigrants, and make decisions that brought the greatest good to the greatest number of Aryans. "To the average German, Hitler was a take-charge leader who was reviving Germany's world status," Denlinger reminded readers. He or she believed "God was on Hitler's side."

Bonhoeffer, on the other hand, recognized the Nazis' repudiation of Christian values and believed that both church and nation would be judged according to how they treated the poor and weak. This compelled him to speak out, Denlinger wrote, "excoriat[ing]

Hitler's nationalism and racial supremacy." How would Bonhoeffer have responded to Trump? Denlinger asked. His chief concerns would be Trump's attitude toward illegal immigrants, his assumption that economic growth is a sign that America is favored by God, and his conviction that "winning is the ultimate moral virtue."

Responding to evangelical pastors who reassured their congregants that Trump was a spiritually weak man whose "heart is right with God," Denlinger called him "a dramatic departure from what evangelical Christians claimed they wanted in a President." His conclusion was that American evangelicals had "reincarnated a blasphemous, Republican Jesus." And like Christians in Germany, "they'll be held accountable for the millions of people he may annihilate in a thermonuclear war." Who would listen to American evangelicals, Denlinger wondered, in the nuclear winter that followed?[20]

In this environment of escalating outrage and terror, Bonhoeffer scholars Lori Brandt Hale and Reggie L. Williams wrote a cover article for the February 2018 issue of *Sojourners* titled "Is This a Bonhoeffer Moment?" After recalling that Trump's bid for the presidency had been steeped in racial scapegoating and messages of ableism and misogyny, the authors rehearsed a litany of moral disgraces from Trump's first year in office, including his Muslim travel bans, his declaration that neo-Nazis were "very fine people," and his toleration of "police brutality and racial profiling." In all this, the authors noted, the Trump administration had acted with the explicit support of many white Christians.

Does all this mean we are living in a Bonhoeffer moment? Hale and Williams asked. While they stressed that drawing historical analogies is perilous work, they also claimed that Bonhoeffer provides "a helpful lens for reflecting on our current situation." As an example, they cited a catechism Bonhoeffer wrote for confirmands in 1931 in which he declared German "ethnic pride" a sin and implied that white nationalism was an affront to the human family's God-given unity.

Nevertheless, Hale and Williams warned that appealing to Bonhoeffer's role in the conspiracy to assassinate Hitler could lead to "nefarious conclusions" if one is not careful to "do the arduous work of discernment that pays attention to his context and our own." In fact, to ask if the times we live in call for violence "is to miss the point of Bonhoeffer's witness" and "the deep truth his life conveys." For the question that was always Bonhoeffer's guiding concern—"Who is Christ for us today?"—compels us to ask whether "we recognize Christ in everyone othered by political structures in ways that push minoritized people to the margins and crush them against walls[.] Do we acknowledge that God has made from one blood all people that dwell on the Earth? Are we attempting to make ourselves into 'good people,' defined by our weekly Sunday morning communities, ones that draw the boundaries of our social responsibilities quite narrowly, or are we looking to serve the Christ we meet in social encounters with real humans every day?" According to Hale and Williams, Bonhoeffer encourages Christians to contemplate these questions while recognizing that "in the midst of this current political maelstrom . . . everything is at stake."[21]

FREQUENT APPEALS to Bonhoeffer during Trump's first year in the White House suggest that the life and writings of the German pastor-theologian have helped many Americans navigate an uncharted cultural landscape by illuminating how principled opponents of the Trump administration might think about resistance. As this book goes to press, this desire to learn from and be inspired by Bonhoeffer is repeatedly demonstrated in tweets, blog posts, op-ed pieces, and magazine articles.

The International Bonhoeffer Society's February 2017 statement expressed the view that the best way to understand Bonhoeffer's contemporary message was not to draw "direct political analogies" but to focus on "how he understood his faith and his responsibilities" and discern where his words "might resonate for us today." This is a helpful distinction, to be sure. But for Americans who have experienced the past year as a slowly unfolding, increasingly terrifying Bonhoeffer moment, it has been difficult to keep in mind.

More thoughtful admirers of Bonhoeffer have resisted facile Trump-Hitler comparisons while honestly assessing the features of Trump's America that commend them. Like Lori Brandt Hale and Reggie Williams, Wes Granberg-Michaelson concedes that there is no "simplistic parallel" between the rise of the Third Reich and today's political realities, but notes that "the similarities of forceful appeals to nationalistic chauvinism, racial bigotry, and cultural exclusivism as manipulative reactions to economic anxieties . . . are chilling." Unfortunately, it has been difficult for this sort of restrained analysis to find an audience in an increasingly polarized rhetorical environment.[22]

Significantly, those who have come to regard Bonhoeffer as a model of resistance in Trump's America are looking to him not to justify antityrannical violence but to help them discern how citizens of a civilized nation should behave when established cultural norms seem no longer to apply. In this atmosphere, Bonhoeffer's warning about idolizing strong leaders, his commentary on "stupidity," and his words on truthfulness as an antidote to "skillful manipulations of reality" are among the aspects of his legacy that are helping Americans calibrate their moral compasses. Whether one believes that the United States is ruled by a "repressive kleptocracy," that Americans are just "flirting with fascism," or that all Nazi allusions are counterproductive, there is no doubt that in 2018 Bonhoeffer has found a deeper resonance in the American imagination than ever before.

CHAPTER TEN

The Battle for Bonhoeffer, circa 2018

DESPITE INCREASED RELIANCE on Bonhoeffer among liberals and moderates since Donald Trump's election, conservatives have certainly not relinquished their own claim on the man. In October 2017, for instance, a blog called *The Reformed Sojourner* offered an in-depth exploration of "progressive Christianity's strange Bonhoeffer compulsion"—strange because, the article claimed, Bonhoeffer was "a vocal, and sometimes outraged opponent" of progressive Christianity.[1]

Given this opposition, the author wondered what could motivate progressive Christians to ignore the "unbridgeable theological and political chasm" that separates them from Bonhoeffer. His answer was that, for Christian progressives, "the easiest and surest means of achieving moral superiority . . . is to demonstrate disdain, even hatred, for their own country." Despising their nation for its presumed crimes, these men and women identify with the Bonhoeffer who expressed his patriotism through antigovernment resistance. But pointing out that American progressives reside in a democratic republic that protects their right to criticize the state, the author denounced their moral posturing as "cheap Bonhoeffer-ism."

According to this "reformed sojourner," because liberal Christians have adopted Bonhoefferian opposition as their default posture toward America, "whenever a non-Progressive (usually a Republican) dares to oppose their policies, or worse yet, to win an election, some of them (repeatedly) convince themselves that it is the rise of yet another

Hitler." In this way, they maintain the absurd fantasy that they are "little Bonhoeffers" justified in reviling the nation of their birth. "The consequences of this bizarre derangement," the author concluded, are "becoming clearer with each passing day."[2]

Reading this article, I could only sigh and acknowledge that, despite the shock of Donald Trump's election, the battle for Bonhoeffer is far from over. I have found it difficult to bring this project to a close in the midst of what appears to be an unfolding story. But the time has come to stop reviewing daily "Google Alerts," op-eds, letters to the editor, and blog posts and come to some tentative conclusions about the ongoing contest for Bonhoeffer's legacy. What have I learned?

For one thing, it has become clear to me that looking to Bonhoeffer for guidance and inspiration has been a fairly consistent feature of our public discourse since 9/11. It is hardly surprising that so many Americans are drawn to Bonhoeffer in the twenty-first century, for he exemplifies a remarkable continuity between thought and behavior, a rare combination of academic depth and pastoral concern, a striking transition from pacifism to violent resistance, and a martyr's faithful acceptance of death. Nor can we overlook Bonhoeffer's antagonistic relationship with one of the most notorious dictators of the twentieth century. As a paradigmatic antityrant, Bonhoeffer naturally appeals to those in search of faithful witnesses to human dignity in the darkest days of the twentieth century.

Indeed, this natural affinity for Bonhoeffer appears only to have intensified over the past two decades, as various groups of Americans have suspected their political leaders of harboring totalitarian aims. Even Barack Obama, who generally avoids hyperbolic rhetoric and who has mostly stayed out of the public eye since leaving the White House, warned in December 2017 that Americans "have to tend to this garden of democracy or else things could fall apart quickly. That's what happened in Germany in the 1930s. Adolph Hitler rose to dominate," Obama reminded his audience. "Sixty million people died. . . . So, you've got to pay attention. And vote." In times like ours, when the specter of Hitler is so easily raised, Bonhoeffer, the paradigmatic anti-Nazi, holds obvious appeal.[3]

In fact, although he does not mention Donald Trump, Barack Obama in 2017 sounds remarkably like Eric Metaxas in 2012 (warning of threats to democracy under Obama) and Larry Rasmussen in 2006 (doing the same under George W. Bush), each of whom called forth images of Nazi Germany to remind fellow citizens of their duty to tend the American "garden of democracy." As these examples indicate, the fear that fascism's seeds may be germinating in our cultural soil has intermittently haunted American political discourse throughout the first two decades of the twenty-first century, whether the imagined sower of tyranny is named Bush, Obama, Clinton, or Trump.

Second, I have found it necessary to rethink the meaning of scholarly engagement in these perilous times. Although I believe the distorted picture of Bonhoeffer rendered in Eric Metaxas's biography is irresponsible and dangerous, it is certainly possible to point out flaws in that book without resorting to ad hominem attacks. But given Metaxas's outsized role as an opinion maker and his unflagging support for Donald Trump (confirmed recently by his denial that Trump's reference to "shithole countries" was racist), I have come to wonder how responsible it is to conduct intellectual business as usual, simply agreeing to disagree about Bonhoeffer's meaning for our time.

There is a risk here of being misunderstood. Scholars have been taken to task for their overwhelmingly negative reaction to Metaxas's Bonhoeffer biography, with one blogger observing that scholarly "sourpusses" have been "on the wrong side of a renewed interest in Bonhoeffer among non-academic types" and wondering if our reactions have been more about fear than fact. "Are they just appalled that an outsider like Metaxas has hijacked their role as the gatekeepers of Bonhoeffer's legacy?" he asks.[4]

This is a fair question. I won't deny that the scholarly reaction to Metaxas probably reflects a mixture of spirited disagreement, jealousy, and frustration. The jealousy arises from the fact that Metaxas's shoddy biography of Bonhoeffer has sold more copies than any other study of the man, and by several orders of magnitude. The frustration stems from the difficulty of refuting Metaxas's errors by traditional means, since he refuses to engage in the sort of give-and-take that epitomizes the scholarly vocation. Nevertheless, he wants to be taken seriously as an interpreter of Bonhoeffer. In February 2017, for instance, Metaxas claimed that his depiction of Bonhoeffer was supremely accurate, despite the carping of "liberal critics": "I keep seeing stuff on the Internet and they're very vicious and they act as though I threw something together over a weekend to suit my view of the world. . . . And I do want to say that there's not a syllable in my Bonhoeffer book that isn't true and I think that people who don't like how Bonhoeffer comes out in my book, that's really something that reveals where they're coming from more than where Bonhoeffer or I are coming from because his is such a well-documented life."[5]

Whatever Metaxas has seen "on the Internet," he has clearly not taken time to read and consider reviews of his book by Bonhoeffer scholars. Instead he dismisses their criticisms out of hand and in the process credits the populist assumption that credentialed "experts" cannot be trusted, particularly if they are "liberal." In reality, Metaxas's attack on his critics exposes the bizarre character of the post-truth world we now inhabit. He asserts that those who are unhappy with the way "Bonhoeffer comes out" in his book reveal more about themselves than about him or about Bonhoeffer, whose life is so "well documented." However, it is precisely this documentation—painstakingly established over decades—that has enabled reviewers to identify the ways Metaxas's interpretive agenda misrepresents Bonhoeffer.

The operation of this agenda is indicated in Metaxas's offhand reference to nameless "liberal critics," which suggests he is more concerned with discerning reviewers' political and theological identities than in partnering with them in the quest to better understand Bonhoeffer. Labeling his critics this way allows Metaxas to withdraw from scholarly dialogue and cling to his "alternative facts" while accusing those whose job it is to know something about Bonhoeffer of promoting "fake news." His charge that all unfavorable opinions are the result of "bias" is the worst sort of intellectual populism. And under the current political conditions, it is increasingly dangerous.

Studying Metaxas's portrait of Bonhoeffer and his ongoing attempts to use him for partisan political purposes has caused me to rethink my role as an observer of what might be called the American Bonhoeffer. For the past twenty years or so, I have been engaged in cataloguing items that reflect Bonhoeffer's popular reception, particularly in the United States. This has involved exploring monuments, pilgrimages, novels, dramas, films, screenplays, works of art of all kinds, and, of course, social and political commentary. My goal has been to describe and analyze before critiquing, to sympathetically observe before judging. While this book is a continuation of that descriptive work, I have come to feel that at present much more is called for than description and observation. I have arrived at the conclusion, in fact, that maintaining critical distance from certain attempts to claim Bonhoeffer's legacy may be irresponsible.

It is one thing to remain dispassionate when describing Bonhoeffer's use by men who murder abortion providers (as I did in *The Bonhoeffer Phenomenon*) when those men are deceased or incarcerated and have been repudiated by all but a handful of supporters. It is quite another thing to remain objective about Bonhoeffer's co-optation by opinion makers who are enabling a presidential administration as it actively works to undermine civil rights protections, degrade the natural environment, and normalize white supremacy. So while I will continue to offer "scholarly" criticism of Eric Metaxas's interpretation of Bonhoeffer's relevance for contemporary America, I can no longer do so in the manner of a detached observer.

Speaking from this more engaged perspective, I want to say this to Eric Metaxas:

> You were grossly irresponsible to use your role as an influential interpreter of Bonhoeffer to endorse someone whom Bonhoeffer would have found repulsive. You are entitled to your political opinions, of course. But you used credibility gained largely from your association with Bonhoeffer's estimable humanity to imply that voting for Donald Trump was incumbent on American Christians. You thus gave them permission to ignore their spiritual intuition that the man was a repudiation of everything they held dear. In the process you did a disservice to Bonhoeffer, to Americans, and to the cause of Christ.

My colleagues will recognize some irony here. Until recently I have been the member of the Bonhoeffer guild most likely to suggest that we reach out to Eric Metaxas, take him seriously as an interpreter of Bonhoeffer, and invite him into dialogue with our community. My fellow Bonhoeffer scholars have generally disagreed with these suggestions, often vehemently. But I persisted in the belief that engaging Metaxas as a dissenting "scholar" was the best way to exercise care for Bonhoeffer's legacy. But when Metaxas publicly and enthusiastically endorsed Donald Trump for president after the revelations in the *Access Hollywood* video—appealing to Bonhoeffer in the process—my attitude shifted. Today I no longer believe it is enough to respectfully disagree with someone who relies on Bonhoeffer's moral gravitas to support President Trump and his policies. That does not mean I am opposed to dialogue in the future, only that there is too much at stake to adhere to scholarly niceties in the meantime.

Despite all this, this project has also taught me that going forward scholars will have a limited role to play in determining how Americans understand and deploy Bonhoeffer. In early 2015, Victoria J. Barnett wrote a characteristically sober assessment of Bonhoeffer's conflicted legacy that should have given pause to advocates of the "Bonhoeffer moment." Her goal was to "dial back the hero worship" that had become such a prominent feature of the Bonhoeffer phenomenon.

According to Barnett, Bonhoeffer was a good man and a brilliant theologian, a man who questioned the very legitimacy of the Nazi regime in early 1933 precisely because of its persecution of German Jews—but who then wrote and spoke surprisingly little on the issue in the ensuing years. Although his writings call people to activism, Barnett reminded readers, he seldom took an activist role. In 1936, he filled out the required political questionnaire and provided an "Aryan certificate" in an attempt to keep his teaching position. He was brought into the resistance only as a ploy to keep him out of Hitler's army. Once there, he found himself part of a plot that included a wide range of figures, some of them honorable, others men who had fully participated in Nazi misdeeds before ultimately turning against the regime. One encounters in Bonhoeffer, Barnett concluded, "an ongoing and striking tension between silence and speaking, between compromise and protest, between the moments when he acted and those in which he did not."

This tension is conspicuously absent from popular portraits of Bonhoeffer, Barnett noted, where we find "a striking divide between the faithful and the historians," between history and hagiography, which "establishes the life story as monument, giving it the meaning we would like it to have." Barnett concluded that "if we can understand Bonhoeffer outside the box—not as saint, not as mythological hero, but as someone who reflected poignantly on evil's consequences for the human conscience and spirit, for an entire culture and country, we may begin to uncover the person behind the mythology: a man who tried to face the darkness of his times. In the process, we may discover someone who can speak more directly to the darknesses and failures of our own."[6]

Barnett's ruminations on Bonhoeffer and hero worship are particularly salient in light of the battle for Bonhoeffer described in these pages. But since her article appeared in 2015, the tendency to view Bonhoeffer as a saint and hero has only intensified, fueled by politicized and decontextualized depictions of Bonhoeffer disseminated by commentators like Metaxas, conservative political activists like Rick Scarborough and Mat Staver, and denominational leaders like Ronnie Floyd.[7]

The appeal of this populist Bonhoeffer, safe from the depredations of scholars and absent the internal tensions described by Barnett, was beautifully captured in a 2013 article in the *Houston Chronicle*. "While theologians and academics debate his legacy and impact," the author noted, "everyday Evangelicals . . . appreciate his courage more than his creed, his daring stand more than his doctrine." To illustrate the populist mind-set of these "everyday Evangelicals," the article quoted a Bonhoeffer "fan" who said she appreciated that his "theology did not impede his witness or work."[8]

As long as American admirers of Bonhoeffer perceive his theology as a potential impediment to his "witness," they are likely to remain impervious to the sorts of nuanced critiques scholars can offer. Thus we should prepare for continuing attempts to rally American Christians with a populist Bonhoeffer unmoored from his theological and historical milieux. And so the battle for Bonhoeffer will continue, with the stakes likely to grow.

In the November 2016 op-ed piece that became the germ for this book, I stressed that "Trump is not Hitler." I continue to believe that drawing such parallels is inimical to both rational discussion and thoughtful action. It is also counterproductive, since what Leo Strauss called the *Reductio ad Hitlerum*—the attempt to refute one's opponent by associating him or her with Hitler—is a rhetorical boomerang.

As we have seen, Hitlerizing our leaders has been a staple of American political discourse throughout the twenty-first century. But while this rhetorical practice seldom changes minds, it almost always provokes attempts to turn it back on its author. This boomerang effect was evident in 2017 with the publication of Dinesh D'Souza's *The Big Lie: Exposing the Nazi Roots of the American Left*. Whatever the book's flaws (and they are many), it made one thing clear: D'Souza was determined to offer a decisive refutation of those who greeted the prospect—and then the reality—of a Trump presidency with comparisons to fascism in general, and Adolf Hitler in particular. He opened his book, in fact, by citing headlines like "Trump's 'Hitler-Level' Rhetoric Could Turn Us into Nazi Germany" and "Donald Trump: The Dress Rehearsal for Fascism." These articles, published around the time of the 2016 election, may have had a reassuring effect in liberal echo chambers, but they did not change anyone's thinking, least of all that of ideologues like D'Souza.

Nevertheless, comparisons between Trump's America and Nazi Germany will keep being made because many Americans, Bonhoeffer scholars among them, find the comparisons too compelling to ignore. When Bonhoeffer scholar Reggie Williams noted that Bonhoeffer opposed German Christians who responded enthusiastically to Hitler's efforts to "make Germany great again by reviving the splendor of Germany's past," the implication that Trumpism reflected Hitlerian rhetoric was strong. When Christoph von Dohnányi, whose father was murdered as part of the resistance cell to which Bonhoeffer belonged, wrote that Dietrich "never could have imagined that this strong, great nation would find itself in the political and ethical crisis it now faces," the invitation to view Trump's America in Nazi terms was almost irresistible.

I have come to believe that these warnings should be taken seriously and that there is more to the anti-Trump "Bonhoeffer moment" than the familiar pattern of rhetorical assassination by Nazi association. If fascist analogies continue to commend themselves, it is largely because, unlike his predecessors, Trump has gained the allegiance of actual fascists—white supremacists and neo-Nazis who find him closer to espousing their own views than any politician in their lifetimes. Nor is the problem limited to sloganeering at organized rallies.

Beyond the frightening echoes of "*Heil* Trump" in the precincts of organized hate, there are a growing number of documented incidents in which "Trump" is employed as a taunt directed at people who look or sound "foreign." In these cases, the president's surname sends the message that people who appear insufficiently "American" have no place in this country. According to several scholars of American history, "the invocation of a president's name as a jaw-jutting declaration of exclusion, rather than inclusion, appears to be unprecedented."[9]

Whether Trump himself is a racist or white supremacist will continue to be debated. What is beyond debate is that Trump's rhetoric and policies have attracted, energized, and emboldened racists, white supremacists, and neo-Nazis in ways that frighten many of their fellow citizens and naturally invite comparisons with history's most notorious ethno-nationalists. These comparisons were lent credibility by Trump's weak response to 2017's "Unite the Right" march in Charlottesville, not to mention his 2018 reference to nonwhite immigrants from "shithole countries." They will become more credible as such incidents multiply.

Thus the Trump era, however long it should last, represents a true test for Christians who regard Bonhoeffer as a model of discipleship. Bonhoeffer never forgot after Hitler came to power that he was not living in ordinary times, no matter how many of his countrymen adjusted and assimilated to Germany's "new normal." We who claim some kinship with Bonhoeffer must similarly resist becoming accustomed to ways of thinking, speaking, and acting that are anti-Christian, and antihuman, in spirit. And we must work to discredit claims on Bonhoeffer by those who do think, speak, and act in these ways. For these things we should be willing to battle.

POSTSCRIPT

Your Bonhoeffer Moment: An Open Letter to Christians Who Love Bonhoeffer but (Still) Support Trump

FRIENDS,

I hope this letter finds you well, despite the distressing times in which we live. Moments like this remind me to give thanks for all we have in common as brothers and sisters in Christ. For that, and for all God's blessings, I am deeply grateful.

I'm writing because I have been thinking about you a lot lately. As I have listened to the news (CNN, MSNBC, Fox, NPR, American Family Network—I try to expose myself to as many perspectives as possible), I have reflected on the phenomenon of Christian support for Donald Trump.

Something of a turning point came for me this past weekend in a hotel room in Boston in November 2017, where I was attending the annual meeting of the American Academy of Religion. Resting between sessions on Bonhoeffer's theology, I was listening to the latest news reports on Roy Moore and his troubled candidacy for the US Senate. A journalist being interviewed on one of the cable channels reported that in his conversations with evangelical pastors in Alabama, several conceded that even if it turned out that Judge Moore was guilty of seeking out and molesting underage women, they would continue to support him, presumably because sending a Republican child molester to the US Senate is preferable to electing a Democrat.

Over the next few hours, a lot of the feelings I have had since the 2016 election coalesced and took shape in this letter. What I want to say begins with a word of thanks. The older I get, the more I appreciate my evangelical Christian upbringing. Among the things it inculcated in me as a young teenager were a clear worldview and a conviction that what one claims to believe should be reflected in the way one lives. These and many other dimensions of evangelical culture have formed how I think about my faith and about the world.

I no longer call myself an evangelical, but the break was more cultural than theological. I was a student at an evangelical seminary in 1980 as the Reagan revolution was getting under way. For reasons I did not understand, professors and students were abandoning the Sunday school–teaching Southern Baptist Jimmy Carter for a divorced former actor with no discernible connection to the Christian faith other than a desire for evangelical electoral support. My skepticism about Ronald Reagan's sincerity was rooted partly in personal experience.

I grew up in an evangelical church in Key Biscayne, Florida, where President Richard Nixon occasionally visited. Members of my church community were fans of Nixon in every sense—we liked his politics, and we loved the fact that he was a practicing Christian. We inferred this from his church attendance, his choice of Billy Graham as a "spiritual adviser," and his friendship with our pastor, John Huffman, who on several occasions was Nixon's personal guest at the White House. At the president's request, our church held a special Saturday evening service to honor the Paris Peace Accords. It was televised live on the major networks.

As you can imagine, Nixon's fall from grace and the disclosure of how duplicitous he had been, how caught up he was in the means-justify-ends world of politics, were devastating for all of us. No one was devastated more than John Huffman, who, after the Watergate scandal came to light, asked Nixon directly if he had known about the break-in. When Nixon swore to him that he had not, Huffman continued to support him.

But when the transcripts of Nixon's White House recordings were released, Huffman was understandably shocked and outraged. "If President Nixon claims to be a Christian," he told *Time*, "he needs to repent of both the language used and the attitudes expressed toward people in those tapes." In an interview with the *New York Times*,

Huffman went further, questioning "the moral qualifications for the presidency of a person who cannot be trusted to tell the truth."[1]

I learned two things from this experience. First, I saw how embarrassing and demoralizing it was for a pastor I trusted and loved to realize that he had been "played" by a master manipulator who masked his quest for power with the veneer of evangelical Christianity. As a recent biographer of Nixon concludes, there was always a self-serving element in Nixon's relationships with evangelical leaders. "When he knew he was going to run for president, he wooed them and they wooed him," the author writes.[2] I guess such things are easier to see in hindsight.

Second, I took a lesson in courage from John Huffman, who repudiated Nixon's actions in no uncertain terms, despite the high personal cost of doing so. The whole experience made me suspicious of politicians who make piety part of their public persona, especially if I suspect they are doing so to solicit Christian support. It has also instilled in me an abiding respect for religious leaders who are willing to speak truth to power.

Despite this traumatic early experience (I was fifteen when Nixon resigned in disgrace), I remained part of the evangelical subculture into my midtwenties. Ultimately, however, I felt isolated from my evangelical friends and mentors on too many issues—poverty, injustice, and racism, for example—to stay in the fold. I know that today many evangelicals are deeply concerned with these matters, but I did not find this to be the case at the time.

By my late twenties I was more comfortable in the Protestant mainline than in the evangelical church of my youth. But I have always retained evangelical sensibilities. These have been particularly helpful in my roles as teacher and pastor, although they have sometimes placed me out of step with my more liberal coreligionists.

It's because I retain such an appreciation for evangelical Christianity and what it taught me (good and bad) that I feel obliged to point out some things that many of you seem not to have noticed or have hidden from yourselves. Take them as feedback from a friendly but critical voice, rooted in a combination of gratitude and concern.

First, there is nothing remotely "Christian" about Donald Trump. I try to be charitable in my judgments of people I do not know, but this is the only conclusion I can draw. The question for the moment isn't whether someone's personal moral failings disqualify him or her from holding office, but just how serious and pervasive these failings are in the case of Donald Trump.

I think Amy Sullivan said it best when she wrote that Trump is "pretty much the human embodiment of the question 'What would Jesus not do?'"[3] Indeed, Trump's personal mottoes—"always get even" and "hit back harder than you were hit"—represent the antitheses of Jesus's own, which were "blessed are the merciful" and "love your neighbor as yourself." Furthermore, neither his stable of evangelical advisers nor his White House handlers have had any success in controlling the flow of evidence that Trump's character is animated by the least Christian of qualities—self-aggrandizement, enrichment at the expense of others, getting away with whatever one can, seeking to humiliate others, and spreading hate and suspicion.

You taught me to judge people on the basis of their character, revealed particularly in the way they treat others. By this standard, Donald Trump is the least "Christian" political candidate in recent memory, and everything you taught me about God and the Christian life demands that I despise him. Claims that he is "rough," "inexperienced," "unrefined," or "unused to governing" are all true as far as they go. But they do not address the moral issue you trained me to recognize and take with utmost seriousness: behavior and language reflect character. And we see a bit more of Trump's character every time he bullies, belittles, lashes out, lies, or lies about lying.

Just to be clear, I am not criticizing Trump's specific policies, about which reasonable people, even those who are faithful Christians, can disagree. I could construct spiritually and theologically based arguments that Trump's policies are unchristian, indeed inhuman, but you could defend his positions on similar bases, and in any case this would take us into the realm of partisan politics where people dig in their heels and stop up their ears. So I will simply reiterate the point I want to make: every part of my evangelically shaped heart is revolted by this man whom you voted for and continue to support come hell or high water—or worse. I will sharpen the point by observing the following:

Regardless of how much you try, you cannot turn Donald Trump into a "real" Christian. Putting it this way reflects how you taught me to think about such things. "Being in a church doesn't make you a Christian any more than being in a barn makes you a cow" was a favorite adage in my evangelical youth. The point was that churches are filled with "nominal Christians," while "real Christians," those who regard prayer, worship, evangelism, and discipleship as nonnegotiable duties of the truly committed, are much harder to find.

This way of judging people's religious commitment was deeply inculcated in me, along with the belief that "cultural" Christians embody a form of cheap grace that undermines the church's witness. Even if he sometimes attends church and reads his mother's Bible, Trump has not publicly indicated a desire to follow or honor Christ. Thus I have to conclude that, according to the definition I learned from you, he is not a serious Christian. Those he has co-opted by naming "advisers" have tried to fudge this issue by speaking of Trump as a "baby Christian." But it is difficult to be convincing when the one on whose behalf you are fudging, asked about his personal faith, says things like "our religion is a very important part of me, and I also think it's a very important part of the country."[4]

Many of you were frustrated with Barack Obama's failure to clearly express his faith and demonstrate his Christian bona fides. But Obama showed more familiarity with Christian ideas, language, and culture than Trump has, despite the latter's conscious efforts to court the evangelical vote. It's not just his inability or unwillingness to articulate his beliefs. Nothing about Trump suggests that following Christ is or has ever been important to him, despite the assurances of starstruck evangelical leaders. They want us to trust a "feeling" they had while they were in Trump's presence, while asking us to ignore his public treatment of people, his habits, and his words.

I remember being asked rather pointedly as an evangelical teenager, "If you were accused of being a Christian, would there be enough evidence to convict you?" This was another way of making the point that one's faith must be reflected in one's life or it is ineffectual and bogus. In Trump's case, no objective person would take the accusation seriously.

Based on recent polling data, a majority of you are not concerned by these matters, as you now believe that a candidate's personal behavior should not disqualify him or her from holding public office.

But because this opinion conflicts so profoundly with the evangelical worldview you shaped in me, not to mention the belief you yourselves held until recently, I can only regard this shift as disingenuous and self-serving.[5]

These things mattered to you a great deal when Reagan and the Bushes were in office, and they certainly mattered during the Clinton and Obama years. They mattered during the 2016 primary season as a phalanx of Republican candidates sought your votes by flashing their evangelical credentials. And they mattered when you were campaigning against Hillary. So when, exactly, did character stop mattering in our assessment of political candidates?

Some of you have said this election was too important to let issues of personal morality determine your vote. I might be able to accept this if you had held your nose, pulled the lever for Trump, and then been ready to disclaim him when he began to act in ways no Christian can condone. But so many of you have stayed on the Trump bandwagon, unwilling to acknowledge even to yourselves that you are being taken for a ride by someone with only the most cynical attachment to your faith. Which leads me to observe the following:

Your fierce embrace of Trump has begun to do real damage to American Christianity. At the end of Trump's first year in office, there is evidence that your support for him has taken a toll on the credibility of our faith. This has been pointed out by many secular critics, including a psychologist who recently wondered, based on an election cycle in which he observed "an especially high level of insincerity, shamelessness, poor judgment and pathological egocentricity," whether evangelicalism itself had become "sociopathic."[6]

But your support for Trump is also troubling other evangelicals, some of whom have begun to distance themselves from the brand, as it were. Peter Wehner is a case in point. He recently wrote that support by white evangelicals for President Trump and Roy Moore has caused him to rethink his identification with both evangelicalism and the Republican Party. He accuses prominent Christian leaders of becoming Trump "courtiers" and concludes that the term "evangelical" "has been so distorted that it is now undermining the Christian witness."[7]

An evangelical journalist recently made the credible claim that you actually represent a new religious movement called "Fox evangelicalism." At the heart of this new religion, she writes, is the "nationalistic, race-baiting, fear-mongering form of politics enthusiastically practiced by Mr. Trump and Roy Moore in Alabama." She describes regular Fox News viewers as taking in "a steady stream of messages that conflate being white and conservative and evangelical with being American." The resulting religious identity is then weaponized in support of "virtually any policy, so long as it is promoted by someone Fox evangelicals consider on their side of the culture war."[8]

Increasingly, there is talk of a generational schism within your community based in part on older evangelicals' support for the "debauched pagan" in the White House.[9] Younger evangelicals are rightly appalled by the hypocrisy of their coreligionists who "care a lot about character. Except when they don't." The result is what one evangelical writer has called a generation of "theological orphans" alienated from their immediate forebears, to whom they are saying: we reject "your idolatrous politics, your nationalistic faith, your moral subjectivity, [and] your fear of the alien and the stranger."[10]

In recent weeks the volume has been dialed up on warnings about how support for Trump is damaging evangelicals' credibility. The point of no return may have been reached with reports that Trump carried on an affair with a porn actress while Melania was at home with their newborn child, and then bought the woman's silence. For many of us, this news simply confirmed what we suspected about Trump—that he had used and would use any means necessary to get what he wanted, regardless of who was injured in the process. What has shocked us is how evangelical spokesmen like Tony Perkins and Jerry Falwell Jr. have continued to cover for the president in the aftermath of these latest revelations. I suspect that nothing these men say in the future will carry any credibility beyond the circle of their closest supporters.

These leaders' responses to this latest scandal have led some to claim that we are now seeing evangelicalism's true colors. Support for Trump, they say, expresses not evangelical loyalty to the Republican Party but long-standing commitments to racism and sexism. It is not surprising that contemporary leaders are "blasé" about reports of Trump's infidelity with a porn actress, Michelle Goldberg observes, when we recall evangelical support for segregation. For "despite his louche personal life, Trump, the racist patriarch promising cultural revenge, doesn't threaten the religious right's traditional values. He embodies them." In this view Trump has revealed the evangelical movement's true priorities, which, according to Goldberg, include "the preservation of traditional racial and sexual hierarchies."[11]

In the wake of the same scandal, Michael Gerson writes that Trump evangelicals are "playing a grubby political game for the highest of stakes: the reputation of their faith." He notes that unlike Billy Graham, John Huffman, and others who were "snookered" by Richard Nixon, Trump's "court evangelicals" have made their political bargain with open eyes. According to Gerson, they are "surrendering the idea that character matters in public life in direct exchange for political benefits to Christians themselves."[12]

I believe there will be real long-term damage as your ongoing support for Trump weakens the evangelical movement from within and without. In addition to estranging younger evangelicals, you risk undermining your claims that Christianity stands on the right side of modern movements for righteousness and justice. I suspect this desire to demonstrate Christianity's moral credibility is part of the reason you are attracted to the courage and witness of Dietrich Bonhoeffer, which brings me to my fourth point.

Your embrace of Trump is eerily reminiscent of German Christians' attachment to Hitler in the early 1930s. I make this point not to convince you that Trump is Hitler but to remind you of the troubling ways Christians have compromised themselves in endorsing political movements in which they perceived the hand of God. I developed a scholarly interest in the churches' role during the Nazi era in part so I could help ensure that Christians would never repeat the mistakes they made under Hitler. Similarly, Dietrich Bonhoeffer is one of my heroes in part because he was able to resist the wave of Hitler worship that swept up many German Protestants.

Being familiar with this history, I have been struck by how reminiscent many of your responses to Trump are of the way Christians in Germany embraced a strong leader they were convinced would restore the country's moral order. Despite all the evidence to the contrary, many Christians in Germany let themselves be persuaded that Hitler was a deeply pious man, placed in power by God through a graceful act of intervention in German history. Hitler encouraged these ideas not by claiming any allegiance to Christ but by employing vague religious language, promising a return to the "good old days," and posing for photographs as he left church, prayed, and entertained ecclesiastical leaders.

Here are a few examples of how Protestant Christian leaders in Germany spoke about God's role in Hitler's accession to power:

- "With National Socialism an epoch in German history has begun that is at least as decisive for the German people, as for example the epoch of Martin Luther."
- "No one could welcome January 30, 1933 more profoundly or more joyfully than the German Christian leadership."
- "Adolf Hitler, with his faith in Germany, as the instrument of our God became the framer of German destiny and the liberator of our people from their spiritual misery and division."
- "[Hitler is] the best man imaginable, a man shaped in a mold made of unity, piety, energy and strength of character."
- "[Hitler], the most German man, is also the most faithful, a believing Christian. We know that he begins and ends the course of his day with prayer, that he has found in the Gospel the deepest source of his strength."
- "If the German who truly believed in Jesus could find the Spirit of the kingdom of God anywhere, he could find it in Adolf Hitler's movement."
- "In the pitch-black night of Christian church history, Hitler became like a wonderful transparency for our time, a window through which light fell upon the history of Christianity."
- "[God has granted us an] hour of grace . . . through Adolf Hitler."
- "God has once again raised his voice in a singular individual."[13]

Compare these statements with those made in recent months by American charismatic and evangelical leaders:

- "God raised up . . . Donald Trump" (Michelle Bachman).
- "God has righteously chosen [Trump] to affect the way that this nation goes forward" (Chuck Pierce).

- "Donald Trump represents a supernatural answer to prayer" (James Robison).
- "God had raised up [Trump] for such a time as this" (Stephen Strang).
- "Donald Trump actively seeks God's guidance in his life" (James Dobson).
- Trump's victory "showed clear evidence of 'the hand of God' on the election" (Franklin Graham).
- "[Trump is] a bold man, a strong man, and an obedient man" (Kenneth Copeland).
- "I see this as a last-minute reprieve for America, and the Church" (Rodney Howard-Browne).
- "[Trump] does look like he's the last hope" (Phyllis Schlafly).
- "God was raising up Donald Trump as He did the Persian king Cyrus the Great" (Lance Wallnau).
- "[Trump is] a man of faith . . . truly committed to making America great again through principles that honor God rather than defy Him" (Stephen Strang).
- "In the midst of . . . despair, came November the 8th, 2016. It was on that day . . . that God declared that the people, not the pollsters, were gonna choose the next president of the United States. And they chose Donald Trump" (Robert Jeffress).
- "We thank God every day that He gave us a leader like President Trump" (Robert Jeffress).[14]

How is Trump able to convince these Christian leaders that he is worthy of their support? Mostly by paying attention to them, inviting them to Trump Tower, and indulging their need to be listened to in an increasingly post-Christian culture. It is truly remarkable that they have been taken in by Trump's vague and barely comprehensible statements about his "faith," such as "I've always been spiritual," "belief is very important," and "I'm going to do a great job for religion." Honestly, Hitler was better at pretending to be a Christian.

Given how often many of you have cited the German Church Struggle as a model for church-state relations in recent years, it is ironic that you do not seem bothered by these leaders who are repeating the mistakes so clearly displayed by German Christians in the wake of the Nazi revolution. Like those naive and desperate Germans, these American Christian leaders theologically justify nationalist fervor, fail to stand up for those being scapegoated by the state (including members of the Christian community), and fear being called unpatriotic as if this were worse than denying Christ.

Of course, knowledge of German cultural history provides some insight into why Christians would support Hitler in 1933. Their country had long been mired in economic depression, political dysfunction, and national humiliation. Even if they hadn't supported Hitler when it was possible to do so in a democratic election, once he was appointed chancellor, they were hopeful that his personal charisma and "outsider" identity would allow him to turn the nation around. Hitler's promises to reestablish the country on its religious and moral foundations made it easier to risk supporting him, despite his totalitarian leanings and hateful rhetoric. But once they jumped on the Nazi bandwagon, Germans found it difficult to admit that they had made a mistake. By the time they were pushed to the threshold of resistance, it was too late.

Likewise, evangelicals who voted for Trump can be given the benefit of the doubt for acting in rational self-interest, given the options. Perhaps, as some have argued, initial evangelical support for Trump was driven "by prudential judgment and fear of a Clinton presidency, rather than by blind acceptance." But if evangelical support for Trump was "contingent," surely the time has come to admit that the gamble was a failure.[15] The superficial, curated projections of the candidate to which we had access during the election campaign have now vanished to reveal the character, the spiritual essence, if you will, of the man. I think we can agree that it is not pretty and gets uglier with time.

Looking back, it is painfully obvious that Christians who embraced Hitler as Germany's "last chance" were determined to see what they wanted to see—Hitler as the new Luther, the long-awaited Savior, the God-sent redeemer who would make Germany great again. They clung to these fantasies even as Hitler showed his true colors and exposed his bogus piety. If these things were difficult to see at the time, it was because the alternatives were so bleak. Which leads to my next point:

I accept your claim that you could not, as Christians, vote for Hillary Clinton. I regard this as a principled stance rooted in the belief that behavior and character matter, as well as certain political convictions that for you are nonnegotiable. If you are one of those evangelical Christians who simply could not, *as a Christian*, vote for Hillary, I will not ask you to consider what role Russian propaganda played in your view of the Clintons. I will simply acknowledge that you found yourself in a truly difficult situation in which party loyalty became less important than the moral burden of having to choose between the "lesser of two evils."

But if you truly felt that both candidates might be "evil," I would point out that you were obliged—*as a Christian*—to extricate yourself from this moral quagmire, either by refusing to vote at all, or by risking a vote for one of the candidates and, depending on how that person governed, being prepared to renounce him or her. In other words, you were obligated to do everything in your power to ensure that the evil you had unwittingly helped unleash on the country would be mitigated by people like yourself who still believe in evil and believe it must be resisted.

Or you could have written in the name of someone whom you could support with a clear conscience, even if voting for that person left you open to the charge that you had assisted in electing one of the "evil" candidates. Voting in this way surely would have felt like an abdication of civic responsibility, but you would have had the satisfaction of knowing that you followed your Christ-inspired conscience. In the words of Bonhoeffer, you would have acted in the confidence that your decision to vote for a write-in candidate was an effort not to "extricate [yourself] heroically from a situation" but to take responsibility for how "the coming generation is to go on living."[16]

You would have voted your conscience in a way that placed you out of step with your friends and colleagues, who humility would compel you to admit might be seeing things more clearly than you. But, like Bonhoeffer, you would have demonstrated the courage and foresight to dissent from those around you, not the least of whom were trusted religious authorities, and take a stand for Christ that carried no guarantee of being recognized as such by others. This would have been difficult, but . . .

It would have been a real Bonhoeffer moment. You would no doubt have experienced, as Bonhoeffer did, isolation and loneliness, even tortured uncertainty. But you would have had the spiritual comfort of knowing that you took an unpopular stand based on your effort to discern God's will in that moment. It would have been your private "Bonhoeffer moment," since you would have done the thing Bonhoeffer might do if he were in your place.

Perhaps you failed to seize your first Bonhoeffer moment by voting for someone you suspected did not deserve the support of a serious Christian. Perhaps you have come to regret this decision. But there will be other Bonhoeffer moments ahead. Before they arrive, I hope you will begin to listen to your Christ-inspired gut feeling about political candidates—before co-opted Christian "leaders" give you permission to support them—and consider that your uneasiness might be the way Christians are supposed to feel when confronted with candidates whose words and behaviors suggest deep character flaws, not to mention woeful ignorance of the faith they are supposed to espouse.

If none of the candidates in an election meets your standard, does it matter whose name you write in? I recently browsed through the official results of Alabama's special Senate election. Given the highly Christian populace of the state, I was surprised that among the 22,852 write-in votes—which included votes for Mickey Mouse, Mel Brooks, and Gus Malzahn (Auburn's football coach)—Bonhoeffer's name did not appear even once. One certainly makes a statement by writing in names like Beyoncé, Bugs Bunny, or Buffett (Jimmy and Warren both received multiple votes), but imagine the statement a Christian voter could make by writing in "Bonhoeffer."

So the next time you are presented with a slate of candidates, consider each one on his or her merits. If you find that you cannot—as a Christian and a responsible citizen—vote for any of them, write in "Bonhoeffer." That will be a Bonhoeffer moment you can feel good about.

NOTES

Notes to the Acknowledgments

1. Keith L. Johnson, "Bonhoeffer and the End of the Christian Academy," in *Bonhoeffer, Christ, and Culture*, ed. Keith L. Johnson and Timothy Larsen (Downers Grove: InterVarsity, 2013), 153–73 (esp. 153–54).

Notes to Chapter 1

1. Leon Howell, "A Time of Trials: The Tribulation of Dietrich Bonhoeffer," *Sojourners*, May–June 1995, http://www.sojo.net/index.cfm?action=magazine.article&issue=soj9505&article=950531; George W. Bush, "President Bush Thanks Germany for Support against Terror," Office of the Press Secretary, 2002; Linda Bloom, "United Methodists Give Bonhoeffer Martyr Status," United Methodist News Service, June 17, 2008, http://archives.gcah.org/bitstream/handle/10516/3563/Bonhoeffer-martyr.aspx.htm.

2. https://bonhoeffercapital.com/; http://drkevinbaird.com/wp/2016/03/06/the-bonhoeffer-institute/; http://thebonhoefferproject.com/why-the-bonhoeffer-project.

3. Warren Throckmorton, "The Popular Bonhoeffer Quote That Isn't in Bonhoeffer's Works," *Warren Throckmorton* (blog), *Patheos*, August 25, 2016, http://www.patheos.com/blogs/warrenthrockmorton/2016/08/25/the-popular-bonhoeffer-quote-that-isnt-in-bonhoeffers-works/; Patricia McCormick, *The Plot to Kill Hitler: Dietrich Bonhoeffer; Pastor, Spy, Unlikely Hero* (New York: Balzer and Bray, 2016); "The Top 10 Best Dietrich Bonhoeffer Quotes," *Strength Awakening*, December 10, 2017, https://strengthawakening.com/top-10-best-dietrich-bonhoeffer-quotes/.

According to Vicki Barnett, the origins of this common solecism are unknown. Barnett writes: "I think the closest quotes are from the passage in *Ethics* on p. 139–40 ('The church . . . has become guilty of the lives of the weakest and most defenseless brothers and sisters of Jesus Christ, . . . confesses that it has looked on silently'), and the 1934 letter in *DBWE* [Dietrich Bonhoeffer Works in English] 13 (p. 217) where he says the church must 'speak out for those who cannot speak.' And then of course there are passages from 'After Ten Years' in *Letters and Papers* ('We have been silent witnesses of evil deeds . . .') and the reflections on who has the courage to act in the section on 'Who stands firm' and his statement 'Inactive waiting and dully looking on are not Christian responses' (p. 49)." E-mail correspondence, June 10, 2016.

4. "Called to Resist Bigotry: A Statement of Faithful Obedience," April 29, 2016, http://www.calledtoresist.org/. See also Brian Tashman, "Rafael Cruz Brings Up Nazi Germany in Rant against Marriage Equality," *Right Wing Watch*, March 11, 2016, http://www.rightwingwatch.org/content/rafael-cruz-brings-nazi-germany-rant-against-marriage-equality.

5. Eric Metaxas, *Bonhoeffer: Pastor, Martyr, Prophet, Spy; A Righteous Gentile vs. the Third Reich* (Nashville: Nelson, 2010), 466.

6. Michael Van Dyke, *Dietrich Bonhoeffer: Opponent of the Nazi Regime*, Heroes of the Faith (Ulrichsville, OH: Barbour Publishing, 2001); Susan Martins Miller, *Dietrich Bonhoeffer*, Men of Faith (Minneapolis: Bethany House, 2002); Elizabeth Raum, *Dietrich Bonhoeffer: Called by God* (New York: Continuum, 2002); Theodore J. Kleinhans, *Till the Night Be Past: The Life and Times of Dietrich Bonhoeffer* (Saint Louis: Concordia, 2002).

7. Mary Glazener, *The Cup of Wrath: A Novel Based on Dietrich Bonhoeffer's Resistance to Hitler* (Macon, GA: Smith and Helwys, 1992); Denise Giardina, *Saints and Villains* (New York: Fawcett, 1998); Paul Barz, *I Am Bonhoeffer: A Credible Life—a Novel*, trans. Douglas W. Stott (Minneapolis: Fortress, 2008); Michael Phillips, *The Eleventh Hour* (Wheaton, IL: Tyndale House, 1993); Suzanne Woods Fisher, *Copper Fire* (Goose Creek, SC: Vintage Romance, 2008).

8. Robert Ellsberg, *All Saints: Daily Reflections on Saints, Prophets, and Witnesses for Our Time* (New York: Crossroad, 1997); James C. Howell, *Servants, Misfits, and Martyrs: Saints and Their Stories* (Nashville: Upper Room Books, 1999); Jim Wallis and Joyce Hollyday, eds., *Cloud of Witnesses*, rev. ed. (Maryknoll, NY: Orbis, 1991); William D. Apel, *Witnesses before Dawn: Exploring the Meaning of Christian Life* (Valley Forge, PA: Judson, 1984); Bernard Christensen, *The Inward Pilgrimage: Spiritual Classics from Augustine to Bonhoeffer* (Minneapolis: Augsburg Fortress, 1976); Malcolm Muggeridge, *A Third Testament* (Boston: Little, Brown, 1976), 14, 196. See also David P. Gushee, *Only Human: Christian Reflections on the Journey toward Wholeness*, Enduring Questions in Christian Life (San Francisco: Jossey-Bass, 2005), where Bonhoeffer is presented as one of four Christians exemplifying "moral greatness" (the others are William Wilberforce, Florence Nightingale, and Martin Luther King Jr.).

9. *Dietrich Bonhoeffer: Memories and Perspectives*, directed by Bain Boehlke, Trinity Films, 1983; *Hanged on a Twisted Cross*, directed by T. N. Mahan, Gateway Films, 1996; *Bonhoeffer: Agent of Grace*, directed by Eric Till, Gateway Films, 1999; *Bonhoeffer*, directed by Martin Doblmeier, Journey Films, 2003.

Notes to Chapter 2

1. Harvey Cox, "Using and Misusing Bonhoeffer," *Christianity and Crisis* 24 (October 19, 1964): 199–201; 199; Carl J. Ridd, "A Message from Bonhoeffer," *Christian Century* 83 (June 29, 1966): 827–29; 827.

2. John Shelby Spong, *A New Christianity for a New World: Why Traditional Faith Is Dying and How a New Faith Is Being Born* (San Francisco: HarperSanFrancisco, 2002); DC Talk, *Jesus Freaks: DC Talk and the Voice of the Martyrs—Stories of Those Who Stood for Jesus, the Ultimate Jesus Freaks* (Bloomington, MN: Bethany House, 1999).

3. Stephen R. Haynes, *The Bonhoeffer Phenomenon: Portraits of a Protestant Saint* (Minneapolis: Fortress, 2004); *The Bonhoeffer Legacy: Post-Holocaust Perspectives* (Minneapolis: Fortress, 2006).

4. Daniel Berrigan, "The Passion of Dietrich Bonhoeffer," *Saturday Review*, May 30, 1970, 17–22; 17, 22.

5. Robert McAfee Brown, "ABC—Assy, Bonhoeffer, Carswell," *Christian Century* 88 (March 24, 1971): 369–71; 369.

6. Geffrey B. Kelly, *Liberating Faith: Bonhoeffer's Message for Today* (Minneapolis: Augsburg, 1984), 154, 98; Larry Rasmussen, with Renate Bethge, *Dietrich Bonhoeffer—His Significance for North Americans* (Minneapolis: Fortress, 1990), 74.

7. G. Clarke Chapman, "What Would Bonhoeffer Say to Christian Peacemakers Today?" in *Theology, Politics, and Peace*, ed. Theodore Runyan (Maryknoll, NY: Orbis, 1989), 167–75.

8. Geffrey B. Kelly, "The Idolatrous Enchainment of Church and State: Bonhoeffer's Critique of Freedom in the United States," in *Bonhoeffer for a New Day: Theology in a Time of Transition*, ed. John W. de Gruchy (Grand Rapids: Eerdmans, 1997), 298–318; 311.

9. Rasmussen, *Dietrich Bonhoeffer*, 37, 35.

10. Doris Bergen, "Contextualizing Dietrich Bonhoeffer: Nazism, Christianity and the Question of Silence," in *Interpreting Bonhoeffer: Historical Perspectives, Emerging Issues*, ed. Clifford J. Green and Guy C. Carter (Minneapolis: Fortress, 2013), 112.

11. Franklin H. Littell and Hubert G. Locke, eds., *The German Church Struggle and the Holocaust* (San Francisco: Mellen Research Press, 1990); Israel Gutman, ed., *Encyclopedia of the Holocaust* (New York: Macmillan, 1990), 230–31.

12. John S. Conway, "Coming to Terms with the Past: Interpreting the German Church Struggles 1933-1990," *German History* 16, no. 3 (1998): 377–96; Jürgen Fangmeier and Hinrich Stoevesandt, eds., *Karl Barth, Letters, 1961–1968*, trans. Geoffrey W. Bromiley (Edinburgh: T. & T. Clark, 1981), 250.

13. Dietrich Bonhoeffer, *Berlin: 1932–1933*, ed. C. Nicolaisen, E.-A. Scharffenorth, and L. L. Rasmussen, trans. I. Best, D. Higgins, and D. W. Stott, Dietrich Bonhoeffer Works in English, vol. 12 (Minneapolis: Fortress, 2009), 367, 426.

14. Haynes, *The Bonhoeffer Legacy*; John W. de Gruchy, *Daring, Trusting Friend: Bonhoeffer's Friend Eberhard Bethge* (Minneapolis: Fortress, 2005), 176.

15. Information about the Righteous Among the Nations program can be found at http://www.yadvashem.org/yv/en/holocaust/resource_center/item.asp?gate=1-10.

16. Marilyn Henry, "Who, Exactly, Is a 'Righteous Gentile'?" *Righteous-Jews.org*, April 22, 1998, https://www.righteousjews.org/article2.html.

17. Geffrey B. Kelly and F. Burton Nelson, *The Cost of Moral Leadership: The Spirituality of Dietrich Bonhoeffer* (Grand Rapids: Eerdmans, 2003), 118; Janet Benge and Geoff Benge, *Dietrich Bonhoeffer: In the Midst of Wickedness* (Seattle: YWAM Publishing, 2012), 164; Dave Jackson and Neta Jackson, *Hero Tales: A Family Treasury of True Stories from the Lives of Christian Heroes*, vol. 2 (Minneapolis: Bethany House, 1997), 17.

18. Michael Phillips, *The Eleventh Hour* (Wheaton, IL: Tyndale House, 1993), 120, 193.

19. Michael Van Dyke, *Dietrich Bonhoeffer: Opponent of the Nazi Regime*, Heroes of the Faith (Ulrichsville, OH: Barbour Publishing, 2001), 30.

20. Greg Ligon, ed., *Bonhoeffer's Cost of Discipleship*, Shepherd's Notes Christian Classics (Nashville: Holman, 1998), 2, 5; Van Dyke, *Dietrich Bonhoeffer*, 77.

21. Denise Giardina, *Saints and Villains* (New York: Fawcett, 1998), 12.

22. Giardina, *Saints and Villains*, 216, 225, 270, 301, 272, 298, 480.

23. Mary Glazener, *The Cup of Wrath: A Novel Based on Dietrich Bonhoeffer's Resistance to Hitler* (Macon, GA: Smith and Helwys, 1992), 140.

24. Kelly and Nelson, *Cost of Moral Leadership*, 40, 42.

25. Robert Coles, *Dietrich Bonhoeffer*, Modern Spiritual Masters (Maryknoll, NY: Orbis, 1998), 31, 41; Robert Coles, *Lives of Moral Leadership: Men and Women Who Have Made a Difference* (New York: Random House, 2000).

26. James W. Fowler, *Stages of Faith: The Psychology of Human Development and the Quest for Meaning* (New York: Harper and Row, 1981), 201, and Josh Gressel, "Faith Development: Stage Six," *Pleasant Hill Patch*, August 7, 2013, https://patch.com/california/pleasanthill/faith-development--stage-six. In another study in this genre, Robin W. Lovin and Jonathan P. Gosser claim that Bonhoeffer belongs in this select company of the spiritually mature by applying faith development theory to what is known of his life. See

Robin W. Lovin and Jonathan P. Gosser, "Dietrich Bonhoeffer: Witness in an Ambiguous World," in *Trajectories in Faith: Five Life Stories*, ed. James W. Fowler and Robin W. Lovin (Nashville: Abingdon, 1980), 147–84.

27. Robert L. Hunter, "Dietrich Bonhoeffer: A Vision and a Voice for Our Times," *Saturday Evening Post*, September/October 1997, 50–51; "Hitler's Would-Be Assassin," *Saturday Evening Post*, November/December 1997, 44–47, 51; Keith W. Clements, *What Freedom? The Persistent Challenge of Dietrich Bonhoeffer* (Bristol, UK: Bristol Baptist College, 1990), 2, 11.

28. Dennis Covington, "Christopher Hitchens: God Is Not Great," *Paste*, May 9, 2007, https://www.pastemagazine.com/articles/2007/05/christopher-hitchens-god-is-not-great.html.

29. Nancy Koehn, *Forged in Crisis: The Power of Courageous Leadership in Turbulent Times* (New York: Scribner, 2017), 3, 2, 4, 6.

30. Koehn, *Forged in Crisis*, 284–85.

31. Koehn, *Forged in Crisis*, 291, 316, 319.

32. Koehn, *Forged in Crisis*, 346, 366.

33. Koehn, *Forged in Crisis*, 2, 9.

Notes to Chapter 3

1. Timothy Larsen, "The Evangelical Reception of Dietrich Bonhoeffer," in *Bonhoeffer, Christ, and Culture*, ed. Keith L. Johnson and Timothy Larsen (Downers Grove: InterVarsity, 2013), 39–57; 46.

2. Larsen, "Evangelical Reception," 56–57; 41.

3. Larsen, "Evangelical Reception," 43–44.

4. Larsen, "Evangelical Reception," 44–45.

5. Richard Weikart, *The Myth of Dietrich Bonhoeffer: Is His Theology Evangelical?* (San Francisco: International Scholars Publications, 1997), 27, 43, 77, 28, 105.

6. Weikart, *Myth of Dietrich Bonhoeffer*, 139.

7. Larsen, "Evangelical Reception," 50; "The Ten Most Influential Christians," *Christian History* 65 (2000), http://www.christianitytoday.com/history/issues/issue-65/.

8. *Christian History* 32 (1991), http://www.ctlibrary.com/ch/1991/issue32/; Michael Van Dyke, *Dietrich Bonhoeffer: Opponent of the Nazi Regime*, Heroes of the Faith (Ulrichsville, OH: Barbour Publishing, 2001); Janet Benge and Geoff Benge, *Dietrich Bonhoeffer: In the Midst of Wickedness* (Seattle: YWAM Publishing, 2012); Susan Martins Miller, *Dietrich Bonhoeffer: The Life and Martyrdom of a Great Man Who Counted the Cost of Discipleship*, Men of Faith (Minneapolis: Bethany House, 2002).

9. *Bonhoeffer: The Cost of Freedom*, written and directed by Paul McCusker (Colorado Springs: Focus on the Family, 1997, 1999).

10. Michael Phillips, *The Eleventh Hour* (Wheaton, IL: Tyndale House, 1993), 462; Suzanne Woods Fisher, *Copper Fire* (Ladson, SC: Vintage Inspirations, 2008).

11. Larsen, "Evangelical Reception," 52; Miller, *Dietrich Bonhoeffer*, 131.

12. Mark DeVine, "Bonhoeffer Is Still Speaking," *Baptist Press*, May 5, 2006, http://www.bpnews.net/23201/firstperson-bonhoeffer-still-speaking; Miller, *Dietrich Bonhoeffer*, 129.

13. Larsen, "Evangelical Reception," 53. Dietrich Bonhoeffer, *Discipleship*, ed. and trans. Martin Kuske and Ilse Tödt, Dietrich Bonhoeffer Works in English, vol. 4 (Minneapolis: Fortress, 2003), 178.

14. Weikart, *Myth of Dietrich Bonhoeffer*, 127; *Christian Reader*, September/October 1997. "Books of the Century," *Christianity Today* 46 (April 24, 2000), http://www.christianitytoday.com/ct/2000/april24/5.92.html; Dale Larsen and Sandy Larsen, *Dietrich Bonhoeffer: Costly Grace*, Christian Classics Bible Studies (Downers Grove: InterVarsity, 2002); Greg Ligon, ed., *Bonhoeffer's Cost of Discipleship*, Shepherd's Notes Christian Classics (Nashville: Holman, 1998).

15. Theodore J. Kleinhans, *Till the Night Be Past: The Life and Times of Dietrich Bonhoeffer* (Saint Louis: Concordia, 2002), 36.

16. Rubel Shelly, "Biographers Needed! Please Apply," RubelShelly.com, accessed February 21, 2018, http://rubelshelly.com/content.asp?CID=16342; Weikart, *Myth of Dietrich Bonhoeffer*, 127.

17. Phillips, *Eleventh Hour*, 461.

18. Fisher, *Copper Fire*.

19. Van Dyke, *Dietrich Bonhoeffer*, 47, 55; Benge and Benge, *Dietrich Bonhoeffer*, 62–63.

20. Charles Colson, "Caesar and Christ: Should We Disobey Our Government?" *BreakPoint*, November 28, 2000.

21. James Dobson, "The New Cost of Discipleship," *Christianity Today* 43 (September 6, 1999), http://www.christianitytoday.com/ct/1999/september6/9ta056.html.

22. *Focus on the Family Newsletter*, May 2000.

23. Michael Westmoreland-White, Glen H. Stassen, and David P. Gushee, "Disciples of the Incarnation: The Witness of Dietrich Bonhoeffer, Martin Luther King, Jr., and Christian Rescuers of Jews Informs Our Discipleship Today," *Sojourners* 23, no. 4 (May 1994), http://www.sojo.net/index.cfm?action=magazine.article&issue=soj9405&article=940520.

24. David P. Gushee, "Following Jesus to the Gallows," *Christianity Today* 39 (April 3, 1995): 26–27.

25. Jim Wallis, "When I First Met Bonhoeffer," *Sojourners*, December 2005, https://sojo.net/magazine/december-2005/when-i-first-met-bonhoeffer.

26. Charles Marsh, *Wayward Christian Soldiers: Freeing the Gospel from Political Captivity* (Oxford: Oxford University Press, 2007), 3, 119.

27. Chris Rice, "Dietrich Bonhoeffer as We Understand Him at JPUSA," *ADKF (A Desperate Kind of Faithful)* (blog), accessed February 21, 2018, https://justthischris.wordpress.com/dietrich-bonhoeffer-articles/dietrich-bonhoeffer-as-we-understand-him/.

28. Andrew D. Rowell, "Innovative Ecclesiological Practices: Emerging Churches in Dialogue with Dietrich Bonhoeffer" (unpublished manuscript, January 31, 2007), http://www.andyrowell.net/andy_rowell/files/bonhoeffer_and_emerging_church_sample_paper_5.pdf. See also Steve Bezner, "Bonhoeffer and the Emerging Church," *Citizen Bezner*, January 9, 2007, http://citizenbezner.blogspot.com/2007/01/bonhoeffer-and-emerging-church.html.

29. Ray S. Anderson, *An Emergent Theology for Emerging Churches* (Downers Grove: InterVarsity, 2006), 46, 152.

30. Anderson, *Emergent Theology*, 192, 194.

31. Anderson, *Emergent Theology*, 140.

32. Larsen, "Evangelical Reception," 42.

Notes to Chapter 4

1. Karen V. Guth, "Claims on Bonhoeffer: The Misuse of a Theologian," *Christian Century*, May 13, 2015, https://www.christiancentury.org/article/2015-05/claims-bonhoeffer.

2. Robert O. Smith, "Bonhoeffer, Bloggers, and Bush: Uses of a 'Protestant Saint' in the Fog of War" (paper delivered at the annual meeting of the Academy of Religion, Philadelphia, November 2005), 2; graciously shared with the author.

3. Walter Wink, "The Bonhoeffer Assumption," *Sojourners* 31, no. 1 (January–February 2002), https://sojo.net/magazine/january-february-2002/bonhoeffer-assumption.

4. Smith, "Bonhoeffer, Bloggers, and Bush," 3; Richard Land, "What Would King Have Said about Saddam?" *Beliefnet* 4 (February 2003). In October 2002, Land was the lead author in a letter to President George W. Bush that defended an invasion of Iraq as warranted according to the Christian tradition of "just war." See the so-called Land Letter at http://www.drrichardland.com/press/entry/the-so-called-land-letter.

5. The reader's comment can be found at http://www.beliefnet.com/boards_mini/index.asp?boardID=50687.

6. Smith, "Bonhoeffer, Bloggers, and Bush," 3, 5–6, 7.

7. Al Staggs, "The Parallels to Hitler's Germany Are Abundantly Clear: Dietrich Bonhoeffer and the Iraq Crisis," *Baptist Standard*, March 3, 2003, http://levantium.com/2010/06/20/the-parallels-to-hitlers-germany-are-abundantly-clear/.

8. Geffrey B. Kelly and F. Burton Nelson, *The Cost of Moral Leadership: The Spirituality of Dietrich Bonhoeffer* (Grand Rapids: Eerdmans, 2003), 120.

9. "What Would Dietrich Do?" *Photon Courier*, January 18, 2003, http://photoncourier.blogspot.com/2003_01_01_photoncourier_archive.html.

10. Jean Bethke Elshtain, "Thinking about War and Justice," *The Religion and Culture Web Forum*, May 2003, https://divinity.uchicago.edu/sites/default/files/imce/pdfs/webforum/052003/commentary.pdf.

11. Michael Cromartie, "Dirty Hands and Concrete Action: A Conversation with Jean Bethke Elshtain," *Books and Culture*, September 1, 2003, http://www.ctlibrary.com/bc/2003/sepoct/12.18.html; Alan Johnson, "Just War, Humanitarian Intervention and Equal Regard: An Interview with Jean Bethke Elshtain," *Dissent*, Summer 2005, https://www.dissentmagazine.org/wp-content/files_mf/1390329368d1Inteview.pdf.

12. Stanley Hauerwas, *Performing the Faith: Bonhoeffer and the Practice of Nonviolence* (Grand Rapids: Brazos, 2004), 19, 202.

13. See http://www.j-n-v.org/Other_aw_documents/Voices_US_VCNV.htm.

14. Mark Devine, *Bonhoeffer Speaks Today: Following Jesus at All Costs* (Nashville: Broadman and Holman, 2005), 139–40.

15. Michael Van Dyke, *Dietrich Bonhoeffer: Opponent of the Nazi Regime*, Heroes of the Faith (Ulrichsville, OH: Barbour Publishing, 2001), 205.

16. See David Alan Black, "Do We Need a New Barmen Declaration?" *Dave Black Online*, July 16, 2003, http://www.daveblackonline.com/do_we_need_a_new_barmen_declarat.htm. Although Black mentions Bonhoeffer and his opposition to "statism," he does not figure largely in the article.

17. Raymond A. Schroth, "Bonhoeffer Was Wrong," *National Catholic Reporter*, January 27, 2006, http://natcath.org/NCR_Online/archives2/2006a/012706/012706r.php.

18. In a 2006 article titled "The Bonhoeffer Debate," the *Kansas City Star* reported that local Christians' religious attitudes on assassination were fairly divided: 53 percent would personally try to assassinate someone like Hitler, while only 37.5 percent thought their religion would permit them to do so. For a range of negative responses to Schroth's article, see "19 Responses to 'Raymond A. Schroth: Bonhoeffer Was Wrong,'" *Titusonenine*, February 5–6, 2006, http://titusonenine.classicalanglican.net/?p=11262. See also Martin E. Marty, "Bonhoeffer Now," Martin Marty Center for the Public Understanding of Religion, February 6, 2006, https://divinity.uchicago.edu/sightings/bonhoeffer-now-martin-e-marty.

19. Larry Rasmussen, "The Steep Price of Grace," *Sojourners*, February 2006, https://sojo.net/magazine/february-2006/steep-price-grace.

20. Charles Marsh, *Wayward Christian Soldiers: Freeing the Gospel from Political Captivity* (Oxford: Oxford University Press, 2007), 47.

21. Marsh, *Wayward Christian Soldiers*, 110.

22. See comments posted in reaction to the program "Ethics and the Will of God: The Legacy of Dietrich Bonhoeffer," https://onbeing.org/programs/martin-doblmeier-ethics-and-the-will-of-god-the-legacy-of-dietrich-bonhoeffer/.

23. Ben Domenech, "The Last Ship," *BenDomenech.com*, July 21, 2003.

24. "Pat Robertson Clarifies His Statement regarding Hugo Chavez," Pat Robertson, news release, August 24, 2005, http://www.patrobertson.com/pressreleases/hugochavez.asp; Christian Platt, "Mideast Tensions Wind toward Morally Tight Conclusion," *Pueblo (CO) Chieftain*, May 6, 2006, https://www.chieftain.com/editorial/mideast-tensions-wind-toward-morally-tight-conclusion/article_de089045-898e-5b5f-b573-de0cd5ea0ada.html.

25. Loose Cannon [Charlotte Hayes], "The T-Shirt Two: Why They're Not Alike . . . ," *Beliefnet*, February 2, 2006; Swami Uptown [Jesse Kornbluth], "Cindy Sheehan and Dietrich Bonhoeffer: Two of a Kind," *Beliefnet*, February 6, 2006.

26. See "About Voices," *Voices for Creative Nonviolence*, accessed February 22, 2018, http://vcnv.org/about-voices/; Jeff Leys, "Our Bonhoeffer Moment," *Voices for Creative Nonviolence*, October 2, 2007, http://old.vcnv.org/our-bonhoeffer-moment.

Notes to Chapter 5

1. Dan Barry and John Eligon, "'Trump, Trump, Trump!' How a President's Name Became a Racial Jeer," *New York Times*, December 16, 2017, https://www.nytimes.com/2017/12/16/us/trump-racial-jeers.html.

2. John W. Whitehead, founder of the right-leaning Rutherford Institute, in 2006 cited examples of American schools' "totalitarian mindset" and concluded with an "ominous parallel" from German history: "On January 30, 1933, Adolf Hitler was elected chancellor of Germany. Two days later, a 26-year-old minister named Dietrich Bonhoeffer gave a national radio address protesting Hitler's election in a radio sermon/speech entitled 'The Younger Generation's Changed View of the Concept of Fuhrer.' Throughout his speech, Bonhoeffer warned the people of Germany that the 'Fuhrer' (leader) could very easily become a '*Verführer*' (seducer), noting that the two words are only three letters different from each other. While Bonhoeffer was remarking that a leader who makes himself an idol mocks God, the broadcast was cut off in mid-sentence and the station returned to playing classical German music—music that would soon accompany goose-stepping Nazis as they ripped a gaping hole in the fabric of the twentieth century." See John W. Whitehead, "Turning Our Schools into Enclaves of Totalitarianism," *The Rutherford Institute*, July 3, 2006, https://www.rutherford.org/publications_resources/john_whiteheads_commentary/turning_our_schools_into_enclaves_of_totalitarianism.

3. As an expression of hysterical anti-Obamaism, it is difficult to surpass the rumor that began circulating in March 2008 claiming not only that Obama was a Muslim but also that he was the antichrist foretold in the book of Revelation. "According to The Book of Revelations," an online version of the rumor went, "the anti-Christ will be a man, in his 40s, of MUSLIM descent, who will deceive the nations with persuasive language . . . will promise false hope and world peace, and when he is in power, will destroy everything. Is it OBAMA??" Some who endorsed this claim pointed out that the beast of "Revelations" is given authority for forty-two months, which is "almost a four-year term to a Presidency." A commentator on these rumors noted that "outgoing Antichrist designee George W. Bush must be thrilled to see a newcomer wearing the ungodly mantle." See "Is Barack Obama the Antichrist?" *ThoughtCo*, updated March 18, 2017, https://www.thoughtco.com/is-barack-obama-the-antichrist-3298948.

4. "Billboard Shows Obama as Hitler, Demands President's Impeachment," *Huffington Post*, October 15, 2013, https://www.huffingtonpost.com/entry/obama-hitler-billboard-indiana_n_4101322.html.

5. David Weigel "Ted Cruz: Funding Obamacare Is Basically Like Appeasing Hitler," *Slate*, September 24, 2013, http://www.slate.com/blogs/weigel/2013/09/24/ted_cruz_funding_obamacare_is_basically_like_appeasing_hitler.html.

6. Luke Brinker, "Seven Conservatives Who Have Compared Obama to Hitler," *Salon*, January 13, 2015, https://www.salon.com/2015/01/13/7_conservatives_who_have_compared_obama_to_hitler/; Matthew O'Brien, "Why Do the Super-Rich Keep Comparing Obama to Hitler?" *Atlantic*, January 29, 2014, https://www.theatlantic.com/business/archive/2014/01/why-do-the-super-rich-keep-comparing-obama-to-hitler/283404/; and Jamelle Bouie, "You Know Who Else Said That? My Favorite Examples of Conservatives Comparing Obama to Hitler," *Slate*, January 13, 2015, http://www.slate.com/articles/news_and_politics/politics/2015/01/republicans_comparing_barack_obama_to_hitler_my_favorite_examples_of_the.html.

7. Erwin W. Lutzer, *Hitler's Cross: The Revealing Story of How the Cross of Christ Was Used as a Symbol of the Nazi Agenda* (Chicago: Moody Press, 1995), 160; "Christian v. America," *Christianity Today* 40, no. 5 (1996): 64.

8. See "Confessing Movement," *Wikipedia*, last edited February 18, 2018, https://en.wikipedia.org/wiki/Confessing_Movement. It is no coincidence that the largest of these movements, the Confessing Church Movement in the Presbyterian Church (USA), operated within a denomination that in the 1980s adopted the Barmen Declaration as one of its confessional documents.

9. William Stacy Johnson, "Regaining Perspective," *Presbyterian Outlook*, May 21, 2001, 11.

10. Daniel K. Williams, *Defenders of the Unborn: The Pro-Life Movement before Roe v. Wade* (New York: Oxford University Press, 2016), 38, 263. Some

pro-life thinkers have taken a deeper look at Bonhoeffer's relevance for their movement. For instance, George Grant argues that Bonhoeffer opposed the Nazi eugenics program on the basis of the regime's active promotion of abortion and that, after he was banned from preaching and teaching, he continued his pro-life ministries covertly. See George Grant, *Third Time Around: A History of the Prolife Movement* (Brentwood, TN: Wolgemuth and Hyatt, 1991), 145.

11. *Focus on the Family Newsletter*, May 2000.

12. Amanda Ripley, "Terrorists and Saints," *Washington City Paper*, February 5, 1999, https://www.washingtoncitypaper.com/news/article/13017079/terrorists-and-saints; John Yewell, "Straight Shooters," *Colorado Springs Independent Online*, February 8, 2001, https://www.csindy.com/coloradosprings/straight-shooters/Content?oid=1110788. The American Coalition of Life Activists (ACLA) was successfully sued in 1999 over their "Nuremberg Files Project," a website that identified abortion doctors. The project's goal, according to ACLA national director David Crane, was "to gather all available information on abortionists and their accomplices for the day when they may be formally charged and tried at Nuremberg-type trials for their crimes." See Skipp Porteous, "Banquet of the White Rose," *Albion Monitor*, February 18, 1996, http://www.albionmonitor.com/abortion/whiterose.html.

13. *Brockhoeft Report* 1, no. 4 (December 1993). "John Brockhoeft, a defender of the unborn, has completed serving several years in prison for closing down abortuaries by means of fire. While he was incarcerated, he wrote what has become known as *The Brockhoeft Report*. *The Brockhoeft Report* was originally in newsletter format and edited by Shelley Shannon until her subsequent arrest and conviction for shooting late term abortionist George Tiller. After Shelley's trial *The Brockhoeft Report* was published in the Prayer & Action News, edited by Dave and Dorothy Leach. John Brockhoeft is a signer of Paul Hill's Defensive Action statement. He was released from prison under severe restrictions placed on his personal liberties" (www.armyofgod.com, accessed January 2003).

14. Timothy George, "A Tale of Two Declarations," *Beeson*, Spring 2011, https://www.beesondivinity.com/assets/1346/2011_beeson_final_copy.pdf.

15. "Manhattan Declaration: A Call of Christian Conscience," November 20, 2009, 1, http://manhattandeclaration.org/man_dec_resources/Manhattan_Declaration_full_text.pdf.

16. "Manhattan Declaration," 2, 3, 7, 8.

17. "Manhattan Declaration," 8, 9, 9, 2.

18. "Manhattan Declaration," 3, 1. On the God who "has laid total claim on our lives," cf. Barmen Declaration, para. 2: "Jesus Christ is . . . God's vigorous announcement of his claim upon our whole life"; and para. 5: "we reject the false doctrine that beyond its special commission the State should and could become the sole and total order of human life and so fulfil the vocation of the

Church as well." On "those who have been entrusted with temporal power . . . fulfill the first responsibility of government," cf. Barmen Declaration, para. 5's reference to the "responsibility of those who rule and those who are ruled."

19. George, "Tale of Two Declarations," 2.

20. George, "Tale of Two Declarations," 2.

21. George, "Tale of Two Declarations," 2.

22. George, "Tale of Two Declarations," 2, 3; Betsy Childs, "Costly Grace and Christian Witness: Revisiting the Manhattan Declaration," *Beeson*, Spring 2011, 12–15; 15.

23. Eric Metaxas, *Bonhoeffer: Pastor, Martyr, Prophet, Spy; A Righteous Gentile vs. the Third Reich* (Nashville: Nelson, 2010), 60, 61, 400.

24. Transcript of *Glenn Beck*, August 5, 2010, http://www.foxnews.com/story/0,2933,598764,00.html.

25. Mark Joseph, "The President and the Prophet: Obama's Unusual Encounter with Eric Metaxas," *National Review*, February 7, 2012, http://www.nationalreview.com/corner/290393/president-prophet-obamas-unusual-encounter-eric-metaxas-mark-joseph.

26. Scott Horton, "On Dietrich Bonhoeffer—Six Questions for Eric Metaxas," *Browsings: The Harper's Blog*, December 23, 2010, http://harpers.org/archive/2010/12/hbc-90007864.

27. Clifford Green, "Hijacking Bonhoeffer," *Christian Century*, October 4, 2010, https://www.christiancentury.org/reviews/2010-09/hijacking-bonhoeffer; Eric Metaxas, "CPAC 2013 Speech on Religious Freedom," Eric Metaxas, March 16, 2013, http://ericmetaxas.com/writing/essays/cpac-2013-speech-religious-freedom/#sthash.C3Tlsgtk.dpuf.

28. Clifford Green, "Hijacking Bonhoeffer"; Lauren Green, "New Bio of Executed WWII Pastor/Spy Reveals U.S. Influence," *FoxNews.com*, April 9, 2010, http://www.foxnews.com/world/2010/04/09/new-bio-executed-wwii-pastorspy-reveals-influence.html.

Notes to Chapter 6

1. Sara Pulliam Bailey, "Is Eric Metaxas the Next Chuck Colson?" *Religious News Service*, July 29, 2013, https://religionnews.com/2013/07/29/is-eric-metaxas-the-next-chuck-colson/.

2. Eric Metaxas, *Seven Men and the Secret of Their Greatness* (Nashville: Nelson, 2013), 96.

3. Eric Metaxas, *Bonhoeffer: Pastor, Martyr, Prophet, Spy; A Righteous Gentile vs. the Third Reich* (Nashville: Nelson, 2010), 466.

4. Metaxas, *Bonhoeffer*, 95. "The Authentic Bonhoeffer," interview of Eric Metaxas, *Christianity Today*, July 7, 2010, http://www.christianitytoday.com/ct/2010/july/7.54.html.

5. Kathryn Jean Lopez, "Bonhoeffer the Brave: A New Look at a 20th-Century Hero," *National Review Online*, December 10, 2010, http://www.nationalreview.com/article/255411/bonhoeffer-brave-interview. See also David Heim, "Alan Wolfe on Metaxas's Bonhoeffer," *Christian Century*, February 10, 2011, http://www.christiancentury.org/blogs/archive/2011-02/alan-wolfe-metaxass-bonhoeffer.

6. Lopez, "Bonhoeffer the Brave."

7. Joseph Loconte, "Belief in Action," *Wall Street Journal*, April 23, 2010, http://online.wsj.com/article/SB10001424052702303491304575189132952513158.html. Other reviews of the book that emphasized features of Bonhoeffer's life appealing to social and religious conservatives include Cal Thomas, "Bonhoeffer and a Christian's 'Privilege to Suffer,'" *Washington Examiner*, June 22, 2010, http://www.washingtonexaminer.com/cal-thomas-bonhoeffer-and-a-christians-privilege-to-suffer/article/32076, and Rebecca Bynum, "Dietrich Bonhoeffer Rediscovered," *New English Review*, April 2010, http://www.newenglishreview.org/print.cfm?pg=custpage&frm=1641&sec_id=86067.

8. *Glenn Beck*, Fox News Channel, May 1, 2011, http://video.foxnews.com/v/4446987/?#sp=show-clips.

9. Lopez, "Bonhoeffer the Brave"; *Glenn Beck*, December 3, 2010.

10. Paul Lehmann, "Review of *The Communion of Saints* and *No Rusty Swords*," *Union Seminary Quarterly* Review 21, no. 3 (March 1966): 364–69; 365.

11. Metaxas, *Bonhoeffer*, 465, 468.

12. Metaxas, *Bonhoeffer*, 467. See Ralf K. Wüstenberg, *A Theology of Life: Dietrich Bonhoeffer's Concept of Religionless Christianity*, trans. Douglas Stott (Grand Rapids: Eerdmans, 1998). Although this book is listed in the book's bibliography, it appears not to have informed Metaxas's understanding of the prison letters.

13. Metaxas, *Bonhoeffer*, 467, 84.

14. Nancy Lukens, "Misrepresenting the Life of Dietrich Bonhoeffer," *Sojourners*, February 2011, https://sojo.net/magazine/february-2011/how-eric-metaxas-agenda-driven-biography-fails-capture-true-bonhoeffer; Clifford Green, "Hijacking Bonhoeffer," *Christian Century*, October 4, 2010, https://www.christiancentury.org/reviews/2010-09/hijacking-bonhoeffer; Victoria Barnett, "Review of Eric Metaxas, *Bonhoeffer: Pastor, Martyr, Prophet, Spy: A Righteous Gentile vs. the Third Reich*," *Association of Contemporary Church Historians Quarterly* 15, no. 3 (September 2010), https://contemporarychurchhistory.org/2010/09/review-of-eric-metaxas-bonhoeffer-pastor-martyr-prophet-spy-a-righteous-gentile-vs-the-third-reich/. See also "Review of *Bonhoeffer: Pastor, Martyr, Prophet, Spy*," *Kirkus Reviews*, December 15, 2010, https://www.kirkusreviews.com/book-reviews/eric-metaxas/bonhoeffer/.

15. Green, "Hijacking Bonhoeffer"; Metaxas, *Bonhoeffer*, 265, 318.

16. Metaxas, *Bonhoeffer*, 95, 169,

17. Andy Rowell, "Bonhoeffer: The Evangelical Hero," *Books and Culture*,

June 2010, http://www.booksandculture.com/articles/webexclusives/2010/june/bonhoeffer.html.

18. Richard Weikart, "Metaxas's Counterfeit Bonhoeffer: An Evangelical Critique," Stanislaus State, Department of History, accessed February 21, 2018, http://www.csustan.edu/history/faculty/weikart/metaxas.htm; e-mail to the author, February 4, 2011.

19. Weikart, "Metaxas's Counterfeit Bonhoeffer."

20. Tim Challies, "Counterfeit Bonhoeffer," *@Challies*, January 18, 2011, http://www.challies.com/articles/counterfeit-bonhoeffer.

21. Carl R. Trueman, "Bonhoeffer and Anonymous Evangelicals," *Mortification of Spin* (blog), Alliance of Confessing Evangelicals, January 18, 2011, http://www.alliancenet.org/mos/postcards-from-palookaville/bonhoeffer-and-anonymous-evangelicals.

22. Michael Hayes, *Bonhoeffer and Evangelicals*, accessed March 12, 2018, https://bonhoeffernowandthen.wordpress.com/about/. See also Frederick Meekins, "Are Evangelicals Too Quick to Embrace Bonhoeffer as One of Their Own?" *WEB Commentary*, August 30, 2015, http://www.webcommentary.com/php/ShowArticle.php?id=meekinsf&date=150830, and William Macleod, "Bonhoeffer—a Reliable Guide?" *Banner of Truth*, September 23, 2016, https://banneroftruth.org/us/resources/articles/2016/bonhoeffer-reliable-guide/.

23. Jason B. Hood, "Redeeming Bonhoeffer (the Book)," *Christianity Today*, February 7, 2011, http://www.christianitytoday.com/ct/2011/februaryweb-only/redeemingbonhoeffer.html.

24. Bailey, "Is Eric Metaxas the Next Chuck Colson?" Metaxas has written that what initially attracted him to Bonhoeffer was his discovery that there really was "a Christian whose faith had led him to heroically stand up against the Nazis at the cost of his own life." Before that time, it seemed all the stories he had heard "of people taking their faith seriously" were negative (*Seven Men*, 89).

25. Scott Horton, "On Dietrich Bonhoeffer—Six Questions for Eric Metaxas," *Browsings: The Harper's Blog*, December 23, 2010, http://harpers.org/archive/2010/12/hbc-90007864.

26. Lopez, "Bonhoeffer the Brave."

27. Metaxas, *Bonhoeffer*, 472, 128; Green, "Hijacking Bonhoeffer."

28. Metaxas, *Seven Men*, 112; Robert Ericksen, "Protestants," in *The Oxford Handbook of Holocaust Studies*, ed. Peter Hayes and John K. Roth (New York: Oxford University Press, 2010), 253.

29. Metaxas, *Bonhoeffer*, 144.

30. Frederick Clarkson, "Christian Right Leaders Escalate Anti-LGBT Threats," *LGBTQ Nation*, May 8, 2015, https://www.lgbtqnation.com/2015/05/christian-right-leaders-escalate-anti-lgbt-threats/, and Frederick Clarkson, "Will Our Prisons Overflow with Christians?," Political Research Associates,

March 1, 2015, http://www.politicalresearch.org/2015/03/01/will-our-prisons-overflow-with-christians/.

31. Timothy Larsen, "The Evangelical Reception of Dietrich Bonhoeffer," in *Bonhoeffer, Christ, and Culture*, ed. Keith L. Johnson and Timothy Larsen (Downers Grove: InterVarsity, 2013), 39–57; 50, 51.

32. Lopez, "Bonhoeffer the Brave."

Notes to Chapter 7

1. http://ericmetaxas.com/media/video/2012-national-prayer-breakfast/.

2. https://www.freeconferencecallhd.com/playback/?n=OYkzo/jbKxc; James Robinson, "James Dobson, Rick Scarborough, Mat Staver Address Supreme Court Same-Sex Marriage Threat," *Charisma News*, March 16, 2015, http://www.charismanews.com/opinion/48754-james-dobson-rick-scarborough-mat-staver-address-supreme-court-same-sex-marriage-threat.

3. "We Pledge in Solidarity to Defend Marriage and the Family and Society Founded upon Them," Freedom Federation, accessed February 21, 2018, http://americandecency.org/article_images/Marriage%20Pledge.pdf; see also Bill Johnson, "A Bonhoeffer Moment—Rick Scarborough," *American Decency*, March 24, 2015, http://www.americandecency.org/full_article.php?article_no=3217.

4. Larry Tomczak, "Church Is Facing a Dietrich Bonhoeffer Moment," *Charisma News*, March 30, 2015, http://www.charismanews.com/opinion/heres-the-deal/48952-church-is-facing-a-dietrich-bonhoeffer-moment. At this time the only opinion outlet on the left to take seriously the declaration of a "Bonhoeffer moment" was *Think Progress*. See Jack Jenkins, "Why This Pastor Who Tried to Assassinate Hitler Has Become a Hero to the Anti-LGBT Movement," *Think Progress*, April 14, 2015, http://thinkprogress.org/lgbt/2015/04/14/3646532/conservatives-comparing-anti-lgbt-crusade-pastors-attempt-assassinate-hitler/.

5. Bob Seidensticker, "Does the Church Face a Bonhoeffer Moment? Maybe It's Just a Case of the Vapours," *Cross Examined* (blog), *Patheos*, April 1, 2015, http://www.patheos.com/blogs/crossexamined/2015/04/does-the-church-face-a-dietrich-bonhoeffer-moment-maybe-its-just-a-case-of-the-vapours/.

6. Robert King, "Pence, GOP Leaders Get Pastors' 'Rebuke' for RFRA Fix," *Indianapolis Star*, April 27, 2015, https://www.indystar.com/story/news/2015/04/27/pence-gop-leaders-get-pastors-rebuke-rfra-fix/26483311/; Amy Hemphill, "Don't Cite Dietrich Bonhoeffer in Support of RFRA," *Indianapolis Star*, April 29, 2015, http://www.indystar.com/story/opinion/readers/2015/04/29/cite-dietrich-bonhoeffer-support-rfra/26593581/; Jack H. Rog-

ers, "American Christians Are Being Persecuted," letter to the editor, *Indianapolis Star*, May 2, 2015, http://www.indystar.com/story/opinion/readers/2015/05/02/american-christians-persecuted/26806147/.

7. Frederick Clarkson, "Christian Right Leaders Escalate Anti-LGBT Threats," *LGBTQ Nation*, May 8, 2015, https://www.lgbtqnation.com/2015/05/christian-right-leaders-escalate-anti-lgbt-threats/. In May two articles in mainstream publications questioned the use of Bonhoeffer by evangelicals, although neither mentioned those who were proclaiming a "Bonhoeffer moment." See Carl R. Trueman, "Vivent les Differences!" *First Things*, May 27, 2015, http://www.firstthings.com/blogs/firstthoughts/2015/05/vivent-les-differences, and Karen V. Guth, "Claims on Bonhoeffer: The Misuse of a Theologian," *Christian Century*, May 13, 2015, http://www.christiancentury.org/article/2015-05/claims-bonhoeffer.

8. JoAnne Viviano, "Southern Baptists Kick Off Conference with Call for Leadership," *Columbus Dispatch*, June 16, 2015, http://www.dispatch.com/article/20150616/NEWS/306169742; "Rev. Ronnie Floyd Speaks to Southern Baptists about Same-Sex Marriage," *YouTube*, June 17, 2015, https://www.youtube.com/watch?v=nEtwogA39eU.

9. Todd Starnes, "Southern Baptists: Supreme Court Is Not Final Authority on Gay Marriage," *Fox News Opinion*, June 16, 2015, http://www.foxnews.com/opinion/2015/06/16/southern-baptists-supreme-court-is-not-final-authority-on-gay-marriage.html.

10. "Southern Baptist President Rages over Marriage Equality," *The Rachel Maddow Show*, June 16, 2015, http://www.msnbc.com/rachel-maddow-show/watch/ronnie-floyd-rages-over-marriage-equality-468054083960. See also Steve Benen, "This Week in God," *The MaddowBlog*, MSNBC, June 20, 2015, http://www.msnbc.com/rachel-maddow-show/week-god-62015.

11. Jeffrey Small, "Southern Baptist Anti-Gay Stance Echoes Its Prior Support of Segregation," *Huffington Post*, June 18, 2015, http://www.huffingtonpost.com/jeffrey-small/southern-baptist-antigay-_b_7607386.html.

12. "America's Largest Protestant Church, Still Basically a Hate Group," *Misanthropology 101*, June 21, 2015.

13. Alyson Miers, "No, You Are Not the Bonhoeffer in This Moment," *The Monster's Ink* (blog), June 28, 2015, https://alysonmiers.com/2015/06/28/no-you-are-not-the-bonhoeffer-in-this-moment/.

14. Chuck Queen, "Breaking Down Southern Baptist Rhetoric against Same-Sex Marriage," *Patheos*, June 30, 2015, http://www.patheos.com/blogs/unfundamentalistchristians/2015/06/breaking-down-southern-baptist-rhetoric-against-same-sex-marriage/.

15. See conservativecurmudgeon, "This Generation's Bonhoeffer Is among Us . . . Tragically," *RedState*, June 28, 2015, http://www.redstate.com/diary/conservativecurmudgeon/2015/06/28/generations-bonhoeffer-among-us-tragically/.

16. "We Pledge in Solidarity to Defend Marriage and the Family and Society Founded upon Them."

17. "We Pledge in Solidarity to Defend Marriage and the Family and Society Founded upon Them"; Michelle Goldberg, "Of Course the Christian Right Supports Trump," *New York Times*, January 26, 2018, https://www.nytimes.com/2018/01/26/opinion/trump-christian-right-values.html. On use of the Bible to defend segregation in the 1950s and '60s, see Stephen R. Haynes, "Distinction and Dispersal: Folk Theology and the Maintenance of White Supremacy," *Journal of Southern Religion* 17 (2015), http://jsreligion.org/issues/vol17/haynes.html.

18. https://www.freeconferencecallhd.com/playback/?n=OYkzo/jbKxc; "We Pledge in Solidarity to Defend Marriage and the Family and Society Founded upon Them." See also Rev. Bo Wagner, "Faith Focus: When Christians Must Practice Disobedience," *Chattanooga Times Free Press*, September 13, 2015, http://www.timesfreepress.com/news/life/entertainment/story/2015/sep/13/when-christians-must-practice-disobedience/324457/.

19. Small, "Southern Baptist Anti-Gay Stance Echoes Its Prior Support of Segregation."

20. "Today's Issues," American Family Radio, May 19, 2015.

21. "Kim Davis," *Wikipedia*, last edited February 14, 2018, https://en.wikipedia.org/wiki/Kim_Davis.

22. Brian Tashman, "Kim Davis' Lawyer Wants Her Named TIME's Person of the Year," *Right Wing Watch*, December 3, 2015, http://www.rightwingwatch.org/content/kim-davis-lawyer-wants-her-named-times-person-year.

23. Wagner, "Faith Focus."

24. Charles Marsh, *Strange Glory: A Life of Dietrich Bonhoeffer* (New York: Knopf, 2014), 237, 240, 253, 308, 384.

25. Diane Reynolds, *The Doubled Life of Dietrich Bonhoeffer: Women, Sexuality, and Nazi Germany* (Eugene, OR: Cascade, 2016), 17, 234, 7.

26. One article picked up on this irony. See David Ferguson, "Anti-LGBT Christians Compare Themselves to Possibly Gay German Priest Who Tried to Kill Hitler," *Raw Story*, April 14, 2015, http://www.rawstory.com/2015/04/anti-lgbt-christians-compare-themselves-to-possibly-gay-german-priest-who-tried-to-kill-hitler.

Notes to Chapter 8

1. David Weigel, "Glenn Beck Got 20,000 People to Turn Out for an 'All Lives Matter' Rally," *Washington Post*, August 31, 2015, https://www.washingtonpost.com/news/post-politics/wp/2015/08/31/glenn-beck-got-20000-people-to-turn-out-for-an-all-lives-matter-rally/.

2. See Warren Throckmorton, "Glenn Beck's Historical Problems at Lib-

erty University: The Purple Triangle and the Jehovah's Witnesses," *Warren Throckmorton* (blog), *Patheos*, May 2, 2014, http://www.patheos.com/blogs/warrenthrockmorton/2014/05/02/glenn-becks-historical-problems-at-liberty-university-the-purple-triangle-and-the-jehovahs-witnesses/.

3. Lael Arrington, "When Politicians Fail Us: A Bonhoeffer Alternative to Doublespeak and Cunning," *Stream*, October 28, 2015, https://stream.org/politicians-fail-us-bonhoeffer-alternative-doublespeak-cunning/.

4. BrandinF, "A New Bonhoeffer Moment: The Acceptance of Guilt," *The Bonhoeffer Center Blog*, September 6, 2015, http://thebonhoeffercenter.org/?p=67&option=com_wordpress&Itemid=206.

5. Molly Worthen, "Donald Trump and the Rise of the Moral Minority," *New York Times*, September 26, 2015, https://www.nytimes.com/2015/09/27/opinion/sunday/donald-trump-and-the-rise-of-the-moral-minority.html.

6. Marian Wright Edelman, "Child Watch Column: Whither America?," Children's Defense Fund, January 1, 2016, http://www.childrensdefense.org/newsroom/child-watch-columns/child-watch-documents/WhitherAmerica.html.

7. "Called to Resist Bigotry: A Statement of Faithful Obedience," April 29, 2016, http://www.calledtoresist.org/; Jim Wallis, "Christians Called to Resist Trump's Bigotry," *Huffington Post*, April 30, 2016, https://www.huffingtonpost.com/jim-wallis/christians-called-to-resi_b_9809222.html.

8. Jack Kerwick, "Bernie Sanders' Cheap Virtue vs. the Real Thing," *Front Page*, April 29, 2016, http://www.frontpagemag.com/fpm/262655/bernie-sanders-cheap-virtue-vs-real-thing-jack-kerwick.

9. Warren Throckmorton, "The Popular Bonhoeffer Quote That Isn't in Bonhoeffer's Works," *Warren Throckmorton* (blog), *Patheos*, August 25, 2016, http://www.patheos.com/blogs/warrenthrockmorton/2016/08/25/the-popular-bonhoeffer-quote-that-isnt-in-bonhoeffers-works/. Throckmorton found a source for the Bonhoeffer "quote" in Robert K. Hudnut's *The Sensitive Man and the Christ* (1971), which on page 21 twice repeats the words "Not to speak is to speak. Not to act is to act," the second time in introducing Martin Niemöller's quote "They came first for the Communists . . ." See Warren Throckmorton, "Update on a Spurious Bonhoeffer Quote: Not to Speak Is to Speak, Not to Act Is to Act," *Warren Throckmorton* (blog), *Patheos*, November 11, 2016, http://www.patheos.com/blogs/warrenthrockmorton/2016/11/11/update-on-a-spurious-bonhoeffer-quote-not-to-speak-is-to-speak-not-to-act-is-to-act/.

10. Warren Throckmorton, "Eric Metaxas: We Need Virtue in Our Leaders and We Must Vote for Donald Trump," Patheos, June 17, 2016, http://www.patheos.com/blogs/warrenthrockmorton/2016/06/17/eric-metaxas-we-need-virtue-in-our-leaders-and-we-must-vote-for-donald-trump/; Casey Harper, "Leading Evangelical Makes Case for Christian Support of Trump," *The Daily Caller*, July 18, 2016, http://dailycaller.com/2016/07/18/leading-evangelical-makes-the-case-for-christian-support-of-trump/.

11. Samuel Smith, "Eric Metaxas: Why Christians Should Vote for Donald Trump," *Christian Post*, July 20, 2016, http://www.christianpost.com/news/eric-metaxas-why-christians-should-vote-for-donald-trump-166714/.

12. "A Bonhoeffer Moment: Q&A with Eric Metaxas," *Decision*, September 15, 2016, https://billygraham.org/decision-magazine/september-2016/a-bonhoeffer-moment-qa-with-eric-metaxas/.

13. Janet Porter, "Not to Vote Is to Vote," *WorldNetDaily.com*, August 23, 2016, http://www.wnd.com/2016/08/not-to-vote-is-to-vote/.

14. Mark DeVine, "Bonhoeffer's Dirty Hands and the 2016 Presidential Election," *Hillbilly Politics* (blog), October 28, 2016, http://hillbillypolitics.com/blog/2016/10/26/bonhoeffers-dirty-hands-and-the-2016-presidential-election/.

15. "Week in Politics: Hillary Clinton Makes History," *NPR.com*, June 10, 2016, https://www.npr.org/2016/06/10/481590351/week-in-politics-hillary-clinton-makes-history.

16. Eric Metaxas, "Should Christians Vote for Trump?" *Wall Street Journal*, October 12, 2016, https://www.wsj.com/articles/should-christians-vote-for-trump-1476294992.

17. Jonah Goldberg, "Vote God-Trump 2016," *National Review*, October 17, 2016, http://www.nationalreview.com/corner/441143/ignore-your-conscience-and-vote-trump.

18. Charles Marsh, "Eric Metaxas's Bonhoeffer Delusions," *Religion and Politics*, October 18, 2017, http://religionandpolitics.org/2016/10/18/eric-metaxas-bonhoeffer-delusions/.

19. Rob Schenck, "Eric Metaxas Wrong for Using Bonhoeffer to Support Trump," *Christian Post*, November 3, 2016, http://www.christianpost.com/news/eric-metaxas-wrong-for-using-bonhoeffer-to-support-trump-171268/.

20. Gregory A. Smith and Jessica Martínez, "How the Faithful Voted: A Preliminary 2016 Analysis," Pew Research Center, November 9, 2016, http://www.pewresearch.org/fact-tank/2016/11/09/how-the-faithful-voted-a-preliminary-2016-analysis/.

Notes to Chapter 9

1. Stephen R. Haynes, "Has the Bonhoeffer Moment Finally Arrived?" *Huffington Post*, November 28, 2016, https://www.huffingtonpost.com/stephen-r-haynes/has-the-bonhoeffer-moment_b_13275278.html.

2. J. W. Wartick, "Against the Idolatry of the State—Dietrich Bonhoeffer," *JWWartick.com*, February 4, 2017, https://jwwartick.com/2017/02/04/idolatry-state-bonhoeffer/; Rachel Stoltzfoos, "Martin O'Malley Compares Trump to Hitler, KKK," *Daily Caller*, January 17, 2017, http://dailycaller.com/2017/01/14/martin-omalley-compares-trump-to-hitler-and-the-kkk

-in-one-tweet/; hesterprynne, "Dietrich Bonhoeffer Subtweets PEOTUS," *Blue Mass Group*, January 13, 2017, http://bluemassgroup.com/2017/01/diet rich-bonhoeffer-subtweets-peotus/.

3. David Brooks, "How Should One Resist the Trump Administration?" *New York Times*, February 14, 2017, https://www.nytimes.com/2017/02/14 /opinion/how-should-one-resist-the-trump-administration.html. A letter in the *Tampa Bay Times* on February 22 called Brooks a "hypocrite" and took him to task for attempting "to destroy President Donald Trump by quoting Dietrich Bonhoeffer and St. Benedict, both of whom," the author wrote, "would be appalled by Brooks's column." The author of the letter quoted Bonhoeffer's *Discipleship* to the effect that "by judging others we blind ourselves to our own evil and to the grace which others are just as entitled to as we are." See Thomas Newcomb Hyde, "Character Assassination," letter to the editor, *Tampa Bay Times*, February 22, 2017, http://www.tampabay.com /opinion/letters/thursdays-letters-breaking-down-barriers-between-police -community/2314149.

4. Mark Edington, "Our Bonhoeffer Moment," *Huffington Post*, February 4, 2017, http://www.huffingtonpost.com/entry/our-bonhoeffer-moment_us _5895eaa0e4b061551b3dff0b.

5. "Dietrich Bonhoeffer Speaks Powerfully to the Trump Age!" *Englewood Review of Books*, February 3, 2017, http://englewoodreview.org/dietrich-bon hoeffer-speaks-powerfully-to-the-trump-age/.

6. Norman Lebrecht, "Just In: Christoph von Donyani Warns against the New US Intolerance," *Slipped Disc*, February 6, 2017, http://slippedisc.com/2017 /02/just-in-christoph-von-dohnanyi-warns-against-the-new-us-intolerance/.

7. According to longtime society members, the only other such statement by the IBS-ELS was released at the time of the Gulf War in 1991.

8. International Bonhoeffer Society, "Statement Issued by the Board of Directors of the International Bonhoeffer Society—English Language Section, February 1, 2017," Bonhoeffer Center, http://thebonhoeffercenter.org/index .php?option=com_content&view=article&id=148&catid=12&Itemid=208.

9. "Reflections on Bonhoeffer and Politics in Our Time—Rev. Dr. Reggie Williams," *We Talk, We Listen*, April 3, 2017, https://wetalkwelisten.word press.com/2017/04/03/reflections-on-bonhoeffer-and-politics-in-our-time -rev-dr-reggie-williams/.

10. Joseph Hartropp, "Would Bonhoeffer Have Resisted Donald Trump?" *Christian Today*, February 7, 2017, http://www.christiantoday.com/article /would.dietrich.bonhoeffer.have.resisted.donald.trump/104498.htm. Hartropp does not answer the question posed in his title, but writes: "Broad comparisons to Hitler and the Nazis are probably not always helpful, even if sometimes containing some truth. Bonhoeffer may be best understood not as someone who can tell us whether Donald Trump or Hillary Clinton is most like Hitler, but rather points us to God in Jesus Christ who lives and gives his

life 'for others,' and calls his disciples to make a radical, costly choice, and do the same."

11. Taylor S. Brown, "The Political Ideology of Eric Metaxas," *Christian Revolution* (blog), *Patheos*, January 31, 2017, http://www.patheos.com/blogs/thechristianrevolution/2017/01/political-idolatry-eric-metaxas/.

12. W. Travis McMaken, "Not Another 'Bonhoeffer Moment,'" *DET*, May 15, 2017, http://derevth.blogspot.com/2017/05/not-another-bonhoeffer-moment.html.

13. Emma Green, "An Evangelical Christian Defends Trump's First Week in Office," *Atlantic*, January 30, 2017, https://www.theatlantic.com/politics/archive/2017/01/eric-metaxas-trump/514898/.

14. "Trump, Truth and the First 100 Days," *Up Front*, April 22, 2017, http://www.aljazeera.com/programmes/upfront/2017/04/trump-truth-100-days-170421103041654.html. Responding to Metaxas's claim that Christianity is more about forgiveness than morality, blogger John Fea wondered whether Metaxas listened to his own radio show or read his own books. See Fea, "Jim Wallis and Eric Metaxas Discuss Evangelicals and Trump," *The Way of Improvement Leads Home*, April 22, 2017, https://thewayofimprovement.com/2017/04/22/jim-wallis-and-eric-metaxas-discuss-evangelicals-and-trump/, and Napp Nazworth, "Eric Metaxas and Jim Wallis' Horrible Debate on Evangelicals and Trump," *Christian Post*, April 28, 2017, http://www.christianpost.com/news/eric-metaxas-and-jim-wallis-horrible-debate-on-evangelicals-and-trump-181907/.

15. Joe Scarborough's Facebook page, accessed February 27, 2018, https://www.facebook.com/JoeNBC/posts/10155580094186880; Dietrich Bonhoeffer, *Letters and Papers from Prison*, ed. C. Gremmels et al., trans. I. Best et al., Dietrich Bonhoeffer Works in English, vol. 8 (Minneapolis: Fortress, 2010), 43.

16. See the discussion on Christian Forums at https://www.christianforums.com/threads/bonhoeffer-on-human-stupidity-and-political-power.8020839/; Tim Suttle, "America's Wisdom Problem," *Huffington Post*, August 30, 2017, http://www.huffingtonpost.com/entry/americas-wisdom-problem_us_59a6f0f5e4b08299d89d0b79. Like Scarborough, Suttle did not directly implicate Trump, but he did compare Bonhoeffer's critique of those who disbelieve "facts that contradict one's own prejudice" to climate change skepticism; see also Glenn Beck, "Glenn: Bonhoeffer's Warning about Stupidity Applies Today," *Glenn Beck Program*, recording, August 4, 2017, http://www.glennbeck.com/2017/08/04/glenn-bonhoeffers-warning-about-stupidity-applies-today/.

17. Stephanie Potter, "In Solidarity: Community Gathers for Candlelight Vigil," *Pittsburg (KS) Morning Sun*, August 14, 2017, http://www.morningsun.net/news/20170814/in-solidarity-community-gathers-for-candlelight-vigil; Members of the Cape Ann Clergy, "Standing Up to Hate," letter to the editor, *Gloucester (MA) Times*, August 17, 2017, http://www.gloucestertimes.com

/opinion/letters_to_the_editor/letter-standing-up-to-hate/article_95eac3fc-5824-5d96-bdaf-e72b5af5637d.html.

18. Tony Macula, "Charlottesville Exposed the Risk Taken in Voting for Trump," letter to the editor, *Livingston (NY) County News*, August 17, 2017, http://www.thelcn.com/lcn06/charlottesville-exposed-the-risk-taken-in-voting-for-trump-20170817; Brad Gibbens, "People of Faith Stand against Hate," letter to the editor, *Grand Forks (ND) Herald*, September 1, 2017, http://www.grandforksherald.com/opinion/letters/4320293-letter-people-faith-stand-against-hate.

19. Sean Russell, "What Does Our Silence Say?," *Fort Worth Weekly*, January 24, 2018, https://www.fwweekly.com/2018/01/24/what-does-our-silence-say/.

20. Stephen L. Denlinger, "Dietrich Bonhoeffer: Wrestling with Faith in the Age of Trump," *Huffington Post*, January 6, 2018, https://www.huffingtonpost.com/entry/dietrich-bonhoeffer-wrestling-with-faith-in-the-age_us_5a516ca8e4b0ee59d41c0b6a.

21. Lori Brandt Hale and Reggie L. Williams, "Is This a Bonhoeffer Moment?," *Sojourners*, February 2018, https://sojo.net/magazine/february-2018/this-bonhoeffer-moment-American-Christians.

22. Wes Granberg-Michaelson, "When Seminary Becomes a Threat," *Sojourners*, February 2018, https://sojo.net/magazine/february-2018/when-underground-seminary-becomes-threat-bonhoeffer.

Notes to Chapter 10

1. Mark Birchler, "Progressive Christianity's Strange Bonhoeffer Compulsion (1)," *The Reformed Sojourner* (blog), October 25, 2017, https://thereformedsojourner.wordpress.com/2017/10/25/progressive-christianitys-strange-bonhoeffer-compulsion-1/. As further evidence that the Right's willingness to wield Bonhoeffer as a weapon has not been diminished by his increasing embrace by the Left, when Carl Lentz of Hillsong Church in New York City sidestepped a question about the sinfulness of abortion during an appearance on *The View*, a commentator wrote that Lentz had fallen into the trap of "cheap grace." Quoting from *Discipleship*, Tre Goins-Phillips opined that "pastors should be pointing nonbelievers and believers alike toward 'costly grace,' which according to Bonhoeffer, 'is costly because it calls us to follow' Jesus's teachings, no matter what." See Tre Goins-Phillips, "Matt Walsh to Pastors 'Afraid' of Condemning Abortion: 'Find a New Job. You Aren't Qualified,'" *Independent Journal Review*, November 8, 2017, http://ijr.com/the-declaration/2017/11/1014211-matt-walsh-pastors-afraid-condemning-abortion-find-new-job-arent-qualified/.

2. Mark Birchler, "Progressive Christianity's Strange Bonhoeffer Compul-

sion (2)," *The Reformed Sojourner* (blog), October 29, 2017, https://thereformedsojourner.wordpress.com/2017/10/29/progressive-christianitys-strange-bonhoeffer-compulsion-2/.

3. Julia Manchester, "Obama Warns of Complacency, Notes Rise of Hitler," *Hill*, December 6, 2017, http://thehill.com/blogs/blog-briefing-room/news/363555-obama-warns-of-complacency-notes-rise-of-hitler.

4. Joel Willitts, "Portraits of Dietrich Bonhoeffer—Metaxas and Schlingensiepen," *Euangelion* (blog), *Patheos*, April 13, 2011, http://www.patheos.com/blogs/euangelion/2011/08/portraits-of-dietrich-bonhoeffer-metaxas-and-schlingensiepen/.

5. Warren Throckmorton, "Eric Metaxas to Bonhoeffer Scholars: Every Syllable of My Biography Is True," *Warren Throckmorton* (blog), *Patheos*, February 9, 2017, http://www.patheos.com/blogs/warrenthrockmorton/2017/02/09/eric-metaxas-bonhoeffer-scholars-every-syllable-bonhoeffer-bio-true/.

6. Victoria J. Barnett, "Bonhoeffer Is Widely Beloved: But to Fully Understand Him We Should First Dial Back the Hero Worship," *Washington Post*, April 9, 2015, https://www.washingtonpost.com/news/acts-of-faith/wp/2015/04/09/bonhoeffer-is-widely-beloved-but-to-fully-understand-him-we-should-first-dial-back-the-hero-worship/.

7. The tension between "silence and speaking" Barnett notes in Bonhoeffer's life is particularly relevant given the widespread use of the manufactured "Bonhoeffer quote" about "silence in the face of evil" in the months after her article appeared.

8. See Ken Chitwood, "Decades after Execution, Bonhoeffer's Legacy Lives On," *Houston Chronicle*, April 9, 2013, http://blog.chron.com/sacredduty/2013/04/decades-after-execution-bonhoeffers-legacy-lives-on/.

9. Dan Barry and John Eligon, "'Trump, Trump, Trump!' How a President's Name Became a Racial Jeer," *New York Times*, December 16, 2017, https://www.nytimes.com/2017/12/16/us/trump-racial-jeers.html.

Notes to the Postscript

1. John A. Huffman Jr., *A Most Amazing Call: One Pastor's Reflections on a Ministry Full of Surprises* (n.p., 2011).

2. Kelsey Dallas, "Q&A: Did Richard Nixon Have a Religious Side?," *Salt Lake City Deseret News*, May 26, 2017, https://www.deseretnews.com/article/865680780/QA-Did-Richard-Nixon-have-a-religious-side.html. This description of Nixon's religiosity is by John A. Farrell, author of *Richard Nixon: The Life* (New York: Doubleday, 2017).

3. Amy Sullivan, "America's New Religion: Fox Evangelicalism," *New York Times*, December 15, 2017, https://www.nytimes.com/2017/12/15/opinion/sunday/war-christmas-evangelicals.html.

4. Stephen E. Strang, *God and Donald Trump* (Lake Mary, FL: FrontLine, 2017), 102.

5. While in 2011 only 30 percent of American evangelicals believed "an elected official who commits an immoral act in their personal life can still behave ethically and fulfill their duties in their public and professional life," the number was 70 percent in October 2016 (Danielle Kurtzleben, "POLL: White Evangelicals Have Warmed to Politicians Who Commit 'Immoral' Acts," *NPR .com*, October 23, 2016, https://www.npr.org/2016/10/23/498890836/poll-white-evangelicals-have-warmed-to-politicians-who-commit-immoral-acts.

6. Tim Rymel, "Has Evangelical Christianity Become Sociopathic,?" *Huffington Post*, May 11, 2017, https://www.huffingtonpost.com/entry/has-evangelical-christianity-become-sociopathic_us_5914ce6fe4b02d6199b2ed92.

7. Peter Wehner, "Why I Can No Longer Call Myself an Evangelical Republican," *New York Times*, December 9, 2017, https://www.nytimes.com/2017/12/09/opinion/sunday/wehner-evangelical-republicans.html.

8. Sullivan, "America's New Religion."

9. Ross Douthat, "Is There an Evangelical Crisis?," *New York Times*, November 25, 2017, https://www.nytimes.com/2017/11/25/opinion/sunday/trump-evangelical-crisis.html.

10. Jerrod C. Wilson, "This Theologically Orphaned Generation," *The Gospel Coalition*, November 14, 2017, https://www.thegospelcoalition.org/blogs/jared-c-wilson/theologically-orphaned-generation/.

11. Michelle Goldberg, "Of Course the Christian Right Supports Trump," *New York Times*, January 26, 2018, https://www.nytimes.com/2018/01/26/opinion/trump-christian-right-values.html.

12. Michael Gerson, "The Trump Evangelicals Have Lost Their Gag Reflex," *Washington Post*, January 22, 2018, https://www.washingtonpost.com/opinions/the-trump-evangelicals-have-lost-their-gag-reflex/2018/01/22/761d1174-ffa8-11e7-bb03-722769454f82_story.html.

13. Mary Solberg, ed., *A Church Undone: Documents from the German Christian Faith Movement, 1932–1940* (Minneapolis: Fortress, 2015), 125, 145, 197, 246, 302, 333, 347, 353, 358.

14. Strang, *God and Donald Trump*, 4, 15, 17, 22, 25, 30, 64, 65, 65, 73, 107, 169, 176.

15. Darren Guerra, "Trump, Evangelicals, Religion, and the 2016 Exit Polls," *First Things*, November 9, 2016, https://www.firstthings.com/blogs/firstthoughts/2016/11/trump-evangelicals-religion-and-the-2016-exit-polls.

16. Dietrich Bonhoeffer, *Letters and Papers from Prison*, ed. C. Gremmels et al., trans. I. Best et al., Dietrich Bonhoeffer Works in English, vol. 8 (Minneapolis: Fortress, 2010), 42.

BIBLIOGRAPHY

"America's Largest Protestant Church, Still Basically a Hate Group." *Misanthropology 101*, June 21, 2015.

Anderson, Ray S. *An Emergent Theology for Emerging Churches.* Downers Grove: InterVarsity, 2006.

Apel, William D. *Witnesses before Dawn: Exploring the Meaning of Christian Life.* Valley Forge, PA: Judson, 1984.

Arrington, Lael. "When Politicians Fail Us: A Bonhoeffer Alternative to Doublespeak and Cunning." *Stream*, October 28, 2015. https://stream.org/politicians-fail-us-bonhoeffer-alternative-doublespeak-cunning/.

Bailey, Sara Pulliam. "Is Eric Metaxas the Next Chuck Colson?" *Religious News Service*, July 29, 2013. https://religionnews.com/2013/07/29/is-eric-metaxas-the-next-chuck-colson/.

Barnett, Victoria J. "Bonhoeffer Is Widely Beloved: But to Fully Understand Him We Should First Dial Back the Hero Worship." *Washington Post*, April 9, 2015. https://www.washingtonpost.com/news/acts-of-faith/wp/2015/04/09/bonhoeffer-is-widely-beloved-but-to-fully-understand-him-we-should-first-dial-back-the-hero-worship/.

———. "Review of Eric Metaxas, *Bonhoeffer: Pastor, Martyr, Prophet, Spy: A Righteous Gentile vs. the Third Reich.*" *Association of Contemporary Church Historians Quarterly* 15, no. 3 (September 2010). https://contemporarychurchhistory.org/2010/09/review-of-eric-metaxas-bonhoeffer-pastor-martyr-prophet-spy-a-righteous-gentile-vs-the-third-reich/.

Barry, Dan, and John Eligon. "'Trump, Trump, Trump!' How a President's Name Became a Racial Jeer." *New York Times*, December 16, 2017. https://www.nytimes.com/2017/12/16/us/trump-racial-jeers.html.

Barz, Paul. *I Am Bonhoeffer: A Credible Life—a Novel.* Translated by Douglas W. Stott. Minneapolis: Fortress, 2008.

Beck, Glenn. "Glenn: Bonhoeffer's Warning about Stupidity Applies Today." *Glenn Beck Program*, recording, August 4, 2017. http://www.glennbeck.com/2017/08/04/glenn-bonhoeffers-warning-about-stupidity-applies-today/.

Benen, Steve. "This Week in God." *The MaddowBlog*, MSNBC, June 20, 2015. http://www.msnbc.com/rachel-maddow-show/week-god-62015.

Benge, Janet, and Geoff Benge. *Dietrich Bonhoeffer: In the Midst of Wickedness*. Seattle: YWAM Publishing, 2012.

Bergen, Doris. "Contextualizing Dietrich Bonhoeffer: Nazism, Christianity and the Question of Silence." In *Interpreting Bonhoeffer: Historical Perspectives, Emerging Issues*, edited by Clifford J. Green and Guy C. Carter, 111–26. Minneapolis: Fortress, 2013.

Berrigan, Daniel. "The Passion of Dietrich Bonhoeffer." *Saturday Review*, May 30, 1970, 17–22.

Bezner, Steve. "Bonhoeffer and the Emerging Church." *Citizen Bezner*, January 9, 2007. http://citizenbezner.blogspot.com/2007/01/bonhoeffer-and-emerging-church.html.

"Billboard Shows Obama as Hitler, Demands President's Impeachment." *Huffington Post*, October 15, 2013. https://www.huffingtonpost.com/entry/obama-hitler-billboard-indiana_n_4101322.html.

Birchler, Mark. "Progressive Christianity's Strange Bonhoeffer Compulsion (1)." *The Reformed Sojourner* (blog), October 25, 2017. https://thereformedsojourner.wordpress.com/2017/10/25/progressive-christianitys-strange-bonhoeffer-compulsion-1/.

———. "Progressive Christianity's Strange Bonhoeffer Compulsion (2)." *The Reformed Sojourner* (blog), October 29, 2017. https://thereformedsojourner.wordpress.com/2017/10/29/progressive-christianitys-strange-bonhoeffer-compulsion-2/.

Black, David Alan. "Do We Need a New Barmen Declaration?" *Dave Black Online*, July 16, 2003. http://www.daveblackonline.com/do_we_need_a_new_barmen_declarat.htm.

Bloom, Linda. "United Methodists Give Bonhoeffer Martyr Status." United Methodist News Service, June 17, 2008. http://archives.gcah.org/bitstream/handle/10516/3563/Bonhoeffer-martyr.aspx.htm.

Bonhoeffer, Dietrich. *Berlin: 1932–1933*. Edited by C. Nicolaisen, E.-A. Scharffenorth, and L. L. Rasmussen. Translated by I. Best, D. Higgins, and D. W. Stott. Dietrich Bonhoeffer Works in English, vol. 12. Minneapolis: Fortress, 2009.

———. *Discipleship*. Edited and translated by Martin Kuske and Ilse Tödt. Dietrich Bonhoeffer Works in English, vol. 4. Minneapolis: Fortress, 2003.

———. *Letters and Papers from Prison*. Edited by C. Gremmels, E. Bethge, R. Bethge, I. Tödt, and J. W. de Gruchy. Translated by I. Best, L. E. Dahill, R. Krauss, N. Lukens, B. Rumscheidt, M. Rumscheidt, and D. W.

Stott. Dietrich Bonhoeffer Works in English, vol. 8. Minneapolis: Fortress, 2010.

Bonhoeffer. Directed by Martin Doblmeier. Journey Films, 2003.

Bonhoeffer: Agent of Grace. Directed by Eric Till. Gateway Films, 1999.

Bonhoeffer: The Cost of Freedom. Written and directed by Paul McCusker. Colorado Springs: Focus on the Family, 1997, 1999.

"A Bonhoeffer Moment: Q&A with Eric Metaxas." *Decision*, September 15, 2016. https://billygraham.org/decision-magazine/september-2016/a-bonhoeffer-moment-qa-with-eric-metaxas/.

"Bonhoeffer on Human Stupidity and Political Power." Christian Forums, accessed February 20, 2018. https://www.christianforums.com/threads/bonhoeffer-on-human-stupidity-and-political-power.8020839/.

"Books of the Century." *Christianity Today* 46 (April 24, 2000). http://www.christianitytoday.com/ct/2000/april24/5.92.html.

Bouie, Jamelle. "You Know Who Else Said That? My Favorite Examples of Conservatives Comparing Obama to Hitler." *Slate*, January 13, 2015. http://www.slate.com/articles/news_and_politics/politics/2015/01/republicans_comparing_barack_obama_to_hitler_my_favorite_examples_of_the.html.

BrandinF. "A New Bonhoeffer Moment: The Acceptance of Guilt." *The Bonhoeffer Center Blog*, September 6, 2015. http://thebonhoeffercenter.org/?p=67&option=com_wordpress&Itemid=206.

Brinker, Luke. "Seven Conservatives Who Have Compared Obama to Hitler." *Salon*, January 13, 2015. https://www.salon.com/2015/01/13/7_conservatives_who_have_compared_obama_to_hitler/.

Brockhoeft Report 1, no. 4 (December 1993). Accessed December 2003. www.saltshaker.us.

Brooks, David. "How Should One Resist the Trump Administration?" *New York Times*, February 14, 2017. https://www.nytimes.com/2017/02/14/opinion/how-should-one-resist-the-trump-administration.html.

Brown, Robert McAfee. "ABC—Assy, Bonhoeffer, Carswell." *Christian Century* 88 (March 24, 1971): 369–71.

Brown, Taylor S. "The Political Ideology of Eric Metaxas." *Christian Revolution* (blog), *Patehos* January 31, 2017. http://www.patheos.com/blogs/thechristianrevolution/2017/01/political-idolatry-eric-metaxas/.

Bush, George W. "President Bush Thanks Germany for Support against Terror." Office of the Press Secretary, 2002.

Bynum, Rebecca. "Dietrich Bonhoeffer Rediscovered." *New English Review*, April 2010. http://www.newenglishreview.org/print.cfm?pg=custpage&frm=1641&sec_id=86067.

"Called to Resist Bigotry: A Statement of Faithful Obedience." April 29, 2016. http://www.calledtoresist.org/.

Challies, Tim. "Counterfeit Bonhoeffer." *@Challies*, January 18, 2011. http://www.challies.com/articles/counterfeit-bonhoeffer.

Chapman, G. Clarke. "What Would Bonhoeffer Say to Christian Peacemakers Today?" In *Theology, Politics, and Peace*, edited by Theodore Runyan, 167–75. Maryknoll, NY: Orbis, 1989.

Chitwood, Ken. "Decades after Execution, Bonhoeffer's Legacy Lives On." *Houston Chronicle*, April 9, 2013. http://blog.chron.com/sacredduty/2013/04/decades-after-execution-bonhoeffers-legacy-lives-on/.

Christensen, Bernard. *The Inward Pilgrimage: Spiritual Classics from Augustine to Bonhoeffer*. Minneapolis: Augsburg Fortress, 1976.

Christian Reader. September/October 1997.

Clarkson, Frederick. "Christian Right Leaders Escalate Anti-LBGT Threats." *LGBTQ Nation*, May 8, 2015. https://www.lgbtqnation.com/2015/05/christian-right-leaders-escalate-anti-lgbt-threats/.

———. "Will Our Prisons Overflow with Christians?" Political Research Associates, March 1, 2015. http://www.politicalresearch.org/2015/03/01/will-our-prisons-overflow-with-christians/.

Clements, Keith W. *What Freedom? The Persistent Challenge of Dietrich Bonhoeffer*. Bristol, UK: Bristol Baptist College, 1990.

Coles, Robert. *Dietrich Bonhoeffer*. Modern Spiritual Masters. Maryknoll, NY: Orbis, 1998.

———. *Lives of Moral Leadership: Men and Women Who Made a Difference*. New York: Random House, 2000.

Colson, Charles. "Caesar and Christ: Should We Disobey Our Government?" *BreakPoint*, November 28, 2000.

———. "Christian v. America." *Christianity Today* 40, no. 5 (1996): 64.

conservativecurmudgeon. "This Generation's Bonhoeffer Is among Us . . . Tragically." *RedState*, June 28, 2015. http://www.redstate.com/diary/conservativecurmudgeon/2015/06/28/generations-bonhoeffer-among-us-tragically/.

Conway, John S. "Coming to Terms with the Past: Interpreting the German Church Struggles 1933–1990." *German History* 16, no. 3 (1998): 377–96.

Covington, Dennis. "Christopher Hitchens: God Is Not Great." *Paste*, May 9, 2007. https://www.pastemagazine.com/articles/2007/05/christopher-hitchens-god-is-not-great.html.

Cox, Harvey. "Using and Misusing Bonhoeffer." *Christianity and Crisis* 24 (October 19, 1964): 199–201.

Cromartie, Michael. "Dirty Hands and Concrete Action: A Conversation with Jean Bethke Elshtain." *Books and Culture*, September 1, 2003. http://www.ctlibrary.com/bc/2003/sepoct/12.18.html.

Dallas, Kelsey. "Q&A: Did Richard Nixon Have a Religious Side?" *Salt Lake City Deseret News*, May 26, 2017. https://www.deseretnews.com/article/865680780/QA-Did-Richard-Nixon-have-a-religious-side.html.

DC Talk. *Jesus Freaks: DC Talk and the Voice of the Martyrs—Stories of Those*

Who Stood for Jesus, the Ultimate Jesus Freaks. Bloomington, MN: Bethany House, 1999.

Denlinger, Stephen L. "Dietrich Bonhoeffer: Wrestling with Faith in the Age of Trump." *Huffington Post*, January 6, 2018. https://www.huffingtonpost.com/entry/dietrich-bonhoeffer-wrestling-with-faith-in-the-age_us_5a516ca8e4b0ee59d41c0b6a.

DeVine, Mark. "Bonhoeffer Is Still Speaking." *Baptist Press*, May 5, 2006. http://www.bpnews.net/23201/firstperson-bonhoeffer-still-speaking.

———. *Bonhoeffer Speaks Today: Following Jesus at All Costs*. Nashville: Broadman and Holman, 2005.

———. "Bonhoeffer's Dirty Hands and the 2016 Presidential Election." *Hillbilly Politics* (blog), October 28, 2016. http://hillbillypolitics.com/blog/2016/10/26/bonhoeffers-dirty-hands-and-the-2016-presidential-election/.

Dietrich Bonhoeffer: Memories and Perspectives. Directed by Bain Boehlke. Trinity Films, 1983.

"Dietrich Bonhoeffer: Theologian in Nazi Germany." *Christian History* 32 (1991). http://www.ctlibrary.com/ch/1991/issue32/.

"Dietrich Bonhoeffer and Evangelicals: Bonhoeffer from an Evangelical Perspective." *Bonhoeffer Now and Then* (blog). https://bonhoeffernowandthen.wordpress.com/about/.

"Dietrich Bonhoeffer Speaks Powerfully to the Trump Age!" *Englewood Review of Books*, February 3, 2017. http://englewoodreview.org/dietrich-bonhoeffer-speaks-powerfully-to-the-trump-age/.

Dobson, James. Audio interview. Free Conference Call, HD. Accessed February 20, 2018. https://www.freeconferencecallhd.com/playback/?n=OYkzo/jbKxc.

———. "The New Cost of Discipleship." *Christianity Today* 43 (September 6, 1999). http://www.christianitytoday.com/ct/1999/september6/9ta056.html.

Domenech, Ben. "The Last Ship." *BenDomenech.com*, July 21, 2003.

Douthat, Ross. "Is There an Evangelical Crisis?" *New York Times*, November 25, 2017. https://www.nytimes.com/2017/11/25/opinion/sunday/trump-evangelical-crisis.html.

Edelman, Marian Wright. "Child Watch Column: Whither America?" Children's Defense Fund, January 1, 2016. http://www.childrensdefense.org/newsroom/child-watch-columns/child-watch-documents/WhitherAmerica.html.

Edington, Mark. "Our Bonhoeffer Moment." *Huffington Post*, February 4, 2017. http://www.huffingtonpost.com/entry/our-bonhoeffer-moment_us_5895eaa0e4b061551b3dff0b.

Ellsberg, Robert. *All Saints: Daily Reflections on Saints, Prophets, and Witnesses for Our Time*. New York: Crossroad, 1997.

Elshtain, Jean Bethke. "Thinking about War and Justice." *The Religion and Culture Web Forum*, May 2003. https://divinity.uchicago.edu/sites/default/files/imce/pdfs/webforum/052003/commentary.pdf.

Emery, David. "Is Barack Obama the Antichrist?" *ThoughtCo*, updated March 18, 2017. https://www.thoughtco.com/is-barack-obama-the-antichrist-3298948.

Ericksen, Robert. "Protestants." In *The Oxford Handbook of Holocaust Studies*, edited by Peter Hayes and John K. Roth, 250–64. New York: Oxford University Press, 2010.

"Ethics and the Will of God: The Legacy of Dietrich Bonhoeffer." December 2004. https://onbeing.org/programs/martin-doblmeier-ethics-and-the-will-of-god-the-legacy-of-dietrich-bonhoeffer/.

Fangmeier, Jürgen, and Hinrich Stoevesandt, eds. *Karl Barth, Letters, 1961–1968*. Translated by Geoffrey W. Bromiley. Edinburgh: T. & T. Clark, 1981.

Fea, John. "Jim Wallis and Eric Metaxas Discuss Evangelicals and Trump." *The Way of Improvement Leads Home*, April 22, 2017. https://thewayofimprovement.com/2017/04/22/jim-wallis-and-eric-metaxas-discuss-evangelicals-and-trump/.

"Federal Judge Orders Fine against U.S. Citizens for Bringing Medicine to Iraq: Voices in the Wilderness Will Refuse to Comply with Order." Accessed August 2005. http://vitw.org/archives/978.

Ferguson, David. "Anti-LGBT Christians Compare Themselves to Possibly Gay German Priest Who Tried to Kill Hitler." *Raw Story*, April 14, 2015. http://www.rawstory.com/2015/04/anti-lgbt-christians-compare-themselves-to-possibly-gay-german-priest-who-tried-to-kill-hitler.

Fisher, Suzanne Woods. *Copper Fire*. Ladson, SC: Vintage Inspirations, 2008.

Focus on the Family Newsletter. May 2000.

Fowler, James W. *Stages of Faith: The Psychology of Human Development and the Quest for Meaning.* New York: Harper and Row, 1981.

George, Timothy. "A Tale of Two Declarations." *Beeson*, Spring 2011. https://www.beesondivinity.com/assets/1346/2011_beeson_final_copy.pdf.

Gerson, Michael. "The Trump Evangelicals Have Lost Their Gag Reflex." *Washington Post*, January 22, 2018. https://www.washingtonpost.com/opinions/the-trump-evangelicals-have-lost-their-gag-reflex/2018/01/22/761d1174-ffa8-11e7-bb03-722769454f82_story.html.

Giardina, Denise. *Saints and Villains*. New York: Fawcett, 1998.

Gibbens, Brad. "People of Faith Stand against Hate." Letter to the editor, *Grand Forks (ND) Herald*, September 1, 2017. http://www.grandforksherald.com/opinion/letters/4320293-letter-people-faith-stand-against-hate.

Glazener, Mary. *The Cup of Wrath: A Novel Based on Dietrich Bonhoeffer's Resistance to Hitler*. Macon, GA: Smith and Helwys, 1992.

Goins-Phillips, Tre. "Matt Walsh to Pastors 'Afraid' of Condemning Abortion:

'Find a New Job. You Aren't Qualified.'" *Independent Journal Review*, November 8, 2017. http://ijr.com/the-declaration/2017/11/1014211-matt-walsh-pastors-afraid-condemning-abortion-find-new-job-arent-qualified/.

Goldberg, Jonah. "Vote God-Trump 2016." *National Review*, October 17, 2016. http://www.nationalreview.com/corner/441143/ignore-your-conscience-and-vote-trump.

Goldberg, Michelle. "Of Course the Christian Right Supports Trump." *New York Times*, January 26, 2018. https://www.nytimes.com/2018/01/26/opinion/trump-christian-right-values.html.

Granberg-Michaelson, Wes. "When Seminary Becomes a Threat." *Sojourners*, February 2018. https://sojo.net/magazine/february-2018/when-underground-seminary-becomes-threat-bonhoeffer.

Grant, George. *Third Time Around: A History of the Prolife Movement*. Brentwood, TN: Wolgemuth and Hyatt, 1991.

Green, Clifford. "Hijacking Bonhoeffer." *Christian Century*, October 4, 2010. https://www.christiancentury.org/reviews/2010-09/hijacking-bonhoeffer.

Green, Emma. "An Evangelical Christian Defends Trump's First Week in Office." *Atlantic*, January 30, 2017. https://www.theatlantic.com/politics/archive/2017/01/eric-metaxas-trump/514898/.

Gressel, Josh. "Faith Development: Stage Six." *Pleasant Hill Patch*, August 7, 2013. https://patch.com/california/pleasanthill/faith-development--stage-six.

Gruchy, John W. de. *Daring, Trusting Friend: Bonhoeffer's Friend Eberhard Bethge*. Minneapolis: Fortress, 2005.

Guerra, Darren. "Trump, Evangelicals, Religion, and the 2016 Exit Polls." *First Things*, November 9, 2016. https://www.firstthings.com/blogs/firstthoughts/2016/11/trump-evangelicals-religion-and-the-2016-exit-polls.

Gushee, David P. "Following Jesus to the Gallows." *Christianity Today* 39 (April 3, 1995): 26–27.

———. *Only Human: Christian Reflections on the Journey toward Wholeness*. Enduring Questions in Christian Life. San Francisco: Jossey-Bass, 2005.

Guth, Karen V. "Claims on Bonhoeffer: The Misuse of a Theologian." *Christian Century*, May 13, 2015. https://www.christiancentury.org/article/2015-05/claims-bonhoeffer.

Gutman, Israel, ed., *Encyclopedia of the Holocaust*. New York: Macmillan, 1990.

Hale, Lori Brandt, and Reggie L. Williams. "Is This a Bonhoeffer Moment?" *Sojourners*, February 2018. https://sojo.net/magazine/february-2018/this-bonhoeffer-moment-American-Christians.

Hanged on a Twisted Cross. Directed by T. N. Mahan. Gateway Films, 1996.

Hansen, Collin. "The Authentic Bonhoeffer." Interview of Eric Metaxas. *Christianity Today*, July 7, 2010. http://www.christianitytoday.com/ct/2010/july/7.54.html.

Hartropp, Joseph. "Would Bonhoeffer Have Resisted Donald Trump?" *Christian Today*, February 7, 2017. http://www.christiantoday.com/article/would.dietrich.bonhoeffer.have.resisted.donald.trump/104498.htm.

Hauerwas, Stanley. *Performing the Faith: Bonhoeffer and the Practice of Nonviolence*. Grand Rapids: Brazos, 2004.

Haynes, Stephen R. *The Bonhoeffer Legacy: Post-Holocaust Perspectives*. Minneapolis: Fortress, 2006.

———. *The Bonhoeffer Phenomenon: Portraits of a Protestant Saint*. Minneapolis: Fortress, 2004.

———. "Distinction and Dispersal: Folk Theology and the Maintenance of White Supremacy." *Journal of Southern Religion* 17 (2015). http://jsreligion.org/issues/vol17/haynes.html.

———. "Has the Bonhoeffer Moment Finally Arrived?" *Huffington Post*, November 28, 2016. https://www.huffingtonpost.com/stephen-r-haynes/has-the-bonhoeffer-moment_b_13275278.html.

Heim, David. "Alan Wolfe on Metaxas's Bonhoeffer." *Christian Century*, February 10, 2011. http://www.christiancentury.org/blogs/archive/2011-02/alan-wolfe-metaxass-bonhoeffer.

Hemphill, Amy. "Don't Cite Dietrich Bonhoeffer in Support of RFRA." *Indianapolis Star*, April 29, 2015. http://www.indystar.com/story/opinion/readers/2015/04/29/cite-dietrich-bonhoeffer-support-rfra/26593581/.

Henry, Marilyn. "Who, Exactly, Is a 'Righteous Gentile'?" *RighteousJews.org*, April 22, 1998. https://www.righteousjews.org/article2.html.

Hesterprynne. "Dietrich Bonheffer Subtweets PEOTUS." *Blue Mass Group*, January 13, 2017. http://bluemassgroup.com/2017/01/dietrich-bonhoeffer-subtweets-peotus/.

Hood, Jason B. "Redeeming Bonhoeffer (the Book)." *Christianity Today*, February 7, 2011. http://www.christianitytoday.com/ct/2011/februaryweb-only/redeemingbonhoeffer.html.

Horton, Scott. "On Dietrich Bonhoeffer—Six Questions for Eric Metaxas." *Browsings: The Harper's Blog*, December 23, 2010. http://harpers.org/archive/2010/12/hbc-90007864.

Howell, James C. *Servants, Misfits, and Martyrs: Saints and Their Stories*. Nashville: Upper Room Books, 1999.

Howell, Leon. "A Time of Trials: The Tribulation of Dietrich Bonhoeffer." *Sojourners*, May–June 1995. http://www.sojo.net/index.cfm?action=magazine.article&issue=soj9505&article=950531.

Huffman, John A., Jr. *A Most Amazing Call: One Pastor's Reflections on a Ministry Full of Surprises*. N.p, 2011.

Hunter, Robert L. "Dietrich Bonhoeffer: A Vision and a Voice for Our Times." *Saturday Evening Post*, September/October 1997, 50–51.

———. "Hitler's Would-Be Assassin." *Saturday Evening Post*, November/December 1997, 44–47.

Hyde, Thomas Newcomb. "Character Assassination." Letter to the editor, *Tampa Bay Times*, February 22, 2017. http://www.tampabay.com/opinion/letters/thursdays-letters-breaking-down-barriers-between-police-community/2314149.

International Bonhoeffer Society. "Statement Issued by the Board of Directors of the International Bonhoeffer Society—English Language Section, February 1, 2017." Bonhoeffer Center. http://thebonhoeffercenter.org/index.php?option=com_content&view=article&id=148&catid=12&Itemid=208.

Jackson, Dave, and Neta Jackson. *Hero Tales: A Family Treasury of True Stories from the Lives of Christian Heroes*. Vol. 2. Minneapolis: Bethany House, 1997.

Jenkins, Jack. "Why This Pastor Who Tried to Assassinate Hitler Has Become a Hero to the Anti-LGBT Movement." *Think Progress*, April 14, 2015. http://thinkprogress.org/lgbt/2015/04/14/3646532/conservatives-comparing-anti-lgbt-crusade-pastors-attempt-assassinate-hitler/.

Johnson, Alan. "Just War, Humanitarian Intervention and Equal Regard: An Interview with Jean Bethke Elshtain." *Dissent*, Summer 2005. https://www.dissentmagazine.org/wpcontent/files_mf/1390329368d1Inteview.pdf.

Johnson, Bill. "A Bonhoeffer Moment—Rick Scarborough." *American Decency*, March 24, 2015. http://www.americandecency.org/full_article.php?article_no=3217.

Johnson, William Stacy. "Regaining Perspective." *Presbyterian Outlook*, May 21, 2001, 11.

Kelly, Geffrey B. "The Idolatrous Enchainment of Church and State: Bonhoeffer's Critique of Freedom in the United States." In *Bonhoeffer for a New Day: Theology in a Time of Transition*, edited by John W. de Gruchy, 298–318. Grand Rapids: Eerdmans, 1997.

———. *Liberating Faith: Bonhoeffer's Message for Today*. Minneapolis: Augsburg, 1984.

Kelly, Geffrey B., and F. Burton Nelson. *The Cost of Moral Leadership: The Spirituality of Dietrich Bonhoeffer*. Grand Rapids: Eerdmans, 2003.

Kerwick, Jack. "Bernie Sanders' Cheap Virtue vs. the Real Thing." *Front Page*, April 29, 2016. http://www.frontpagemag.com/fpm/262655/bernie-sanders-cheap-virtue-vs-real-thing-jack-kerwick.

King, Robert. "Pence, GOP Leaders Get Pastors' 'Rebuke' for RFRA Fix." *Indianapolis Star*, April 27, 2015. https://www.indystar.com/story/news/2015/04/27/pence-gop-leaders-get-pastors-rebuke-rfra-fix/26483311/.

Kleinhans, Theodore J. *Till the Night Be Past: The Life and Times of Dietrich Bonhoeffer*. Saint Louis: Concordia, 2002.

Koehn, Nancy. *Forged in Crisis: The Power of Courageous Leadership in Turbulent Times*. New York: Scribner, 2017.

Kurtzleben, Danielle. "POLL: White Evangelicals Have Warmed to Politicians Who Commit 'Immoral' Acts." *NPR.com*, October 23, 2016. https://www.npr.org/2016/10/23/498890836/poll-white-evangelicals-have-warmed-to-politicians-who-commit-immoral-acts.

Land, Richard. "What Would King Have Said about Saddam?" *Beliefnet* 4 (February 2003).

Larsen, Dale, and Sandy Larsen. *Dietrich Bonhoeffer: Costly Grace*. Christian Classics Bible Studies. Downers Grove: InterVarsity, 2002.

Larsen, Timothy. "The Evangelical Reception of Dietrich Bonhoeffer." In *Bonhoeffer, Christ, and Culture*, edited by Keith L. Johnson and Timothy Larsen, 39–57. Downers Grove: InterVarsity, 2013.

Lebrecht, Norman. "Just In: Christoph von Donyani Warns against the New US Intolerance." *Slipped Disc*, February 6, 2017. http://slippedisc.com/2017/02/just-in-christoph-von-dohnanyi-warns-against-the-new-us-intolerance/.

Lehmann, Paul. "Review of *The Communion of Saints* and *No Rusty Swords*." *Union Seminary Quarterly Review* 21, no. 3 (March 1966): 364–69.

Leys, Jeff. "Our Bonhoeffer Moment." *Voices for Creative Nonviolence*, October 2, 2007. http://old.vcnv.org/our-bonhoeffer-moment.

Ligon, Greg, ed. *Bonhoeffer's Cost of Discipleship*. Shepherd's Notes Christian Classics. Nashville: Holman, 1998.

Littell, Franklin H., and Hubert G. Locke, eds. *The German Church Struggle and the Holocaust*. San Francisco: Mellen Research Press, 1990.

Loconte, Joseph. "Belief in Action." *Wall Street Journal*, April 23, 2010. http://online.wsj.com/article/SB10001424052702303491304575189132952513158.html.

Loose Cannon [Charlotte Hayes]. "The T-Shirt Two: Why They're Not Alike . . ." *Beliefnet*, February 2, 2006.

Lopez, Kathryn Jean. "Bonhoeffer the Brave: A New Look at a 20th-Century Hero." *National Review Online*, December 10, 2010. http://www.nationalreview.com/article/255411/bonhoeffer-brave-interview.

Lovin, Robin W., and Jonathan P. Gosser. "Dietrich Bonhoeffer: Witness in an Ambiguous World." In *Trajectories in Faith: Five Life Stories*, edited by James W. Fowler and Robin W. Lovin, 147–84. Nashville: Abingdon, 1980.

Lukens, Nancy. "Misrepresenting the Life of Dietrich Bonhoeffer." *Sojourners*, February 2011. https://sojo.net/magazine/february-2011/how-eric-metaxas-agenda-driven-biography-fails-capture-true-bonhoeffer.

Macleod, William. "Bonhoeffer—a Reliable Guide?" *Banner of Truth*, September 23, 2016. https://banneroftruth.org/us/resources/articles/2016/bonhoeffer-reliable-guide/.

Macula, Tony. "Charlottesville Exposed the Risk Taken in Voting for Trump." Letter to the editor, *Livingston (NY) County News*, August 17, 2017. http://

www.thelcn.com/lcn06/charlottesville-exposed-the-risk-taken-in-voting-for-trump-20170817.

Manchester, Julia. "Obama Warns of Complacency, Notes Rise of Hitler." *Hill*, December 6, 2017. http://thehill.com/blogs/blog-briefing-room/news/363555-obama-warns-of-complacency-notes-rise-of-hitler.

"Manhattan Declaration: A Call of Christian Conscience." November 20, 2009. http://manhattandeclaration.org/man_dec_resources/Manhattan_Declaration_full_text.pdf.

Marsh, Charles. "Eric Metaxas's Bonhoeffer Delusions." *Religion and Politics*, October 18, 2017. http://religionandpolitics.org/2016/10/18/eric-metaxas-bonhoeffer-delusions/.

———. *Strange Glory: A Life of Dietrich Bonhoeffer*. New York: Knopf, 2014.

———. *Wayward Christian Soldiers: Freeing the Gospel from Political Captivity*. Oxford: Oxford University Press, 2007.

McCormick, Patricia. *The Plot to Kill Hitler: Dietrich Bonhoeffer; Pastor, Spy, Unlikely Hero*. New York: Balzer and Bray, 2016.

McMaken, W. Travis. "Not Another 'Bonhoeffer Moment.'" *DET*, May 15, 2017. http://derevth.blogspot.com/2017/05/not-another-bonhoeffer-moment.html.

Meekins, Frederick. "Are Evangelicals Too Quick to Embrace Bonhoeffer as One of Their Own?" *WEB Commentary*, August 30, 2015. http://www.webcommentary.com/php/ShowArticle.php?id=meekinsf&date=150830.

Members of the Cape Ann Clergy. "Standing Up to Hate." Letter to the editor, *Gloucester (MA) Times*, August 17, 2017. http://www.gloucestertimes.com/opinion/letters_to_the_editor/letter-standing-up-to-hate/article_95eac3fc-5824-5d96-bdaf-e72b5af5637d.html.

Metaxas, Eric. *Bonhoeffer: Pastor, Martyr, Prophet, Spy; A Righteous Gentile vs. the Third Reich*. Nashville: Nelson, 2010.

———. *Seven Men and the Secret of Their Greatness*. Nashville: Nelson, 2013.

———. "Should Christians Vote for Trump?" *Wall Street Journal*, October 12, 2016. https://www.wsj.com/articles/should-christians-vote-for-trump-1476294992.

Miers, Alyson. "No, You Are Not the Bonhoeffer in This Moment." *The Monster's Ink* (blog), June 28, 2015. https://alysonmiers.com/2015/06/28/no-you-are-not-the-bonhoeffer-in-this-moment/.

Miller, Susan Martins. *Dietrich Bonhoeffer: The Life and Martyrdom of a Great Man Who Counted the Cost of Discipleship*. Men of Faith. Minneapolis: Bethany House, 2002.

Muggeridge, Malcolm. *A Third Testament*. Boston: Little, Brown, 1976.

Nazworth, Napp. "Eric Metaxas and Jim Wallis' Horrible Debate on Evangelicals and Trump." *Christian Post*, April 28, 2017. http://www.christianpost.com/news/eric-metaxas-and-jim-wallis-horrible-debate-on-evangelicals-and-trump-181907/.

"19 Responses to 'Raymond A. Schroth: Bonhoeffer Was Wrong.'" *Titusonenine*, February 5–6, 2006. http://titusonenine.classicalanglican.net/?p=11262.

O'Brien, Matthew. "Why Do the Super-Rich Keep Comparing Obama to Hitler?" *Atlantic*, January 29, 2014. https://www.theatlantic.com/business/archive/2014/01/why-do-the-super-rich-keep-comparing-obama-to-hitler/283404/.

"Pat Robertson Clarifies His Statement Regarding Hugo Chavez." Pat Robertson, news release, August 24, 2005. http://www.patrobertson.com/pressreleases/hugochavez.asp.

Phillips, Michael. *The Eleventh Hour*. Wheaton, IL: Tyndale House, 1993.

Platt, Christian. "Mideast Tensions Wind toward Morally Tight Conclusion." *Pueblo (CO) Chieftain*, May 6, 2006. https://www.chieftain.com/editorial/mideast-tensions-wind-toward-morally-tight-conclusion/article_de089045-898e-5b5f-b573-de0cd5ea0ada.html.

Porteous, Skipp. "Banquet of the White Rose." *Albion Monitor*, February 18, 1996. http://www.albionmonitor.com/abortion/whiterose.html.

Porter, Janet. "Not to Vote Is to Vote." *WorldNetDaily.com*, August 23, 2016. http://www.wnd.com/2016/08/not-to-vote-is-to-vote/.

Potter, Stephanie. "In Solidarity: Community Gathers for Candlelight Vigil." *Pittsburg (KS) Morning Sun*, August 14, 2017. http://www.morningsun.net/news/20170814/in-solidarity-community-gathers-for-candlelight-vigil.

Queen, Chuck, "Breaking Down Southern Baptist Rhetoric against Same-Sex Marriage." *Patheos*, June 30, 2015. http://www.patheos.com/blogs/unfundamentalistchristians/2015/06/breaking-down-southern-baptist-rhetoric-against-same-sex-marriage/.

Rasmussen, Larry. "The Steep Price of Grace." *Sojourners*, February 2006. https://sojo.net/magazine/february-2006/steep-price-grace.

Rasmussen, Larry, with Renate Bethge. *Dietrich Bonhoeffer—His Significance for North Americans*. Minneapolis: Fortress, 1990.

Raum, Elizabeth. *Dietrich Bonhoeffer: Called by God*. New York: Continuum, 2002.

"Reflections on Bonhoeffer and Politics in Our Time—Rev. Dr. Reggie Williams." *We Talk, We Listen*, April 3, 2017. https://wetalkwelisten.wordpress.com/2017/04/03/reflections-on-bonhoeffer-and-politics-in-our-time-rev-dr-reggie-williams/.

"Review of *Bonhoeffer: Pastor, Martyr, Prophet, Spy*." *Kirkus Reviews*, December 15, 2010. https://www.kirkusreviews.com/book-reviews/eric-metaxas/bonhoeffer/.

"Rev. Ronnie Floyd Speaks to Southern Baptists about Same-Sex Marriage." *YouTube*, June 17, 2015. https://www.youtube.com/watch?v=nEtw0gA39eU.

Reynolds, Diane. *The Doubled Life of Dietrich Bonhoeffer: Women, Sexuality, and Nazi Germany*. Eugene, OR: Cascade, 2016.

Rice, Chris L. "Dietrich Bonhoeffer as We Understand Him at JPUSA." *ADKF (A Desperate Kind of Faithful)* (blog), accessed February 21, 2018. https://justthischris.wordpress.com/dietrich-bonhoeffer-articles/dietrich-bonhoeffer-as-we-understand-him/.

Ridd, Carl J. "A Message from Bonhoeffer." *Christian Century* 83 (June 29, 1966): 827–29.

Ripley, Amanda. "Terrorists and Saints." *Washington City Paper*, February 5, 1999. https://www.washingtoncitypaper.com/news/article/13017079/terrorists-and-saints.

Robison, James. "James Dobson, Rick Scarborough, Mat Staver Address Supreme Court Same-Sex Marriage Threat." *Charisma News*, March 16, 2015. http://www.charismanews.com/opinion/48754-james-dobson-rick-scarborough-mat-staver-address-supreme-court-same-sex-marriage-threat.

Rogers, Jack H. "American Christians Are Being Persecuted." Letter to the editor, *Indianapolis Star*, May 2, 2015. http://www.indystar.com/story/opinion/readers/2015/05/02/american-christians-persecuted/26806147/.

"Ronnie Floyd Rages over Marriage Equality." *The Rachel Maddow Show*, June 16, 2015. http://www.msnbc.com/rachel-maddow-show/watch/ronnie-floyd-rages-over-marriage-equality-468054083960.

Rowell, Andrew D. "Innovative Ecclesiological Practices: Emerging Churches in Dialogue with Dietrich Bonhoeffer." Unpublished manuscript, January 31, 2007. http://www.andyrowell.net/andy_rowell/files/bonhoeffer_and_emerging_church_sample_paper_5.pdf.

Rowell, Andy. "Bonhoeffer: The Evangelical Hero." *Books and Culture*, June 2010. http://www.booksandculture.com/articles/webexclusives/2010/june/bonhoeffer.html.

Russell, Sean. "What Does Our Silence Say?" *Fort Worth Weekly*, January 24, 2018. https://www.fwweekly.com/2018/01/24/what-does-our-silence-say/.

Rymel, Tim. "Has Evangelical Christianity Become Sociopathic?" *Huffington Post*, May 11, 2017. https://www.huffingtonpost.com/entry/has-evangelical-christianity-become-sociopathic_us_5914ce6fe4b02d6199b2ed92.

Schenck, Rob. "Eric Metaxas Wrong for Using Bonhoeffer to Support Trump." *Christian Post*, November 3, 2016. http://www.christianpost.com/news/eric-metaxas-wrong-for-using-bonhoeffer-to-support-trump-171268/.

Schroth, Raymond A. "Bonhoeffer Was Wrong." *National Catholic Reporter*, January 27, 2006. http://natcath.org/NCR_Online/archives2/2006a/012706/012706r.php.

Seidensticker, Bob. "Does the Church Face a Bonhoeffer Moment? Maybe It's Just a Case of the Vapours." *Cross Examined* (blog), *Patheos*, April 1,

2015. http://www.patheos.com/blogs/crossexamined/2015/04/does-the-church-face-a-dietrich-bonhoeffer-moment-maybe-its-just-a-case-of-the-vapours/.

Shelly, Rubel. "Biographers Needed! Please Apply." RubelShelly.com, February 21, 2018. http://rubelshelly.com/content.asp?CID=16342.

Small, Jeffrey. "Southern Baptist Anti-Gay Stance Echoes Its Prior Support of Segregation." *Huffington Post*, June 18, 2015. http://www.huffingtonpost.com/jeffrey-small/southern-baptist-antigay-_b_7607386.html.

Smith, Gregory A., and Jessica Martínez. "How the Faithful Voted: A Preliminary 2016 Analysis." Pew Research Center, November 9, 2016. http://www.pewresearch.org/fact-tank/2016/11/09/how-the-faithful-voted-a-preliminary-2016-analysis/.

Smith, Robert O. "Bonhoeffer, Bloggers, and Bush: Uses of a 'Protestant Saint' in the Fog of War." Paper delivered at the annual meeting of the Academy of Religion, Philadelphia, November 2005.

Smith, Samuel. "Eric Metaxas: Why Christians Should Vote for Donald Trump." *Christian Post*, July 20, 2016. http://www.christianpost.com/news/eric-metaxas-why-christians-should-vote-for-donald-trump-166714/.

Solberg, Mary, ed. *A Church Undone: Documents from the German Christian Faith Movement, 1932–1940*. Minneapolis: Fortress, 2015.

Spong, John Shelby. *A New Christianity for a New World: Why Traditional Faith Is Dying and How a New Faith Is Being Born*. San Francisco: HarperSanFrancisco, 2002.

Staggs, Al. "The Parallels to Hitler's Germany Are Abundantly Clear: Dietrich Bonhoeffer and the Iraq Crisis." *Baptist Standard*, March 3, 2003. http://levantium.com/2010/06/20/the-parallels-to-hitlers-germany-are-abundantly-clear/.

Stoltzfoos, Rachel. "Martin O'Malley Compares Trump to Hitler, KKK." *Daily Caller*, January 17, 2017. http://dailycaller.com/2017/01/14/martin-omalley-compares-trump-to-hitler-and-the-kkk-in-one-tweet/.

Strang, Stephen E. *God and Donald Trump*. Lake Mary, FL: FrontLine, 2017.

Sullivan, Amy. "America's New Religion: Fox Evangelicalism." *New York Times*, December 15, 2017. https://www.nytimes.com/2017/12/15/opinion/sunday/war-christmas-evangelicals.html.

Suttle, Tim. "America's Wisdom Problem." *Huffington Post*, August 30, 2017. http://www.huffingtonpost.com/entry/americas-wisdom-problem_us_59a6f0f5e4b08299d89d0b79.

Tashman, Brian. "Kim Davis' Lawyer Wants Her Named TIME's Person of the Year." *Right Wing Watch*, December 3, 2015. http://www.rightwingwatch.org/content/kim-davis-lawyer-wants-her-named-times-person-year.

———. "Rafael Cruz Brings Up Nazi Germany in Rant against Marriage Equality." *Right Wing Watch*, March 11, 2016. http://www.rightwingwatch.org/content/rafael-cruz-brings-nazi-germany-rant-against-marriage-equality.

"The Ten Most Influential Christians." *Christian History* 65 (2000). http://www.christianitytoday.com/history/issues/issue-65/.

Throckmorton, Warren. "Eric Metaxas to Bonhoeffer Scholars: Every Syllable of My Biography Is True." *Warren Throckmorton* (blog), *Patheos*, February 9, 2017. http://www.patheos.com/blogs/warrenthrockmorton/2017/02/09/eric-metaxas-bonhoeffer-scholars-every-syllable-bonhoeffer-bio-true/.

———. "Eric Metaxas: We Need Virtue in Our Leaders and We Must Vote for Donald Trump." *Warren Throckmorton* (blog), *Patheos*, June 17, 2016. http://www.patheos.com/blogs/warrenthrockmorton/2016/06/17/eric-metaxas-we-need-virtue-in-our-leaders-and-we-must-vote-for-donald-trump/.

———. "Glenn Beck's Historical Problems at Liberty University: The Purple Triangle and the Jehovah's Witnesses." *Warren Throckmorton* (blog), *Patheos*, May 2, 2014. http://www.patheos.com/blogs/warrenthrockmorton/2014/05/02/glenn-becks-historical-problems-at-liberty-university-the-purple-triangle-and-the-jehovahs-witnesses/.

———. "The Popular Bonhoeffer Quote That Isn't in Bonhoeffer's Works." *Warren Throckmorton* (blog), *Patheos*, August 25, 2016. http://www.patheos.com/blogs/warrenthrockmorton/2016/08/25/the-popular-bonhoeffer-quote-that-isnt-in-bonhoeffers-works/.

———. "Update on a Spurious Bonhoeffer Quote: Not to Speak Is to Speak, Not to Act Is to Act." *Warren Throckmorton* (blog), *Patheos*, November 11, 2016. http://www.patheos.com/blogs/warrenthrockmorton/2016/11/11/update-on-a-spurious-bonhoeffer-quote-not-to-speak-is-to-speak-not-to-act-is-to-act/.

"Today's Issues," American Family Radio, May 19, 2015.

Tomczak, Larry. "Church Is Facing a Dietrich Bonhoeffer Moment." *Charisma News*, March 30, 2015. http://www.charismanews.com/opinion/heres-the-deal/48952-church-is-facing-a-dietrich-bonhoeffer-moment.

"The Top 10 Best Dietrich Bonhoeffer Quotes." *Strength Awakening*, December 10, 2017. https://strengthawakening.com/top-10-best-dietrich-bonhoeffer-quotes/.

Trueman, Carl R. "Bonhoeffer and Anonymous Evangelicals." *Mortification of Spin* (blog), Alliance of Confessing Evangelicals, January 18, 2011. http://www.alliancenet.org/mos/postcards-from-palookaville/bonhoeffer-and-anonymous-evangelicals.

———. "Vivent les Differences!" *First Things*, May 27, 2015. http://www.firstthings.com/blogs/firstthoughts/2015/05/vivent-les-differences.

"Trump, Truth and the First 100 Days." *Up Front*, April 22, 2017. http://www

.aljazeera.com/programmes/upfront/2017/04/trump-truth-100-days-170421103041654.html.

Uptown, Swami [Jesse Kornbluth]. "Cindy Sheehan and Dietrich Bonhoeffer: Two of a Kind." *Beliefnet*, February 6, 2006.

Van Dyke, Michael. *Dietrich Bonhoeffer: Opponent of the Nazi Regime*. Heroes of the Faith. Ulrichsville, OH: Barbour Publishing, 2001.

Viviano, JoAnne. "Southern Baptists Kick Off Conference with Call for Leadership." *Columbus Dispatch*, June 16, 2015. http://www.dispatch.com/article/20150616/NEWS/306169742.

Wagner, Bo. "Faith Focus: When Christians Must Practice Disobedience." *Chattanooga Times Free Press*, September 13, 2015. http://www.timesfreepress.com/news/life/entertainment/story/2015/sep/13/when-christians-must-practice-disobedience/324457/.

Wallis, Jim. "Christians Called to Resist Trump's Bigotry." *Huffington Post*, April 30, 2016. https://www.huffingtonpost.com/jim-wallis/christians-called-to-resi_b_9809222.html.

———. "When I First Met Bonhoeffer." *Sojourners*, December 2005. https://sojo.net/magazine/december-2005/when-i-first-met-bonhoeffer.

Wallis, Jim, and Joyce Hollyday, eds. *Cloud of Witnesses*. Rev. ed. Maryknoll, NY: Orbis, 1991.

Wartick, J. W. "Against the Idolatry of the State—Dietrich Bonhoeffer." *JW-Wartick.com*, February 4, 2017. https://jwwartick.com/2017/02/04/idolatry-state-bonhoeffer/.

"Week in Politics: Hillary Clinton Makes History." *NPR.com*, June 10, 2016. https://www.npr.org/2016/06/10/481590351/week-in-politics-hillary-clinton-makes-history.

Wehner, Peter. "Why I Can No Longer Call Myself an Evangelical Republican." *New York Times*, December 9, 2017. https://www.nytimes.com/2017/12/09/opinion/sunday/wehner-evangelical-republicans.html.

Weigel, David. "Glenn Beck Got 20,000 People to Turn Out for an 'All Lives Matter' Rally." *Washington Post*, August 31, 2015. https://www.washingtonpost.com/news/post-politics/wp/2015/08/31/glenn-beck-got-20000-people-to-turn-out-for-an-all-lives-matter-rally/.

———. "Ted Cruz: Funding Obamacare Is Basically Like Appeasing Hitler." *Slate*, September 24, 2013. http://www.slate.com/blogs/weigel/2013/09/24/ted_cruz_funding_obamacare_is_basically_like_appeasing_hitler.html.

Weikart, Richard. "Metaxas's Counterfeit Bonhoeffer: An Evangelical Critique." Stanislaus State, Department of History, accessed February 21, 2018. http://www.csustan.edu/history/faculty/weikart/metaxas.htm.

———. *The Myth of Dietrich Bonhoeffer: Is His Theology Evangelical?* San Francisco: International Scholars Publications, 1997.

"We Pledge in Solidarity to Defend Marriage and the Family and Society

Founded upon Them." Freedom Federation, accessed February 21, 2018. http://americandecency.org/article_images/Marriage%20Pledge.pdf.

Westmoreland-White, Michael, Glen H. Stassen, and David P. Gushee. "Disciples of the Incarnation: The Witness of Dietrich Bonhoeffer, Martin Luther King, Jr., and Christian Rescuers of Jews Informs Our Discipleship Today." *Sojourners* 23, no. 4 (May 1994). http://www.sojo.net/index.cfm?action=magazine.article&issue=soj9405&article=940520.

"What Would Dietrich Do?" *Photon Courier*, January 18, 2003. http://photoncourier.blogspot.com/2003_01_01_photoncourier_archive.html.

Whitehead, John W. "Turning Our Schools into Enclaves of Totalitarianism." *The Rutherford Institute*, July 3, 2006. https://www.rutherford.org/publications_resources/john_whiteheads_commentary/turning_our_schools_into_enclaves_of_totalitarianism.

Williams, Daniel K. *Defenders of the Unborn: The Pro-Life Movement before Roe v. Wade*. New York: Oxford University Press, 2016.

Willitts, Joel. "Portraits of Dietrich Bonhoeffer—Metaxas and Schlingensiepen." *Euangelion* (blog), *Patheos*, April 13, 2011. http://www.patheos.com/blogs/euangelion/2011/08/portraits-of-dietrich-bonhoeffer-metaxas-and-schlingensiepen/.

Wilson, Jared C. "This Theologically Orphaned Generation." *The Gospel Coalition*, November 14, 2017. https://www.thegospelcoalition.org/blogs/jared-c-wilson/theologically-orphaned-generation/.

Wink, Walter. "The Bonhoeffer Assumption." *Sojourners* 31, no. 1 (January–February 2002). https://sojo.net/magazine/january-february-2002/bonhoeffer-assumption.

Worthen, Molly. "Donald Trump and the Rise of the Moral Minority." *New York Times*, September 26, 2015. https://www.nytimes.com/2015/09/27/opinion/sunday/donald-trump-and-the-rise-of-the-moral-minority.html.

Wüstenberg, Ralf K. *A Theology of Life: Dietrich Bonhoeffer's Concept of Religionless Christianity*. Translated by Douglas Stott. Grand Rapids: Eerdmans, 1998.

Yewell, John. "Straight Shooters." *Colorado Springs Independent Online*, February 8, 2001. https://www.csindy.com/coloradosprings/straight-shooters/Content?oid=1110788.

Index